Guide to Integrating Digital Services

Other Books of Interest from McGraw-Hill

Sarch, *Integrating Voice and Data.* ISBN 0-07-606970-2
Ungaro, *Networking Software.* ISBN 0-07-606969-9
Sarch, Abbatiello, *Telecommunications and Data Communications Fact Book.* ISBN 0-07-606965-6
Nemzow, *Keeping the Link.* ISBN 0-07-046302-6
Ranade, *Introduction to SNA Networking.* ISBN 0-07-051144-6
Ranade, *Advanced SNA Networking.* 0-07-051143-8
Ranade, Ranade, *VSAM: Concepts, Programming, and Design.* ISBN 0-07-051198-5
Ranade, *VSAM: Performance, Design, and Fine Tuning.* ISBN 0-07-583963-6
Knightson, *Standards for Open Systems Connection.* ISBN 0-07-035119-8
Inglis, *Electronic Communications Handbook.* ISBN 0-07-031711-9
Rohde, *Communications Receivers.* ISBN 0-07-053570-1
Sabin, *Single-Sideband Systems and Circuits.* ISBN 0-07-054407-7
Folts, *The McGraw-Hill Compilation of Data Communications Standards.* ISBN 0-07-079965-2
Fthenakis, *Manual of Satellite Communications.* ISBN 0-07-022594-X
Lee, *Mobile Communications Engineering.* ISBN 0-07-037039-7
Owen, *Digital Transmission Systems.* ISBN 0-07-047954-2
Fortier, *Handbook of LAN Technology.* ISBN 0-07-021623-1

Guide to Integrating Digital Services

T1, DDS, and
Voice Integrated
Network Architecture

Robert L. Dayton

Intertext Publications
McGraw-Hill Book Company
New York, N.Y.

Library of Congress Catalog Card Number 88-83065

10 9 8 7 6 5 4 3 2 1

ISBN 0-07-016188-7

Intertext Publications/Multiscience Press, Inc.
One Lincoln Plaza
New York, NY 10023

McGraw-Hill Book Company
1221 Avenue of the Americas
New York, NY 10020

Composed in Ventura Publisher by Context, Inc.

Contents

Preface

Understanding digital communications requires extensive reading and a lot of imagination to fill in the missing information. While that seems like the hard way to learn about anything, the problem is finding documents to read in the first place. When you did locate some information, the technical verbiage left you totally confused.

Turning to seminars to bring you up to speed left you with only part of the information needed. Seminar organizers haven't taken the time to learn themselves and teach only a small portion of the total story. The seminars built around digital telephony material spend an inordinate amount of time on theoretical subjects instead of real life. When you go to one of these sessions, you may find out how much you already know and how much they don't. You also discover how many teach totally wrong information based on their lack of understanding.

Unsatisfied by the available subjects being taught, one returns to the technical documents. Even with a technical background, a lot of writings require repeated readings to understand what the authors meant. Sometimes technical writing runs rampant with clarifying statements. A technocrat wants to make sure that each statement contains every conceivable caveat. Knowing how things work doesn't require a discourse on every nit that needs picking. Nit picking comes when someone wants to know about the fine details.

This book is based on the principle that telecommunications people need to know how their networks function in the total system. The total system includes end-user premise equipment, facilities, and telephone company services. One doesn't build a boat in a basement before finding out if it will fit out the door later. Just as one checks on ways out, one builds telecommunications networks with a total understanding of the surroundings.

Purpose

Over the years, I spent time both as a telecommunications engineer and in the marketing department. Adjusting to the two different disciplines showed that an almost universal problem exists. Engineers and marketing people do not really understand each other. Marketing people supposedly know the end-user's needs but talk in generalities. The engineers need specifics to design the ultimate product to serve the market. It is rare that either one fully understands how the product works in the total end-user network.

The purpose of this book is to provide a solid understanding of all the parts in an integrated digital services world. A good portion of the information concerns telephone company digital services and the integration of end-user equipment.

Dealing with integrated digital services on a private network has few restrictions. One doesn't need to follow many of the standards associated with telephone companies. Nevertheless, the smart ones still follow many of the telephone company transmission constraints.

Other books on digital services have devoted a lot of time to theoretical material gleaned from academic writings. I base our information on years of telecommunications experience. As a result, I include information never seen before in any document.

The information contained here also builds on a background of product development and selection. Selecting telecommunications equipment from many manufacturers develops a keen appreciation for standards. Standards are necessary to assure compatibility in a larger system. They are an absolute requirement for safety and protection against getting a "pig in the poke."

When getting around to making product selections, one often needs to educate oneself about the technical side of the equipment. One problem with technical writings is that they leave some very basic questions after reading them. What are my concerns? What's good and what's bad? Understanding your options before reaching a final decision lessens the surprises later. Instead of requiring the reader to dig for answers or options, we list the end-user advantages and disadvantages.

Audience

During the writing of this book, people asked what I was writing about. Everyone pictures a writer plugging away at the proverbial great American novel. They even understand a person writing a cookbook or some other "how-to" manual. Explaining my intentions to write about integrating digital services led to the usual response of "Oh, I see." It's just not a subject one normally interjects into a conversation.

While not an ice breaker at a party, the subject can save a company many communications dollars. Better yet, an understanding of integrating digital services can save a career from going down the drain.

The best description of this book is that it is a practical technical book about integrating digital services. For the technical person, this book provides the system picture. The sales person can understand how the parts they are selling fit into the total.

Nevertheless, the primary person targeted for this book is the telecommunications end-user. They are the ones that have to make the final decision to spend their company's money. Their employment and future pay increases depends on making intelligent decisions.

Informed end-users make smart selections of products and services. They recognize the need for standards to gauge the value of their decisions. Standards also protect their choice from rapid design changes. Quality standards protect end-users from both physical and financial harm.

Buying that proprietary one-of-a-kind product or service often puts the end-user at risk. If you can't find at least two products that have direct compatibility, you end up in bed with one design. Bed partners are fine if they don't change the way they make the bed each day.

Follow the example of the personal computer manufacturers. Compatible personal computers give the end-user a choice of products at a reduced price. Plug-in circuit boards and software provide the same functions for a myriad number of compatible computers. Telecommunications products and services should have the same flexibility. End-users should have the option to plug any number of services into a variety of products or other services. That is the true meaning of integrated digital services.

1

Introduction to Integrated Digital Services

Digital transmission has a longer telecommunications history than most analog services. It did not obtain prominence until the introduction of digital voice channel banks and T-Carrier systems in 1962. Ten years later, the Bell System launched the digital data system designed for an end-user data network. Eight years later, a major revolution exploded with a magnitude that resulted in a billion dollar business.

Digital Evolution

A revolution in digital transmission started when T-1 telephone company digital services became available to the end-user. Major changes in the telecommunications business prompted a record number of manufacturers to build T-1 equipment. As the original revolution has peaked, a new digital evolution shows promise to spark another major change.

This new evolution is the integrating of digital services over common facilities. What makes this different from combining voice and data circuits over T-1 multiplexers is the use of telephone company services. Telephone companies permitted only one type of service to travel over T-1 facilities when they interfaced with their services.

Watching end-users implement their own networks helped prod the telephone companies into innovative practices. There isn't any greater fear for the major telephone company than the thought of ending up in the cable and wire business. Needless to say, some telephone companies are very happy providing nothing more. They will, in time, also offer integrated digital services to be competitive.

While it has been technically possible for years to integrate digital services, there wasn't an easy way to administer them in a structured environment. Integrating digital services introduces totally new administrative and operational methods for telephone companies.

At best, the change to a totally integrated digital network will take several years. Years of accounting practices and regulation restricts revolutionary offerings. As regulation loosens its grip on telephone companies, innovation will have a freer hand to provide virtual or integrated networks. Operating methods require ways to test the total service from end to end. Preliminary integration of digital services furnishes fragmented testing and a variety of performance support. Mixing apples and oranges has always presented problems to a unified product or service. The goal is to have one maintenance group handling all trouble reports or, better yet, a network control system that automatically reports troubles to the telephone company. After reporting the trouble, the end-user should be compensated for loss of service. The service should also escalate problems up the line quickly after set time intervals.

About the Book

As one might suspect from the title *Guide to Integrating Digital Services*, the main purpose is to give direction. The book includes fundamental information one needs to effectively survive in the digital telecommunications world. Once past the background information, the book advances to the hardware involved with digital services. Completing the major portions of the book is a section on applications.

Chapters Two through Eight deal with information needed to understand digital services. For those individuals who may have a basic knowledge already, we added information that has never appeared in any other publication. Since this information never surfaced before, it also has never appeared in seminars before.

The second part combines services, equipment, and facilities. Chapters Nine through Eleven discuss telephone company interfaces and end-user premise equipment. Chapter Twelve covers the product selection process. Chapter Thirteen introduces concerns about facilities.

Chapters Fourteen through Eighteen cover the applications connecting integrated digital services. Completing the digital story is Chapter Nineteen, which discusses the evolution of digital services.

About the Chapters

Chapter Two — Analog Transmission vs. Digital Transmission describes the differences between analog and digital transmission. It is easier to tell what digital services are all about if you first know what they *aren't*. Many end-users around the country don't understand how a digital service could use analog microwave systems. We present reasons why digital services can use analog transmission equipment.

Chapter Three — Digital Data System Hierarchy covers the various digital signals in use today. The reader gains knowledge about bipolar signals and violation codes. Continuing on, the chapter deals with pulse-shaping considerations and has a review of transmission media. It then details the North American and European digital transmission levels and their differences.

Chapter Four — Digital Data Systems vs. DATAPHONE Digital Services explains the component parts to DATAPHONE Digital Service. Most people lump DATAPHONE Digital Service (DDS) into a general classification of digital service. There are basic differences between the two that create an interface concern. This chapter spells out these differences and points out the end-user concerns. Explaining the fine details about DDS is the only way to understand the principles behind the evolution of digital data.

Chapter Five — Timing Sources discusses the basic clock needs and the various timing accuracy levels used by the telephone companies. It also covers the ways telephone companies deal with timing inaccuracies. Timing remains the principle concern for the end-user, and its importance permeates the book. Manufacturers and end-users have a misconception about the accuracy of some timing. Mathematical examples demonstrate the inaccuracies of certain clock sources.

Chapter Six — Frames, Formats, and Patterns points out the differences between the terms frames, format, and patterns. While these terms often meld into one meaning, they have distinct definitions when used with digital transmission. Formats are sequences of bits or bytes formed in a periodic structure. Frames are periods of the structured format with a framing pattern to designate the period. Pattern bits or bytes appear to delineate the frame. This chapter also details the D4 and Extended Superframe structures. Future digital services depend on the implementation of the Extended Superframe format.

Chapter Seven — Coding Methods explains the digital coding methods used in the practical world to convert analog signal to digital. Spending time learning about theoretical coding schemes is a waste of time to the end-user. Ninety-nine percent of the coding equipment used in the world use only several algorithms. We discuss only the practical methods and leave theory to others. An important section to the end-user is knowing how to subjectively evaluate the various coding methods themselves.

Chapter Eight — Signaling Supervision, Signaling, and Call Processing discusses things like Robbed-Bit, Loop-Start, and Ground-Start Signaling. Signaling states for Loop and Ground-Start Signaling turn up for the first time in published documents. Some end-user multiplexers provide only two states of signaling, whereas some terminal equipment need additional states.

Chapter Nine — Telephone Company Interfaces covers the major telephone company interfaces and their requirements. The Digital Cross-connect System (DCS) unit becomes the greatest telephone company tool to control digital services. One needs to fully understand what it can and cannot do. Some equipment's frame structure cannot pass through a DCS because it requires the same superframe pattern from end to end (superframe integrity). This phenomenon is something the telephone companies don't tell the end-user or manufacturer.

Chapter Ten — End-user Premise Multiplexers devotes itself to T-1 multiplexers. Types of multiplexers and the evolution of end-user premise equipment gives the reader an understanding about their differences. It also covers the low, mid, and high ranges of multiplexers and the end-user's concerns.

Chapter Eleven — Other Premise Digital Terminal Equipment presents concerns about equipment other than multiplexers. Switched 56 kilobit services have several ways of transmitting from the end-user to the telephone company. One method uses dedicated DDS services. Another way uses a T-1 multiplexer to reach a switch location. The third method uses a two-wire method of alternate or ping-pong transmission. Channel Service Units (CSU) are a requirement between the end-user terminal equipment and the telephone company facility. This chapter goes into the CSU as well as other end-user premise interfaces.

Chapter Twelve — Equipment Selection deals with methods of finding the best product with the least repercussions. It discusses how to make effective product selections that withstand the closest scrutiny, get the most out of presentations by venders by planning for the audience and the material presented, and learn about ways to make good decisions.

Chapter Thirteen — Facilities deals with the different transport systems over which the end-user can transmit digital signals. If one doesn't have a background in transmission engineering, it is pot-luck if the service meets the end-user needs. This chapter lists the advantages and disadvantages of each type of facility.

Chapter Fourteen — Digital Transmission Impairments details troubles the end-user will face with timing and jitter problems. It also explains the differences between error-free seconds and bit-error rates for the first time. Comparisons between the error rates provides the understanding needed to evaluate the value of different systems. For example, one digital system has a 95% error-free second performance; it has a better bit-error performance than another service with a 99.5% error-free second level. Comparing just the error-free performance, one assumes the opposite meaning.

Chapter Fifteen — Digital Network Transmission Constraints presents end-user concerns about echo and timing differences. Echo becomes apparent when energy reflects back and there is a long enough transmission delay. This chapter discusses echo and echo cancelers. It also explains the operation of buffers to reduce the effect of timing differences.

Chapter Sixteen — Integrated Services Digital Network presents a different view of ISDN. While other books cover the ISDN message formats, this chapter deals with the hardware side of the issue. ISDN is a telephone company service that has great meaning for that part of the telecommunications world. It is not a panacea for everyone in the future. Basic Access is still under discussion by the ruling standards committees. One system out of several, appears to win out as the North American standard.

Chapter Seventeen — Integrated Telephone Network Architecture lists all the end-user requirements to use telephone company integrated digital services. This chapter shows the connections necessary in a telephone company to provide the various services. Tariff lines describe the boundary lines within the telephone company office. When integrated digital services become virtual networks, the tariff lines become invisible but remain an integral part.

Chapter Eighteen — Combining Networks expands on the applications of integrating digital services. Networking control provides the end-user with an operational handle on their network. Creating networks and restoration plans can lead to other problems. Actual facility distance is often several magnitudes longer than thought. Switching circuits around the end-user network to restore service adds additional delay. This delay affects data response time and may make echo noticeable.

Chapter Nineteen — Digital Evolution reviews the future of integrated digital services. Planning for the future requires unbiased information. When new products are under development, the promises of things to come often surpass the results. This chapter discusses new proposals and their real chances for survival.

Chapter Twenty — Glossary provides a convenient place to look up various digital transmission terms.

Terminology Used

Telephone Companies

When we use the term "telephone companies," we mean all telephone service carriers. Since integrated digital services are not specific to one carrier, we use telephone companies as an all-encompassing term. At one time, everyone considered the Bell System THE telephone company, even though there were hundreds of independent companies. Divestiture divided the Bell System into two major entities — AT&T and the companies supported by Bell Communications Research's documents. Rounding out the major telephone companies are MCI, US Sprint, and many fiber-optic companies.

We use Bell Communications Research as an all-encompassing term meaning the various Bell Operating Companies. Each entity initiates its own plans, but uses Bell Communications Research for research and as the main writer of technical references. After issuing the Bell Communications Research technical references, each operating company can issue small clarifications if they wish.

North American

North American refers to the general standards used by all telephone companies in the United Sates and Canada. Any standard adopted by the Exchange Carriers Association becomes a North American practice. Standards adopted by the Conference of European Postal and Telecommunications Associations become European or CCITT practices.

End-User

Telephone companies always refer to the people that lease their services as customers. It carries over when they refer to equipment at the user's location as Customer Premise Equipment (CPE). Nevertheless, we feel the term end-user describes a more universal entity than does the term customer. An end-user may not be a customer of any telephone company and still have the same concerns.

Registered Service and Trade Marks Used

The following registered trade and service marks are used in the book. Some specific trade or service mark names registered to individual companies not covered below are credited to the particular company in the associated article. Missing credits for trade and service marks or trade names is an oversight and haven't intentionally been omitted from the publication. Additions or corrections in connection with proprietary names will appear in future revisions upon proper notification of the controlling companies.

AT&T's Registered Service Marks:

Dataphone
Accunet
4 ESS
5 ESS
Western Electric
Subscriber-Loop-Carrier

Bell Communications Research Names:

Bellcore
SYNTRAN

NYNEX Registered Service Mark:

INFOPATH

2

Analog Transmission vs. Digital Transmission

Analog Transmission vs. Digital Transmission

To understand digital transmission better, one should first look at the differences between analog and digital technology. A fundamental difference between analog and digital transmission is that analog uses frequency division multiplexing and digital uses time division.

Frequency Division Multiplexing

Frequency Division Multiplexing (FDM) implementation began in the 1930s to place more than one telephone call on a pair of wires. Groups of 12 channels were the transmission limit of the early FDM or carrier systems. In 1939, the first high-capacity system introduced a FDM system that could put 600 telephone circuits over coaxial cable.

Getting more and more channels on the same facilities required many frequency modulations or changes. Frequency modulation uses one constant frequency to interact with voice frequencies to produce a higher set of frequencies. If one frequency interacts with another frequency, two modulation products result in sidebands, or the sum and difference of the two frequencies.

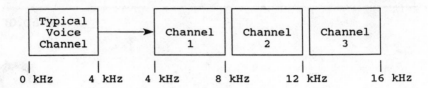

Figure 2-1   Frequency Division Multiplexing (FDM).

```
sin A + sin B = sin (A + B) + sin (A - B)
      Where A = Constant Frequency
            B = Voice or Analog Frequencies
  sin (A + B) = Upper Sideband
  sin (A - B) = Lower Sideband
```

Figure 2-1 shows that Channel 1's frequencies have interacted with a 4 kilohertz (kHz) tone to produce an upper sideband between 4 and 8 kHz. Channel 2's frequencies modulated with an 8 kHz tone and the resultant frequencies, range between 8 and 12 kHz.

When a group of channels are bundled together, they are being multiplexed. At this time, the analog channels modulated with a group of set frequencies and the upper sideband products combine to form a multiplexer output. The aggregate frequency stream combines many sideband frequencies.

Returning the signal to the original 4 kHz channel, the multiplexed frequencies modulate with the same frequencies again. This time, the demultiplexing process combines the modulated analog signal with the frequency constants and retains the lower sideband products.

Time Division Multiplexing

In 1962, the D1 Channel Bank and a digital hierarchy architecture provided a means of reducing telephone company costs. The first time division multiplexers were designed for the voice world, and data rates were not considered. Analog terminal data rates were just creeping up to 2400 bits per second. Revisions came quickly to the original D1 Channel Bank because the quality of the PCM coding did not deliver "toll quality" signals. Toll quality minimum requirements are specified in the Bell System Technical Reference, PUB43801, November 1982.

By 1974, the D4 Bank replaced the older versions of the D1, D1A, D2, and D3 Banks. Most of these revisions were by-products of improved equipment design. D4 Banks put 48 channels in the same physical space in which a D3 Bank provided only 24 channels. In 1982, the D5 Bank equipment design provided 96 channels in the

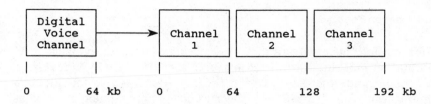

Figure 2-2   Time Division Multiplexing (TDM).

same physical space. While the D4 and D5 channel banks have greater channel capacity, they still emulate the 24-channel D3 Bank.

To use time division multiplexing (TDM), analog signals must change from a frequency domain to a time domain. Instead of talking about hertz per second, we now are in a bits-per-second mode. Figure 2-2 shows time division multiplexing that assigns channel time slots out of the maximum bit-per-second rate transmitted.

Frequency Comparison

Analog signals cannot transmit over a digital system unless they convert to digital pulses first. Digital signals, however, look like high frequency analog signals to analog transmission systems. While one thinks of a digital pulse as being very square, it resembles an analog signal at the receiver end. Before the digital signal goes out on the facility, its characteristic square corners round off by filter action. Further rounding occurs due to transmission characteristics of the facilities.

Digital signals require eight times the frequency bandwidth of their equivalent analog signal. While not efficient, digital pulses can still transmit over analog microwave and cable transmission systems. Figure 2-3 shows a comparison of transmitting 24 4000 hertz-wide channels over a digital and analog facility. You can imagine the reaction upper management had to the first proposal for a digital system that took eight times the analog's bandwidth.

```
|                         768 kilohertz                         |
```
24 Voicegrade Channels – Digital Transmission

```
| 96 kilohertz |
```
24 Voicegrade Channels – Analog Transmission

Figure 2-3   Comparison of Frequency Bandwidths.

Information Theory

Information theory covers the transmission of units or symbols of information and the faithful reconstruction at the receive end. Hartly, Shannon, and Nyquist's work in the late 1920s led to today's communications practices. These theories cover both analog as well as digital transmission.

Analog data modems, no matter how high their bit rates, do not transmit more than 2400 bauds or information symbols per second. Information transfer theory limits the speed of signals transmitting over facilities. A 4000 hertz-wide channel can transfer information just so fast with intelligence. It is like trying to jam two pounds of material into a one-pound bag — the bag will only take so much.

> AXIOM — Bits and bauds do not mean the same thing. Baud defines unit information transfer, whereas bits define the number of binary digits being sent.

A 9600-bit-per-second (bps) modem trasmits at a 2400 baud per second rate. In the case of a 9600 bps modem, it sends 4-bit symbols at a 2400 baud rate. A 14,000 bps modem transmits at the same 2400 baud-per-second rate, but now sends 6-bit symbols.

Nyquist's original work in the 1920s was with telegraph signals. In comparison with today's digital signal transmission, telegraph was very slow. Still, the communication theories that resulted remain appropriate for today's transmission.

Samples or snapshots of an analog signal become binary representations when changed into digital information signals. Shannon's Sampling Theorem stated that the sampling rate must be twice the highest frequency being transmitted. An analog voice channel's bandwidth is 4000 hertz wide. This takes into consideration the guard bands between channels that prevent crosstalk. Nevertheless, the best analog channel's information rates today are usable between 300–3400 hertz.

Using Shannon's sampling theory, the best facility in the world should need a sampling rate of only 6800 bits per second. While some books suggest a higher sampling rate due to filter limitations, there is a basic reason for sampling at 8000 bps. The Bell System had a national network of timing supplies that operated at a 4000 and 64,000 hertz rate. Sampling at a 8000 bps rate was prompted by engineering economics more than any other reason.

Nyquist's frequency designates the highest frequency in the signal being digitized. If the digital rate is 1.544 megabits per second (Mbps), test personnel use a 772 kH frequency to measure the circuit. Test personnel need the frequency generator to verify that the facility meets the engineering design requirements for power loss.

AXIOM — Digital services can use analog facilities without major modifications. Analog services must be digitized before they can use digital facilities.

Advantages of Digital Transmission

Reduction in the Amount and Size of Telephone Company Equipment

Digital transmission reduces the amount of telephone company central office equipment. Analog services go through many stages of frequency modulation and demodulation. All this additional analog equipment occupies a great amount of floor space in a central office. While this may seem to be a minor thing, a telephone company's land, building, and power expenses are prorated over all equipment. Equipment cost almost triples because of the additional loading factors.

Implementing a new analog circuit requires an extensive cross-connection process. Racks of specialized equipment are hardwired to a cross-connect frame. There telephone personnel install and solder wire-pairs between the frame appearances of the various specialized units. All this cross-connection work resulted in tons of copper wire being installed to connect equipment. Analog cross-connections would require several days after completing repetitive paperwork. Digital equipment permitted electronic cross-connections. These connections are made remotely from a central site in minutes.

Connections of digital services into digital switching machines eliminated even more equipment. With analog switching machines, a digital facility used D Banks to recover 24 analog channels. Each of the 24 channels would then connect to the analog switch. Digital switches now have only one input/output port for all 24 channels.

Improved Testing Capabilities

The improved testing capabilities of digital facilities were not fully understood at first. Original testing concepts stayed with the old trusted method of testboards. Each circuit had an appearance at the testboard. Test personnel could access the circuit only if it went through their own office.

Around 1978, AT&T-Long Lines proposed an Automatic Bit Access Test System (ABATS) that remotely tested DATAPHONE Digital Service circuits. Their system allowed test personnel to test digital services anywhere in the country. Previous testing procedures took extensive time to locate troubles. Most of the time involved in trouble sectionalization was spent getting another office to make some tests.

By the time a test person was available, the trouble had usually cleared. ABATS offered the capability to test the circuit at the same time the end-user reported the trouble.

Since digital services are time division multiplexed, test equipment is computer programmed to look at particular time slots. Electronically connecting the test sections and accessing a centralized data base provided even greater testing capabilities.

Immunity to Most Transmission Impairments

Analog transmission suffers from a myriad of impairments. Some impairments result from the modulation process, and others come from external sources. While the following problems can exist on analog facilities, the first three account for 90% of the trouble reports.

1. Open circuits — no continuity
2. Loss — continuity, but at a low power level
3. Noise — induced noise from equipment
4. Impulse noise — peak spikes of noise
5. Phase jitter — alternating current power supply induced
6. Intermodulation distortion — harmonic generation
7. Frequency shift — slightly different modulation frequency sources
8. Single tone interference — induced from other units
9. Envelop delay — time difference between received upper and lower frequencies

Open Circuits

Open circuits were the number one trouble for a number of years. They were also the first trouble that cleared by itself under testing. At one time, the Bell System soldered all connections in the field. The introduction of wire-wrapped connections eliminated the need for hot irons and solder. Nevertheless, wire-wrapped connections corrode, and the circuit appears as an electrical open. Personnel would use a test cord that included an electrical current. This would temporarily seal the electrical connection, and the trouble would clear. Installation of permanent sealing current on the circuit eliminated intermittent opens.

Loss

Loss of power on a circuit resulted from aging equipment and operating procedures. Vacuum tubes accounted for a good portion of power

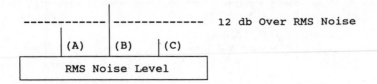

Figure 2-4   Impulse Noise.

loss. The most surprising reason for loss on a circuit was the method used to align carrier systems. Each day, every long-haul carrier office made uncoordinated manual adjustments to the carrier pilot's gain. By the time they completed the daily chore, the end- to-end levels were usually lower than optimum.

Noise

Noise results from deteriorating equipment and induced outside causes. Older radio equipment had an inherent property of getting noisy when the circuits were the busiest. Needless to say, they are no longer in use. Modems that exceeded their authorized power level or high level tones also induced noise on a number of circuits.

Impulse Noise

Impulse noises are very rapid spikes of noise that exceed a threshold 12 db higher that the expected root-mean-square (RMS) noise level. (RMS provides a true picture of the average level of the signals). Figure 2-4 shows three different spikes that exceed the normal RMS level.

The example block for RMS noise is very simplistic since the area really contains many individual noise signals. Expected or RMS noise level is determined from the airline mileage associated with the circuit. After determining the expect RMS level, the impulse noise test set checks for noise spikes greater than 12 decibels (db) over the RMS value. Spike (B) is the only one going past the threshold level. The other spikes, (A) and (C), just figure into the RMS value and do not count as impulse noise.

Phase Jitter

Phase jitter in analog systems is usually a modulation product that results from an alternating current (ac) power supply. Alternating current power supplies generate a direct current to power the com-

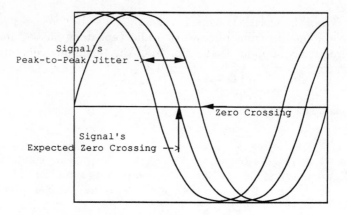

Figure 2-5   Phase Jitter.

munications equipment. Filters on the power line usually remove all hints of the alternating current. When the filter is not effective, the transmitted signal varies back and forth relative to the zero crossing point.

Figure 2-5 shows the variance of a phase-modulated signal crossing from a positive polarity towards the negative. The peak-to-peak jitter measures in degrees away from the expected zero crossing point. Jitter is a descriptive term because the signal looks like it is shaking back and forth. Producing a drawing like Figure 2-5 to show jitter is difficult because it is a dynamic event. One needs an electronic oscilloscope (visual display) to view the phenomenon.

Intermodulation Distortion

Intermodulation Distortion was known as Harmonic Distortion for a number of years. Its measurement specifications still refer to levels of second and third harmonics. Harmonics are multiples of a basic frequency. A second harmonic is twice the basic frequency and a third harmonic is triple. Over the years the method of testing for harmonic distortion changed and so did the name associated with the test. Now, four different tones test the circuit. Combinations of inter-modulation products produce the results for second and third harmonics.

Frequency Shift

Frequency shift is one of several troubles that a tester cannot see on a loopback test. Shifts in frequency in a one-way direction are detected. When the circuit is looped, the frequency shift masks itself. This problem results from microwave radio repeaters having independent frequency supplies that differ from the telephone company's master clock.

Single Tone Interference

Single tone interference is usually induced from another circuit. Either an adjacent circuit has a very high level tone or there is a crosstalk problem in some of the equipment.

Envelop Delay

At one time, envelop delay was a major trouble for data transmission. Frequencies traveling on a facility have different arrival times because impedance (resistance and frequency) slows transmission. Envelop delay is another way of expressing the delays relative to a 1004 hertz tone. Today's modems have dynamic adaptive equalizers, and Envelop Delay is no longer a concern.

Other analog problems that appear occasionally are Phase Hits, Gain Hits, and Dropouts. Fifteen minute measurement periods are specified because these troubles are infrequent. Some analog network management controllers provide instantaneous reports about everything you ever wanted to know about your circuit. At best, they can provide a ballpark view of some impairments. Other measurements may not even be in the same town as the ballpark.

Digital transmission problems reduce to two major impairments. One is the same as the analog service's open circuit problem. The second problem is jitter that occurs in the repeaters (regenerators) and the digital hierarchy time division multiplexers. Other digital impairments are discussed in the chapter on Transmission Impairments.

Standardization

Digital services use a basic building block of 64,000 bits per second. To reach higher bit rates, the basic building blocks combine. This same basic block interfaces with every other basic block in the world. Slight differences in voice coding between Europe and North America standards translate easily.

Standards allow the various telephone company digital services to traverse many networks. Standarization provides an organized approach to internal evolution as well as interaction. Going between

ANALOG MODEM	DIGITAL MODEM
1. Develops a new receive clock every time a different remote modem comes on line.	1. Constant clock recovery of a master clock.
2. Readjusts dynamic equalizer each time a different remote modem comes on line.	2. Fixed equalizer in CSU only.
3. Modulation–demodulation schemes need synchronization.	3. No synchronization needed.
4. Training time 2.4 kb — 5 ms 4.8 kb — 10 ms 9.6 kb — 15 ms	4. Turn-on time 2.4 kb — 5 ms 4.8 kb — 2.5 ms 9.6 kb — 1.875 ms

Table 2-1   Analog vs. Digital Modems.

telephone companies and countries can only occur when everyone closely follows all the standards.

Better Response Time for Data Transmission

One of the best ways to understand the advantages of digital service is to look at data response time. Table 2-1 makes it particularly clear when the differences between an analog modem and a digital modem used on a multipoint circuit are compared. The term "digital modem" refers to a Data Service Unit (DSU) and integrated Channel Service Unit (CSU) combination.

It turns out that the most dramatic thing that a digital modem does is to turn on and off. Turn-on time is the length of time it takes to send two 6-bit data words (noncontrol words) to turn the Receive Line Signal Detector on.

Disadvantages of Digital Transmission

Greater Bandwidth Needed

Nyquist's Frequency is the highest frequency being digitized. This frequency in hertz equals one-half the digital rate in bits per second.

$$F_N = 1/2 \ F_D$$

Where: F_N = Nyquist's Frequency in hertz

F_D = digital rate in bits per Second

Reduced Flexibility Because of Standardization

Data channel rate flexibility found in some multiplexers suffers when using national or worldwide standards. Digital transmission standards are 75% efficient at data rates of 2400, 4800, and 9600 bps. At 56,000 bps, they are 87.5% efficient. Non-standard multiplexers are usually around 90% efficient with 10% going to overhead.

These nonstandard multiplexers can pack a wide range of data rates onto one aggregate high-speed facility. Nevertheless, they use their own proprietary method and cannot communicate with anything but their own clone.

Timing Concerns

Greater concern about clock sources in a digital network is needed. Large analog networks had worries about loop or slave timing units to a master clock. Digital networks that use some telephone company services may find there are several master clocks in the network.

No Secondary, Tertiary, or Additional Channels

For the purpose of this discussion, we are disregarding DATAPHONE Digital Service's announced secondary channel at this time. DDS secondary channel uses a robbed-bit technique that isn't analogous to analog systems. This type of service is covered in the chapter on Digital Data Systems vs. DATAPHONE Digital Service.

There are number of private line circuits that use tones in the spectrum above normal voice transmission. Tones can indicate alarm conditions or turn equipment on or off.

Analog data circuits with a secondary channel usually use the lower end of the frequency bandwidth (approximately 350 Hz). A tertiary channel usually operates around 3200 Hz. If the circuit has any appreciable roll-off on either end of the frequency bandwidth, the second and tertiary channels can suffer.

3

Digital Data System Hierarchy

Digital telephone company networks began as a way to reduce the investment in metallic wire for the Bell Operating Companies. Analog carrier systems of the day didn't meet the needs, and the Bell System took a different approach. Digital transmission itself wasn't new; telephone companies had used telegraph signals for years. What was new was the high-speed capacity of the digital hierarchy.

Interest in a digital transmission hierarchy extended beyond the United States. The Conference of European Postal and Telecommunications Associations (CEPT) also sought a similar answer. Unfortunately, the Bell System and CEPT didn't adopt the same solution. North America opted for efficiency over the advantages of the CEPT design.

Digital Signals

Digital signals vary in characteristics throughout the hierarchy. One shouldn't approach digital transmission thinking its signals are just a string of square pulses. The different signal types play an important role in why certain things happen. This section defines the terms that appear throughout the rest of the book.

Duty Cycles or Return to Zero and Non-Return to Zero Signals

One sometimes finds several terms describing the same aspect of digital signals. Duty cycles and Return or Non-Return to Zero signals

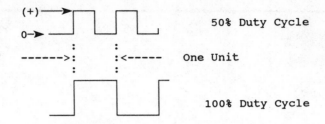

Figure 3-1   100% Duty Cycles.

fit this class. Certain digital signals infer they have a certain duty cycle and never talk about it. After this description, duty cycles also are presumed to be part of the digital signal's description.

Figure 3-1 shows a 50% and 100% duty cycles. The 50% duty cycle rises to a positive value for 50% of the unit's width and returns to zero. It stays at the zero value for the next 50% of the unit's width.

One can see that the signal is on duty for half the time and returns to zero before going on to the next thing. The main reason for a 50% duty cycle is a reduction in intersymbol interference.

The 100% duty cycle works during the whole unit's width and never returns to zero for a rest period. It may return to a zero condition during the next pulse unit, but never during its own time.

Unipolar Signal

Unipolar signals (Figure 3-2) are characteristic of the digital pulses used by electronic equipment. Binary number ones signal a positive voltage above a minimum operational level. Binary zeroes occur when the voltage falls below the minimum positive level. Negative voltages are supressed in the electronic equipment.

Since the electronic equipment's logic circuits only use the unipolar signal, all other digital signal types must change at the interface. After the equipment does its thing, the output drivers deliver the type of signal needed for the next equipment or facility.

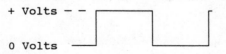

Figure 3-2   Unipolar Signal.

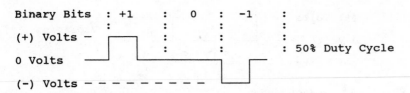

Figure 3-3   Bipolar Return to Zero.

Bipolar Return to Zero Signal or Alternate Mark Inversion (AMI)

Alternate Mark Inversion (AMI) and a Bipolar Return to Zero signals have the same meaning. Figure 3-3 shows an alternating mark inversion pattern of ones bits. A zero or Space bit has zero voltage and only occupies a time division.

Alternating the Mark or ones bit accomplishes three things. One reason is to prevent a direct current (dc) from developing on the circuit. Too many pulses of a positive or negative polarity produce an electrical potential difference. If this happens, a noise signal develops to degrade the transmission. The second reason is to intentionally change or violate the alternating mark bits to send information. Bipolar violations either send control words or alert error detection equipment. A third reason is to provide separation between pulses and make it easier to recover clock references at the far end.

Polar Binary Signal

Polar binary signals use a 100% duty cycle and do not follow any set pattern arrangement. This signal has been around for years at the interface between terminal equipment and modems. Figure 3-4 shows the Space or zero bit as a positive voltage and the Mark or ones bit a negative pulse. Logic engineers rectified this apparent lack of judgment by converting everything to a unipolar signal and making a ones bit positive.

When the Digital Signal Level-4 equipment uses a polar binary signal, it uses the logical positive pulse for a ones bit. Zero bits become negative voltage pulses.

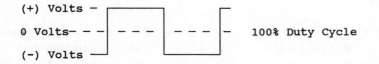

Figure 3-4   Polar Binary Signal (Non-Return to Zero).

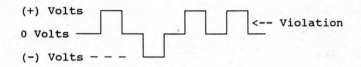

Figure 3-5   Bipolar Violation.

Bipolar Violation

As stated above, bipolar violations serve two functions. One is to send control words and the other is an error indication. Figure 3-5 shows an alternating mark inversion code violation. Instead of continuing the alternating pulse stream, the following mark or ones bit has the same polarity.

DATAPHONE Digital Service (DDS) uses bipolar violations to send control words between the end-user and the local Hub Office. These control words operate loopbacks and provide other information without confusing them with valid end-user data. Controlled bipolar violation codes at higher digital rates replace strings of zero or no pulses.

Bipolar N-Zero Substitution (BNZS)

Bipolar N-Zero Substitution refers to the process of using bipolar violation codes in place of zero bit strings. Timing recovery circuits need pulses to keep the internal clock in synchronization. Stop sending a steady diet of ones bits, and the internal clock wanders or free-runs.

Transmission equipment monitors the data stream for Bipolar violation codes. When it spots N-Zeroes (3, 6, or 8 zeroes), it replaces the zeroes with the violation code. Since monitoring and replacement takes time, the equipment builds in delay to complete the substitution.

B3ZS

The Bipolar Three Zero Substitution (B3ZS) code shows up at the Digital Signal Level-3. Figure 3-6 shows the substitution code sent during a string of six zeroes. Selecting the polarity with which to start the violation code depends on the preceding pulses. The next chapter describes this process for DDS.

```
Zero String ->|  0  |  0  |  0  |  0  |  0  |  0  |
Converts To ->| +1  |  0  | +1  | -1  |  0  | -1  |
```

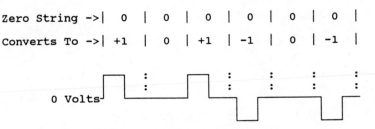

```
          0 Volts
```

Figure 3-6   Bipolar Three Zero Substitution.

B6ZS

Bipolar Six Zero Substitution occurs at the Digital Signal Level-2. A monitor checks the outgoing combined data stream for a string of six zeroes. After sensing a string, the violation code replaces the six zeros time slot shown in Figure 3-7. Polarity of the violation code also depends on the preceding pulse stream.

B8ZS

Bipolar Eight Zero Substitution (B8ZS) appears at the Digital Signal Level-1 and 1C. Its use at these speeds started in 1986; until then a violation was an error. Figure 3-8 shows the replacement code for a string of eight consecutive zeroes. Again, the polarity of the violation pulses depends on the previous pulses.

Bit Stuffing

Compensating for clock differences within the digital network is an ongoing process. When several digital streams combine into the next higher digital level, they add or stuff bits into the data stream. These stuff bits provide the flexibility in the composite data stream for different rates. Stuff bits insert at prescribed points in the data

```
Zero String ---->|  0  |  0  |  0  |  0  |  0  |  0  |
Converts To ---->|  0  | +1  | -1  |  0  | -1  | +1  |
```

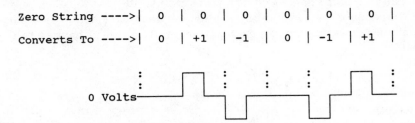

```
            0 Volts
```

Figure 3-7   Bipolar Six Zero Substitution.

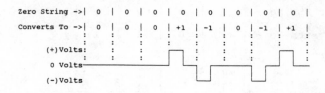

Figure 3-8   Bipolar Eight Zero Substitution.

stream. Figure 3-9 shows a stuff bit (S) added between information bits three and four.

Control words added to the frame pattern tell the receive end if the (S) bit is true or false. If the (S) bit is true, the receive equipment accepts the bit and adds it to the data stream output. Conversely, a false (S) excludes the stuff bit in the output data.

Bit stuffing permits multiplexing different rate data streams into a composite signal. Nevertheless, adding another bit in the data stream at controlled points effects the end-user received data. Voice conversations won't notice any bit-stuffing action. Data circuits will experience a bit error and request retransmission if using an error control process.

Pulse Shape Considerations

Transmission

Digital pulses pictured in documents always have nice clean lines with perfectly formed right angles. Student engineers have all gone through the laborious process of adding multiples of a basic sine wave to arrive at the ultimate square wave. It teaches the engineer that square wave is a composite of many harmonics of a basic analog wave. Consequently, sending a square wave or digital signal down a facility faces the same frequency constraints.

Impedance is resistance with a frequency element. Since impedance goes up when frequency goes up, two things happen to the

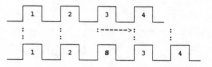

Figure 3-9   Bit Stuffing.

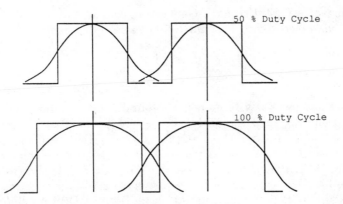

Figure 3-10   Intersymbol Interference.

transmission of the digital signal. First, the very high frequencies used to produce those nice right-angle corners attenuate to a point of disregard. The second impedance action delays the higher frequencies more than the lower ones. Combining the loss at the upper frequencies and delaying their position, the resultant digital signal looks more like analog waveform.

Intersymbol Interference

While those nice square corners disappear, the base of the pulse broadens out. It's just like those hourglass figures after all the sand runs to the bottom. Each digital pulse has room initially and you can identify each one. After transmission, the energy in the pulse bulges out into the next pulse's area. When receive equipment fails to identify which pulse is which, intersymbol interference occurs.

Figure 3-10 shows two different digital signals after transmission. The first example shows two 50% duty cycle pulses, and the second example has two 100% duty cycle pulses. Using the 50% duty cycle signal lessened the intersymbol interference seen with the second example.

Digital Hierarchy Transmission Media

Coaxial Cable and Wire

At one time, the telephone companies only had metallic wire to connect the network together. Coaxial cable introduction in 1939 revolutionized the telecommunications world by providing capacity for 600 high quality circuits. It wasn't until 1962 that metallic wire converted to digital signals. Converting coaxial cables to digital signals took place during the mid-1970s on a limited basis.

Microwave Radio

Analog microwave systems began around 1949 and didn't convert to digital signals until the early 1970s. AT&T's 1A Radio Digital System (1A-RDS) provided a DS-1 signal under the frequency division voice spectrum. Data under voice (DUV) facilities were the main carrier for DATAPHONE Digital Service (DDS)in its initial days.

The 3A-RDS digital microwave furnished a DS-3 level signal in the 11 gigahertz radio band. A digital radio DR 18A-DRS provided a DS-4 level signal in the 18 gigahertz radio band.

Fiber-Optic

Fiber-optic facilities started another telecommunications revolution. Rapid developments in fiber design and transmission methods outpaced the implementer's decision process for many years. While future developments will happen, the pace has leveled off. Bandwidth supply has finally outstripped the demand, and telephone companies' need for new facilities has decreased.

Analog transmission has its frequency division multiplexers. Digital transmission has its time division multiplexers. And now, fiber-optic has the wavelength division multiplexer (WDM). WDMs show up at very high digital rates and combine several optic outputs into one fiber cable. Since frequency and wavelength are inversely proportional, the WDM resembles the frequency division multiplexers used for analog services.

North American Hierarchy

North American's digital network (Figure 3-11) builds from a basic 8-bit block. Each basic block transmits at 8000 times per second equaling a 64,000-bps time slot called the Digital Signal 0 (Zero) Level. A Digital Signal Level-1 time division multiplexer combines 24 basic blocks into the next highest rate.

$$24 \text{ Basic Blocks X } \frac{64,000 \text{ bps}}{\text{Block}} = 1,536,000 \text{ bps}$$

The difference between the total bits per second needed to transmit 24 blocks and the T-1 rate totals 8000 bps. This additional overhead provides synchroniztion between the transmit and receive ter-

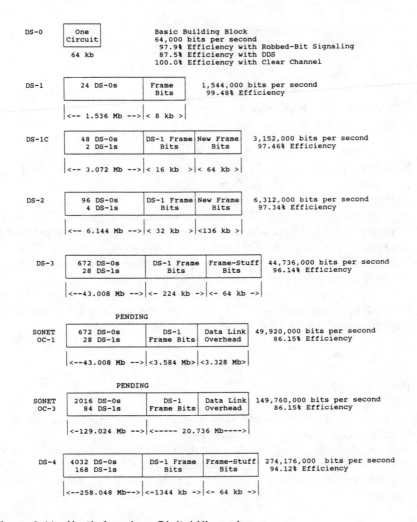

Figure 3-11 North American Digital Hierarchy.

minals. Synchronization control uses a framing pattern that appears in every 193rd bit location.

A step between the Digital Signal Level-1 and Level-2 developed after establishing the digital hierarchy. The T-1C Carrier system became an economic expedient to put more circuits over the local telephone facilities. Local telephone companies installed many T-1C facilities before they realized the system's disadvantages. T-1Cs bit-interleaved two T-1 lines into one new system. Being bit-interleaved, the error detection used for each T-1 line disappeared. There wasn't any way to monitor the T-1C line for errors.

Digital Signal Level-2 combined four T-1 lines into one 6,312,000-bps facility. A DS-2 multiplexer bit-interleaved bits from each T-1

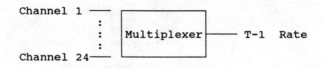

Figure 3-12   DS-1 Multiplexers.

line. Bits from lines number two and four inverted logic states before multiplexing to improve performance.

The next step in the digital signal hierarchy was the DS-3's 44,736,000-bps facility. DS-3 multiplexers combined 28 T-1 lines. Multiplexing 28 separately timed T-1 lines into one system presented problems. T-1 lines bit-interleave into seven separate subframes. Timing differences between the subframes correct by adding or stuffing bits at specific spots in the composite frame.

When laying out the original digital hierarchy, the Digital Signal Level-4 running at 274,176,000 bps became the digital outer limit. Now fiber-optic cables transport seven times that amount.

Digital Multiplexers

Time division multiplexers combine the basic 64,000-bps building blocks into higher rates. Higher-rate multiplexers in turn combine each preceding multiplexer's output. Transmission facilities provide the limit for multiplexing b methods. Fiber-optic developments will require multiplexers beyond the present Digital Signal Level-4 limits.

DS-1 Multiplexers

Digital Signal Level-1 multiplexers (FIgure 3-12) fall into two major categories: the 24-channel Digital Channel Bank, used predominately for voice, and the 23-channel T-1 Digital Multiplexer, used exclusively for digital data. Subsequent chapters cover these multiplexers.

DS-1 multiplexers output a bipolar return-to-zero signal. Some confusion exists in the industry in defining AMI and B8ZS transmission. One gets the impression that they are distinctively different, while in reality one complements the other.

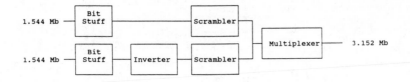

Figure 3-13   DS-1C Multiplexers.

Digital Loop Carrier

AT&T's Subscriber Loop Carrier (SLC — pronounced slick) is similar to the DS-1 multiplexer. Bell Communications Research refers to the system as a Digital Loop Carrier system to get around the Service Mark restrictions. Loop carriers have remote control and testing characteristics not found in the normal DS-1 multiplexer.

DS-1C Multiplexers

DS-1C multiplexers (Figure 3-13) combine two 1,544,000-bps data streams into one. This multiplexer bit-interleaves the two T-1 lines into a 3,152,000-bps line after three stages. The first stage adds stuff bits to compensate for the timing differences between the two T-1 lines. A second stage logically inverts the ones and zeroes from the second T-1 line. All ones bits become zeroes and zeroes become ones to improve the stability of the combined signal. The final stage scrambles the two data streams to strengthen the composite signal.

DS-2 Multiplexers

Digital Signal Level-2 multiplexers (Figure 3-14) also stuff bits to compensate for the timing differences between the four inputs. Next the second and the fourth T-1 line has the binary ones and zeroes logically inverted to improve the statistical properties of the DS-2 signal.

The DS-2 multiplexers use bit-interleaving, and the output is the bipolar signal. This multiplexer checks the output for strings of six zeroes and uses B6ZS violation coding.

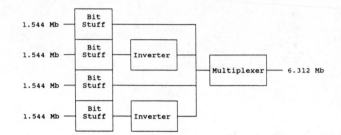

Figure 3-14   DS-2 Multiplexers.

DS-3 Multiplexers

Digital Signal Level-3 multiplexing (Figure 3-15) combines outputs from DS-1, DS-1C, and DS-2 multiplexers. This multiplexer can have two stages of multiplexing. If DS-1 or DS-1C lines are the input, there is a level of multiplexing to raise the aggregate line speed to a DS-2 rate. DS-2 inputs bypass this first level of multiplexing since the lower speed digital signals combined at some other location.

Compensating for timing differences between the T-1 lines happens either with the DS-1C or DS-2 multiplexing. Therefore, further bit stuffing isn't necessary at the DS-3 level. A DS-3 multiplexer bit-interleaves the seven DS-2 level streams into one 44,736,000-bps rate. The output is the bipolar return to zero signal and uses B3ZS code violations.

DS-4 Multiplexers

Digital Signal Level-4 multiplexers (Figure 3-16) bit-interleave six DS-3 Level data streams. Compensation for timing differences between the DS-3 lines calls for bit stuffing again. During the multiplexing, parity bits add for error detection. Also,the information bits combine with a pseudo-random signal to scramble the output. Unlike the lower speed multiplexers, the DS-4 Level uses a polar binary digital signal. Since the output signal is polar binary, zero substitu-

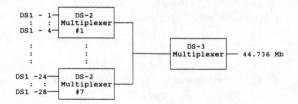

Figure 3-15   DS-3 Multiplexers.

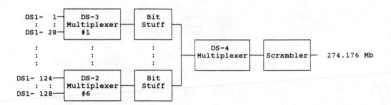

Figure 3-16 DS-4 Multiplexers.

tion violation codes don't exist. Scrambling the information signal assumes that strings of zeroes no longer present a problem.

Conference Of European Postal and Telecommunication Associations (CEPT) Hierarchy

CEPT's digital hierarchy (Figure 3-17) took a course different from the North American direction. They both started with the basic 64,000-bits-per-second building block. What they did from that point on separated the services.

North American — AT&T being the dominant force — chose to use in-band signaling in the DS-0 level. CEPT chose moving the circuit's signaling into a separate channel. They also chose a different Pulse Code Modulation scheme from the North American way.

The CEPT Digital Signal Level-1 includes 30 DS-0 channels for end-user information. One DS-0 block carries the out-of-band signaling for the 30 channels.

Unlike the North American framing pattern, bits that appear in every 193rd bit location, the frame pattern occupies a complete DS-0 block.

Difference Between North American and CEPT Systems

Table 3-1 combines the various digital signal levels and their associated efficiencies. Once past the DS-0 level, the North American method has a higher efficiency.

High-Density Bipolar with a Maximum n-Zero (HDB-n)

CEPT uses a version of Bipolar N-Zero Substitution called High-Density Bipolar with a maximum n-Zero (HDB-n). Selecting which polarity to indicate the violation code depends on preceding pulses.

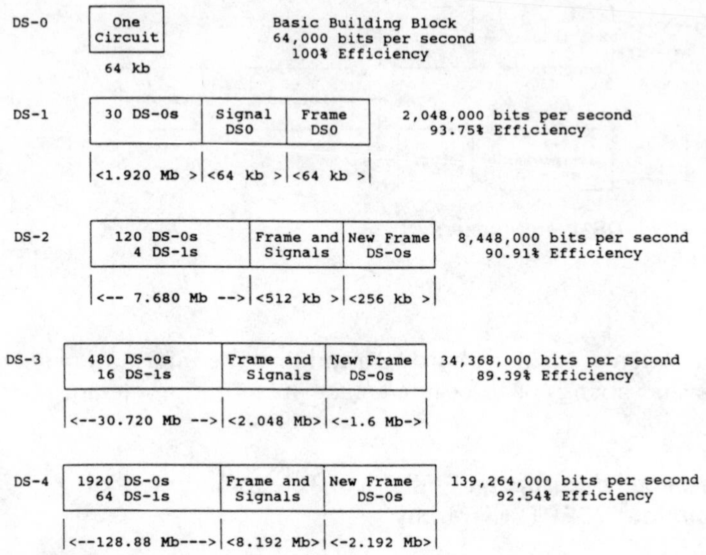

```
DS-0    ┌──────────┐         Basic Building Block
        │ One      │         64,000 bits per second
        │ Circuit  │         100% Efficiency
        └──────────┘
          64 kb


DS-1    ┌──────────────┬────────┬────────┐
        │ 30 DS-0s     │ Signal │ Frame  │  2,048,000 bits per second
        │              │ DS0    │ DS0    │       93.75% Efficiency
        └──────────────┴────────┴────────┘
        |<1.920 Mb >|<64 kb >|<64 kb >|


DS-2    ┌──────────────┬──────────┬──────────┐
        │ 120 DS-0s    │Frame and │New Frame │  8,448,000 bits per second
        │   4 DS-1s    │Signals   │DS-0s     │       90.91% Efficiency
        └──────────────┴──────────┴──────────┘
        |<-- 7.680 Mb -->|<512 kb >|<256 kb >|


DS-3    ┌──────────────┬──────────┬──────────┐
        │ 480 DS-0s    │Frame and │New Frame │  34,368,000 bits per second
        │  16 DS-1s    │Signals   │DS-0s     │       89.39% Efficiency
        └──────────────┴──────────┴──────────┘
        |<--30.720 Mb -->|<2.048 Mb>|<-1.6 Mb->|


DS-4    ┌──────────────┬──────────┬──────────┐
        │ 1920 DS-0s   │Frame and │New Frame │  139,264,000 bits per second
        │   64 DS-1s   │Signals   │DS-0s     │       92.54% Efficiency
        └──────────────┴──────────┴──────────┘
        |<--128.88 Mb--->|<8.192 Mb>|<-2.192 Mb>|
```

Figure 3-17   CEPT Digital Hierarchy.

Digital Level		DS-0s	DS-1s	Data Rate	Efficiency
NA	0	1	—	64 kb	97.90%
CEPT	0	1	—	64 kb	100.00%
NA	1	24	1	1.544 Mb	99.48%
CEPT	1	30	1	2.048 Mb	93.75%
NA	1C	48	2	3.152 Mb	97.46%
CEPT	—	—	—	—	—
NA	2	64	4	6.312 Mb	97.34%
CEPT	2	120	4	8.448 Mb	90.91%
NA	3	672	28	44.736 Mb	94.14%
CEPT	3	480	16	34.368 Mb	89.39%
NA	4	4032	168	274.176 Mb	94.12%
CEPT	4	1920	64	139.264 Mb	92.54%

Table 3-1   Differences Between North American and CEPT Digital
Hierarchy

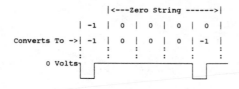

```
                        |<---Zero String ------>|
              | -1  |  0  |  0  |  0  |  0  |
Converts To ->| -1  |  0  |  0  |  0  | -1  |
              :     :     :     :     :     :
     0 Volts
```

Figure 3-18   High Density Bipolar 3-Zero Substitution.

Figure 3-18 shows a HDB 3-Zero code where the preceding pulses ended with a negative pulse and there was an odd number of pulses since the last substitution.

Connections Between Systems

Connections Between North American and CEPT

Interconnecting North American and CEPT networks doesn't have a logical data rate. Crossing over at 64,000 bps makes the most sense if the signaling uses Common Channel Signaling. A simple conversion table between voice-coding methods corrects for any differences. Nevertheless, most digital connections between the Unites States and Europe force the issue of accepting the other's DS-1 signal. Somebody must bite the bullet and accept the six-channel difference between systems. Initially, simple time division multiplexers accepted the two different frame structures and stuffed bits into the data stream for the rate difference.

Trans-Atlantic fiber-optic cable (TAT-8) owner's agreement makes the change between the systems in the United States for the first time. Today's digital switches have both kinds of interfaces and can effectively switch between services. Stuffing bits aren't necessary since the digital switch efficiently packs each line.

Connections Between Facility Types

Telephone companies connect facility types together to provide end-to-end service for end-users. While it may be the only way to get between two points, it often leads to transmission problems. No matter how hard designers try to find that transparent interface, small nuances remain that show up as trouble.

Joining equipment together based on operating speed alone is both naive and foolish. Several large telecommunications ventures failed because they overlooked timing differences, delays, and operating characteristics.

Connections Between Telephone Companies

Beside connecting into different type facilities, the main end-user concern is the timing differences. At one time, the Bell System network used one clock reference point. Divestiture and new telephone companies created many networks with individual clocks. As long as two or more clock sources exist, bit slips happen that affect data transmission.

Digital Data Systems vs. Dataphone Digital Service

Digital Data System was the engineer's name for AT&T's digital data hierarchy in 1972. DATAPHONE Digital Service was a marketing name or Service Mark given to a tariffed service that used the Digital Data System. They unfortunately both use the acronym DDS, which gives the impression they are the same thing.

When we talk about the Digital Data System, we refer to the entire digital hierarchy. DATAPHONE Digital Service (DDS) refers to data of 2.4, 4.8, 9.6, and 56 kb between the user and the Hub Office. A Hub Office is the telephone company's central office where the digital services interconnect.

Figure 4-1 shows the basic building blocks of the existing DDS network. This network is in a transition stage towards equipment that will provide integrated services. Nevertheless, an explanation of the present network provides a better understanding of how the integrated network will operate.

DSU — Data Service Unit

A Data Service Unit (DSU) performs several functions. One is to frequency lock its internal clock to the data stream coming from the DDS Hub Office. Another function is to change the bipolar format to a RS-232C or V.35 interface. The unit responds to Hub Office control commands such as loopback and out of service. It also automatically transmits idle code and zero suppression commands back to the Hub.

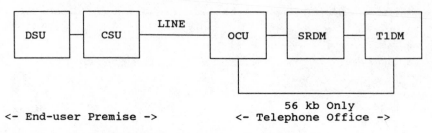

<- End-user Premise ->

56 kb Only
<- Telephone Office ->

Figure 4-1   DATAPHONE Digital Service Equipment.

There was a brief period in the early 1980s that physically separated the DSU circuitry from the Channel Service Unit (CSU). It was AT&T's contention that the CSU was part of the network and was therefore under their control. The Independent Data Communications Manufacturers Association (IDCMA) argued that they were also capable of making a Channel Service Unit. In response, the FCC granted the IDCMA's claim, and the two functions are again enclosed in one unit. DSU user interfaces are RS-232C for data rates up to 9600 bps and a V.35 type for 56 kbps. At 56 kb, the data and clock leads use balanced circuits with CCITT V.35 voltages. All the control leads are RS-232 unbalanced voltages. The DSU's Transmit and receive clocks both come from the network's source. Since DDS is the master clock source, terminal equipment cannot provide external transmit timing to the Data Service Unit.

CSU — Channel Service Unit

In the analog world, the 829 Data Auxiliary Set (DAS) is the termination of the circuit. It provides a variable equalization, a loopback arrangement, sets the transmit level, and provides for a sealing current option. Sealing current eliminates open circuits due to corrosion between wire wrap connections.

In the digital world the CSU is the termination. It provides a fixed equalization, a loopback arrangement, mandatory sealing current, and sets the transmit and receive level. The sealing current has two functions: one for the circuit's electrical continuity, the other to operate the loopback relay. Reversing the current's polarity operates the loopback relay in an open or closed position.

OCU — Office Channel Unit

Office Channel Units (OCU) perform several critical DDS functions. The most important function provides DDS clocking to the data

S	D	D	D	D	D	D	C

S = Stuff bit   D = Data bits   C = Control bit

Figure 4-2   Subrate Bit Structure at the Office Channel Unit.

going towards the user. Extremely accurate nodal clock sources at the Hub Office ensures the user's network will have only one master clock. Second, the OCU changes user control information into a network language. When the DSU sends a control word, it is in the form of a bipolar violation. Bipolar violation can't traverse the digital network and must be changed to a network code. At the other end of the circuit, the distant OCU changes the network code back to a bipolar violation.

Between the user and the OCU, the data rates have been 2400, 4800, 9600, and 56,000 kbps. The OCU treats the three lower or subrate speeds differently than the 56,000 rate. Subrate data is put into blocks of 6 information bits (Figure 4-2). A control bit added to this block tells the DDS network if the 6-bit byte is data or control information. The OCU completes the 8-bit byte or basic building block by inserting an additional or stuff bit.

Control indications use ones-bits when the end-user transmits data and zero bits when in an idle mode. When the end-user sends all-zero bit data, the bipolar violation code tells the OCU the six data bits are all-zeroes. The OCU then changes the violation code back to all zeroes to traverse the DDS network. The ones bit in the Control location maintains ones-density for transport over the network.

56-kb service puts data into 7-bit blocks (Figure 4-3) and adds just the control bit. This completes an 8-bit basic building block of network information.

By adding the Control bit to the 56-kbps data, the resultant 64-kbps signal directly connects to a T1 Data Multiplexer. An OCU output to the network is 64,000 bits per second. It is easy to see how the 56-kb data stream became 64 kbps. Subrate date rates change to 64 kbps by repeating the basic 8-bit byte and multiplying the data rate. Table 4-1 shows how the output of the four different OCUs becomes 64,000 bps.

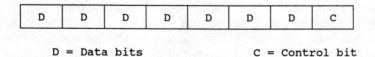

D	D	D	D	D	D	D	C

D = Data bits   C = Control bit

Figure 4-3   56-kb Structure at the Office Channel Unit.

* 56,000 bps + 8000 Control bps = 64,000 bps

* 9600 bps + 3200 Stuff & Control bps = 12,800 bps
         5 × 12,800 Combined bps = 64,000 bps

* 4800 bps + 1600 Stuff & Control bps = 6,400 bps
        10 × 6,400 Combined bps = 64,000 bps

* 2400 bps + 800 Stuff & Control bps = 3,200 bps
         20 × 3,200 Combined bps = 64,000 bps

Table 4-1   Office Channel Unit Output.

SRDM — Subrate Data Multiplexer

Subrate data services can directly connect to a T1DM but would not be economical in most cases. In almost all installations, subrate digital services connect to Subrate Data Multiplexers (SRDM — pronounced sar-dem). They are Time Division Multiplexers devoted to a single data rate. Five 9600-bps digital services multiplex into one 64-kb time slot. Ten 4800-bps and twenty 2400-bps services multiplex into a similar 64-kb time slot.

A 9600 bps OCU repeats a single block of information five times. Some documents explain there is a better error performance because the subrate service repeats and selects only the assumed good data. Its reported value here is overstated since very little can go wrong in the very short distance between the OCU and SRDM. There is an error performance improvement when used with Dataport (see below).

We said the output of one 9600 bps OCU was five repetitions of combined data, stuff, and control bits. A SRDM for 9600 bps digital services can have five different OCU connections to it. As the SRDM scans the five different OCU inputs, it selects one of the five repetitive bytes sent from each input. It places the channel input (12,800 bps) into one of the time slots in the SRDM (Figure 4-4). This process continues through the other four inputs. To identify the individual channels in the SRDM, a framing pattern (Table 4-2) replaces the various zero stuff bits.

Another form of the SRDM is the Integral Subrate Multiplexer (ISMX), referred to as the "is-mux." This unit is a 9600-bps SRDM that has been modified to insert into an OCU mounting. When an end office serves a limited number of users, the ISMX combines the various subrates in a single unit. They were used as an economic alternative when the DDS network was very new.

0	DDDDDDC OCU 1	1	DDDDDDC OCU 2	1	DDDDDDC OCU 3	0	DDDDDDC OCU 4	0	DDDDDDC OCU 5

D = Data Bits   C = Control Bit

Figure 4-4   SRDM Framing Pattern for 9600 bps.

MJU — Multipoint Junction Unit

Not shown in Figure 4-1 is the Multipoint Junction Unit (MJU). This unit, shown in Figure 4-5, is comparable to the analog split-bridge used for multipoint services. MJUs are located at the Hub Office since their input and output is 64 kbps. And since they operate at the DS0 rate or 64 kbps, a common MJU is used for all the DDS rates.

Normal operation of the multipoint circuit has a control point polling outlying terminals. All the data from the control point is fed to all the legs from the MJU. The terminal that answers the poll turns on its Request-to-Sent (RTS) lead, which removes the idle code from the line. Data from the terminal now enters a 1-byte serial buffer in the MJU. This data and the all ones idle code from the other legs are then put through a logic circuit AND gate.

If a streaming terminal (i.e., the terminal doesn't release the RTS lead after transmission) occurs, the access line will not return to an idle code. False data from that access line can add to the other data going to the control point. As soon as one zero bit appears on any input leg to the AND gate, the output will also be a zero. A streaming terminal can stay on the line as long as it doesn't output junk characters or just sends steady ones bits.

T1DM T-1 Data Multiplexer

The last item that distinguishes DATAPHONE Digital Service from the Digital Data System is the T-1 Data Multiplexer (T1DM). A T1DM (pronounced "tid-em") is comparable to the digital channel bank used for voice circuits. It is another time division multiplexer with 24-DS0 time slots. Unlike the digital channel bank (D-Bank), the T1DM only uses 23 time slots for end-user data. Also, unlike the

9600 Bps	0 1 1 0 0
4800 Bps	0 1 1 0 0 1 0 1 0 0
2400 Bps	0 1 1 0 0 1 0 1 0 0 1 1 1 0 0 0 0 1 0 0

Table 4-2   SRDM Framing Format Patterns.

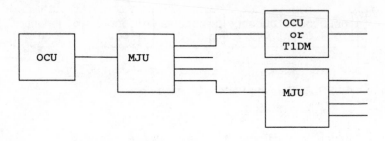

Figure 4-5 Multipoint Junction Units.

digital channel bank, it doesn't use Pulse Code Modulation to return to an analog signal.

T1DMs use the same 1.544 Mbps or D4 framing pattern used by D-Banks. As an added precaution against false framing, the T1DM uses a 6-bit word (101111) in the 24th time slot for synchronization. The 7th bit is a performance indicator, and the 8th bit is spare.

In the analog world, alarm systems monitor carrier pilot frequencies for system outages. DDS presented a problem because carrier pilots were no longer available to the testing personnel. A Digital Transmission Surveillance System (DTSS) monitors the seventh bit in the twenty-fourth time slot and the D4 framing bit. DTSS is not a great measuring device, but it was the best that could be done at the time. When the Extended Superframe (ESF) replaces the D4 framing pattern in the DDS Network, DTSS will phase out. ESF testing capabilities are far superior since they check all the active data instead of 2 out of 193 bits.

DATAPORT — Digital Access Through D4 Banks

End-user locations were often beyond the normal transmission distance for access lines. A DDS service can ride over a DS0 time slot in one of the D-Banks associated with voice circuits. At the end-office, a Dataport card (OCUDP) takes on the function of the OCU at the Hub Office (Figure 4-6). And at the Hub Office, there is another Dataport card (DS0DP) that will interface to the DDS DS0A distributing frame.

A single 2.4, 4.8, or 9.6 kbps DDS service occupies the entire DS0 time slot. The same OCU function of bit stuffing the subrate data up to a 64-kb level occurs. This is the only time repeated data improves the overall error performance.

One 56-kb DDS service usually occupies two DS0 time slots. Since transmission is not the best, Forward Error Correction (FEC) raises the error performance to DDS levels. This algorithm sends an additional 8 parity bits to determine the most probable data bits sent. A

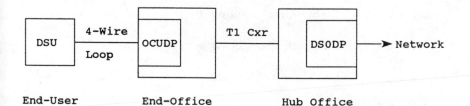

Figure 4-6 DATAPORT Applications.

56-kb DATAPORT card fits into one mounting space, and the next mounting space is empty. Fiber-optic cable for the 1.544-Mb service makes FEC unnecessary. Then the 56-kb DATAPORT unit would disable the FEC option and occupy only one DS0 time slot.

Differences Between Digital Data Systems and DDS

T-1 and DDS digital transmission use the bipolar return-to-zero signal where only the ones bits consecutively invert pulses. When consecutive ones are not inverted (i.e., the same polarity), it is considered a code violation. A major difference between Digital Data System and DATAPHONE Digital Service is that a violation with the first is an error and with the second a control word.

Violation Codes

DDS sends control codes by violating the inverting ones coding method between the DSU and the OCU. A DSU sends a violation code (Figure 4-7) when it is idle and when it senses a string of ones. OCU's send violation codes to put the DSU out of service, loopback interfaces, and to indicate a string of zeroes being sent. Violation codes change at the DSU to control information to the user and at the CSU to transfer control information across the digital network.

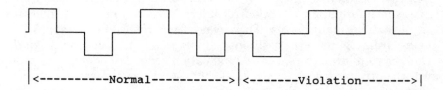

Figure 4-7 Alternate Mark Inversion.

1 1 1 X 0 V — Terminal not sending data

0 0 0 X 0 V — String of zeroes being sent

0 0 1 X 0 V — Facility out of service

0 1 0 X 0 V — Loopback DSU towards Hub Office

Table 4-3   Violation Codes.

Descriptions about the violation codes refer to the process as the "XOV Violation Control Function." To understand the XOV Violation Control, one needs to know what the letter designations are.

X — This designation is for a particular bit position in the 6-bit word for the subrates and the 7-bit word for 56-kbps service. It can be either a positive or a negative polarity ones bit, or zero voltage for a zeros bit depending on the odd or even number of inverting ones bits since the last violation. If there were an even number of ones bits, the X would be an inverted one's bit. Conversely, if there were an odd number of ones, the X bit would be a zero. The purpose of the X bit is to assure an even distribution of positive and negative pulses. This is done to prevent a dc voltage from developing due to energy on the facility being more positive or negative. A dc voltage on the line would lead to noise and other transmission problems.

0 — This is a zero that inserts to provide separation between the X bit and the V bit.

V — While the dictionary describes violation as a transgression, ravishment, or rape, it really is a very helpful thing. This violation is the intentional sending of consecutive ones of the same polarity.

Violation codes for the subrate speeds are shown in Table 4-3.

Control Bits

DDS is also very distinctive by including a control bit with every six or seven information bits. Control information on the digital hierarchy can take many forms. These vary from robbed-bit signaling to using framing pattern positions. Since violation codes on Digital Data System are errors, the DDS violation codes are changed to network control codes at the OCU. Table 4-4 shows the control words sent across the network. The (S) bit location is a stuff or don't-care bit.

S 1 1 1 1 1 1 0 — Terminal not sending data

S 0 0 1 1 0 0 0 — String of zeroes being sent

S 0 0 0 1 1 1 0 — Facility out of service

S 0 1 0 1 1 0 0 — Loopback DSU towards Hub

S = Stuff Bit

Table 4-4   Network Control Codes.

Testing Differences

A major difference between DDS and the Digital Data System is that
DDS has a computer controlled testing device. Automated Bit Access
Test System (ABATS) provides remote access (Figure 4-8) to the individual services across the country. While providing test access to
the circuits, it does not monitor the data being sent on a full time
basis.

When in a test mode, ABATS will automatically sectionalize
troubles on the circuit in a few minutes. Quickly sectionalizing the
trouble condition cuts the average circuit outage time in half when
comparing DDS to analog.

ABATS is one of the dilemmas of divestiture of the Bell System.
Developed by AT&T-Long Lines, it became the maintenance system
for the entire Bell System. At divestiture, AT&T retained ownership
because the Long Lines Department funded its development. A new
operating system will phase out AT&T's ABATS use. Bell Communications Research is working on their own plan to replace
ABATS with a digital access and test system.

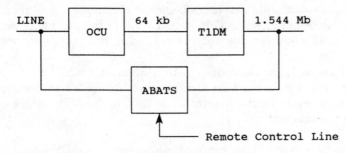

Figure 4-8   Automatic Bit Access Test System.

Equipment Evolution for DDS

Previously, we discussed the DDS network in use for the past 14 years. While there have been advancements in the components used in the network, there has been little evolution in its design. Divestiture of the Bell System dictated radical changes to the overall design. Almost all Hub Offices were assigned to the BOCs. Up to this point, AT&T jointly owned the Hub Offices, but were, for the most part, AT&T controlled. Often, DDS circuits were connected through several Hub Offices. Most AT&T circuits went in and out of the now BOC Hub Office for cross-connection. Each cross-connection meant additional charges that AT&T had to absorb.

Subrate Digital Cross-Connect System

During 1986, the DACS, a Subrate Digital Cross-connect (SRDC), and the Digital Data Multiplexer (DDM) were introduced as equipment replacement. The approach taken not only solves AT&T's economic problem but also leads to a savings to the BOCs and OCCs. Virtual Hub Offices eliminate the need to use other companies' equipment to construct a digital circuit.

This evolution now leads to an easy method to integrate low-speed digital services with other services. Boundary lines disappear when common equipment allows connection to many services.

DDS Secondary Channel

Secondary channel is another DDS evolution. The original concept of a secondary channel was to provide a low-speed diagnostic channel similar to many analog modems. Since the digital transmission didn't permit a frequency band for the diagnostic channel, it meant using part of the bits sent.

Some manufacturers derive a diagnostic channel by multiplexing it with the data being sent. This reduces the data rate being sent by 110 bps and whatever overhead is needed to maintain synchronization.

AT&T chose to create a diagnostic channel by robbing one out of three control bits. It has taken seven years for AT&T to develop and have a very limited implementation of this method. There are disadvantages to this method.

1. The OCU control bit function moves out to the DSU.
2. End-users must buy new DSUs and telephone companies install new Hub Office equipment.

| F | D | D | D | D | D | D | D | C |

F = Frame Bit   D = Data bits   C = Control bit

Figure 4-9   72 Kb Structure at the DSU.

3. Shorter distances happen between end-user and Hub Office due to greater bandwidth requirements.
4. The secondary channel operates at four different odd rates.

Primary	Secondary	Line Rate
2400 bps	133 1/3 bps	3200 bps
4800 bps	266 2/3 bps	6400 bps
9600 bps	533 1/3 bps	12800 bps
56000 bps	2666 2/3 bps	72000 bps

Bandwidth requirements for a 56-kb digital circuit needs a line that can carry 72 kbps. Before, the OCU would count 7 data bits and add a control bit. Now, the new DSU will count 7 data bits, add a control bit, and a framing bit for synchronization (Figure 4-9).

Transmission loss on a cable is a direct function of the frequency being sent. There aren't any repeaters that operate at 36 kHz to extend the circuit distance. Secondly, the nonrepeatered distance is reduced because of the higher loss at 36 kHz.

Integrated Subrate Data Multiplexer (SDM)

Subrate data multiplexing should be viewed from two different aspects. One is an integrated services position using the 1.544-Mbps access to the end-user's premise. The other is a DDS access line from the end-user premise to the Local Exchange Carrier's (LEC) DDS Hub Office. When integrated services are used, the SDM looks like Figure 4-10.

Originally the AT&T M24 Service Function was thought of as only a D-Bank multiplexer in a Central Office. Then the term meant a D-Bank, a Digital Access Cross-Connect System (DACS), or a Digital Interface Frame (DIF) to a 4ESS machine. Digital data requires a DACS that would have at least one of its DS1 ports connected to a

Figure 4-10   Subrate Data Multiplexing with Integrated Services.

DDS Digroup going to the DDS Hub office. Distribution to end-user locations in other LATAs would be sent over the digital network to the distant DDS Hub Office.

Since the end-user may want to fan out digital data to a number of locations, the DACS has to have a Subrate Digital Cross-Connect (SRDC) installed internally to the DACS. Subrate circuits of 2.4, 4.8, and 9.6 kbps transfer from the DACS to the SRDC integrated within a DS-0 signal. The subrate cross-connection occurs in the SRDC, and data circuit returns to the DACS in another DS0 time slot. The reconfigured DS0 (SDM formatted) can now be sent to another end-user premise or to the DDS Network.

This type of service concentrates different types of applications at the end-user's premise and now has direct access to the DDS Network. Direct access can be 1.544 Mbps services provided by the Local Exchange Carrier (LEC), or they may be end-user provided equipment such as microwave radio to the telephone company office.

Subrate Data Multiplexing with DDS

Subrate Data Multiplexing using DDS access lines presents some interesting variations. Figure 4-11 shows a new type DSU attached to multiplexer operating at 64,000 bps. The DSU adds a framing code to the data stream and the new output is 72,000 bps. Office Channel Units capable of DDS Secondary Channel transmission will strip the additional framing pattern and feed a normal 64,000-bps signal to a T1DM for transport. This type of service depends on the local telephone companies installing DDS Secondary Channel equipment.

Only about three vendors have approached the method shown in Figure 4-10. Two of the vendors are the largest providers of D-Bank type of multiplexers and dominate the telephone company market. They have designed cards that will fit into their particular multi-

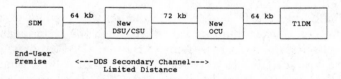

Figure 4-11   Subrate Data Multiplexing with DDS.

plexer and do not appear to address a market that would connect to a myriad of other multiplexers.

Summary

DDS is dependent on a strict frame structure and the use of a control bit. While some people have talked about the use of 64,000-bps data channels, they still will not be able to interconnect into the DDS world. That is, they will not interconnect until the telephone companies adopt a very advanced signaling system. This would require a connection into an ISDN signaling channel or the data channel associated with the Extended Superframe Format.

Bit stuffing at the subrates seems inefficient and uneconomical. The use of common equipment for all data speeds, after they are brought up to 64 kb, overcomes the perceived inefficiencies of bit stuffing.

5

Timing Sources

Timing is by far the most critical part of digital communications. Trying to run a network with poor timing or several sources leads to a calculated disaster. While analog transmission also has timing concerns, they are nothing in comparison to the digital world. An end-user analog network uses a number of individual timed segments. The digital network has only one segment and one clock. An exception to one clock is an operation with several extremely accurate atomic clocks.

Basic Clock Needs

Synchronization vs. Timing

A common misconception involves equipment synchronization and timing. While the band leader uses the baton to keep time, he or she synchronizes the start of the music by saying "a one, a two, etc." Both items are critical to the successful operation but are separate functions.

End-user premise equipment depends on synchronization to remain in step with remote devices and is a function of the framing pattern. Timing controls the internal operation of the end-user's equipment and relies on a master clock source.

Free-Running Clocks

Free-running clocks are like the band member that practices the music without direction. The music gets played in time with the individual's internal clock and sounds great by itself. Putting several band members together succeeds only when the band has a leader to cue the individual clocks.

Remove the external influence of the band leader — or a master clock when it comes to electronic equipment — and the individual clocks free-run. How quickly the free-running clock deviates from a norm depends on the design. The telephone companies use very stable primary frequency supplies. Pull the feed from the master clocking source and the telephone company clocks will not deviate an appreciable amount for many days.

Running Blind

Multiplexers often run asynchronous channels in synchronous circuits with a little magic or smoke. As the term implies, the asynchronous channel runs blind into a closely timed circuit. The one stipulation is that the asynchronous circuit run equal to or slower than 1/8 the speed of the higher-speed synchronous data channel. This stipulation can bend a little, and one can send an asynchronous data stream that is a quarter of the synchronous speed. A problem results when the reconstructed asynchronous pulses distort from their proper position and size. Sending the asynchronous pulses at 1/4 the synchronous rate results in a 25% distortion rate. This is the outer limit of the EIA RS-232C standards. Adding other equipment results in going past the limit.

Figure 5-1 shows asynchronous pulses (A) and (B) running 25 and 50 slower than the synchronous rate. If we logically add the synchronous clock and the (A) asynchronous pulses, only a small portion gets through. At the other end, the equipment reconstructs what it thinks the asynchronous pulse looks like. Pulse (A) ends up with a 25% distortion from where it should be. Logically adding the (B) asynchronous pulse with a synchronous clock source leads to the reconstruction of only a hint of a pulse.

Each asynchronous circuit has an electronic window that has a mythical opening. As the reconstructed asynchronous pulse passes through the equipment, it waits for this window to perform its thing. If the reconstructed pulse is so small that it falls outside the expected window, data will not appear at the terminal.

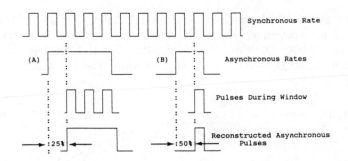

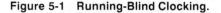

Figure 5-1 Running-Blind Clocking.

Stratum Levels

"Stratum levels" has a pretentious sound. Whoever started the use of stratum levels terminology probably thought that it explained everything. The only problem with using the term stratum level is that one has to spend time describing what it means in the first place. Stratum best describes the telephone company timing layered structure throughout their network. It is easier to think about timing accuracy levels instead of stratum levels. Nevertheless, tons of documents use the term and this book will follow the same trend.

The Trans Canada Telephone system refers to the various levels with letter designations. Stratum Level-1 clocks are Node-A sources. Stratum Level-2 references Node (B) and (C) clocking, Level-3 is a Node-D, and Level-4 is an (E) Node.

Stratum Level-1

Stratum Level-1 is an atomic clock source known for its accuracy. Needless to say, the price of an atomic clock is high and the cost to house the clock somewhere may be just as high. Compounding the price of an atomic clock, add one or two on-line similar clocks to provide active back-up in case of failure. After you place several atomic clocks on line, combine their outputs to produce one averaged clock.

A Stratum Level-1 clock source accuracy stems from the atomic cesium element. The resultant clock is extremely accurate but not perfect. This small bit of inaccuracy shows up in the standards minimum level.

If the atomic clock received no other influence over 10 or 20 years, the clock frequency shouldn't drift more than one part in 100,000,000,000. Looking at the Stratum Level-1 analog clock frequency of 2,048,000 hertz, one can determine the maximum drift allowed.

```
2,048,000 hertz ×         1          = 0.00002048 hertz
                  100,000,000,000
```

As we said, the clock is accurate but not perfect. How one ascertains that the clock frequency drifted off during the past 20 years is beyond the scope of this book. It is also beyond the scope of normal testing equipment. Drifts between two clocking sources would show on dual-trace oscilloscopes over a period of time.

Stratum Level-2

After the telephone companies implement their Stratum Level-1 clock source, they distribute the 2,048,000 analog clock frequency to the first working level. Stratum Level-2 is really the first clock source for the network. The initial clock frequency phase locks the less accurate frequency generators at these main distribution points. Now a primary frequency for the T-1 lines emanating from this telephone company office best describes the maximum clock drift over a long period.

```
1,544,000 hertz ×       1.6        = 0.024704 hertz
                  100,000,000
```

This clock source is still very accurate but is starting to show signs of a measurable difference. At one time, all the regional switching offices (the highest message switch in the switching hierarchy) had a Stratum Level-2 clock. As more telephone companies install their own master clock frequency, these Level-2 locations will increase.

Stratum Level-3

Getting from a Stratum Level-2 to a Level-3 telephone company office is achieved primarily over the digital network. The accuracy of a Stratum Level-3 clock relies on averaging a number of incoming digital lines, which results in a new nodal clock. Using primary and secondary timing sources sets the Level-3 apart from the previous levels.

Telephone company offices with Digital Cross-Connect Systems and DDS Hub Offices also have a Stratum Level-3 nodal clock. AT&T ACCUNET service functions like the M24 and M44 multiplexers all use the Level-3 clock. It is the highest level of timing accuracy accessible to end-user facilities.

$$1,544,000 \text{ hertz} \times \frac{4.6}{1,000,000} = 7.1024 \text{ hertz}$$

Stratum Level-4

Stratum Level-4 is the worst clock frequency in the entire telephone company network and appears at the last office in the chain. Reference frequencies emanating from the original Stratum Level-1 clock have gone through two degrees of inaccuracy. The recovered clock from the incoming T-1 lines frequency locks another frequency generator. This becomes the clock used to transmit digital signals out to the end-user. One of the reasons DATAPHONE Digital Service has greater accuracy is that it uses a Stratum Level-3 clock. Normally, T-1 services emanating from the local telephone company office use the less accurate Stratum Level-4 clock.

$$1,544,000 \text{ hertz} \times \frac{32}{1,000,000} = 49.408 \text{ hertz}$$

This brings us down to the clock internal to the end-user's terminal. Since the terminal relies on phase locking the frequency from an internal crystal, the results are worse than the worst telephone company clock. If the telephone company end-office operated at the outer limits of the T-1 clock, the end-user could expect to exceed the limit.

Telephone Company Distribution

Figure 5-2 shows a typical telephone company timing distribution system. How many Level-1 master clocks exist in a particular telephone company network depends on their basic needs. Trans Canada Telephone selected two master clock locations — one at Ottawa and the other in Calgary. AT&Ts put one master clock at a protected location in a small Missouri town. It's ironic that AT&T

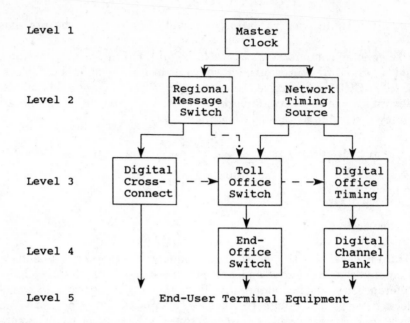

Figure 5-2 Telephone Network Clocking Hierarchy.

clocking must traverse many miles of transmission impairments to get to where it is needed the most.

Other United States telephone companies have opted for independence from AT&T's reference frequency and are installing their own master clocks. As more Stratum Level-1 sources spring up across the country, look for a slight increase in bit slips between networks.

Initially, distribution of the master clock to the Level-2 offices used only analog facilities. Since that early deployment, analog facilities are being phased out in deference to fiber-optic services. Each Level-2 office still remains a regional distribution point.

Level-3 nodal clocks receive their timing frequency over several digital lines. Some of these lines start from other regional timing sources. Nodal clocks average the recovered timing from the different digital facilities and develop a new clock. Deriving a new clock from the various recovered timing clocks depends on the diversity of the received frequencies. If all the recovered clocks were on the plus side, the nodal clock would start off on the high side.

Level-4 clocks locate at the end of the telephone company line. There are exceptions to all rules about timing sources. We show (Figure 5-2) the telephone company end-office switch with a Level-4 timing source. Nevertheless, end-offices that provide switched 56-kb services use a Level-3 clock instead.

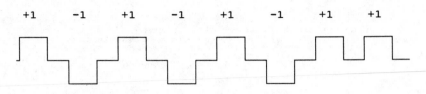

Figure 5-3 Composite Clock.

Composite Frequency Supplies

Telephone company offices have primary frequency generators that phase lock to an incoming master frequency source. The primary operating frequency in any telephone network is 4000 Hz. Multiples of 4000 Hz run everything from the individual channel to the very highest facility carrier system.

A composite clock supply furnishes both 8000 and 64,000 Hz. Timing the Digital Signal Level-0 equipment needs both the 8000- and the 64,000-bps clock. This signal is different from any other digital signal described in Chapter Three. This signal uses a bipolar return- to-zero signal with a violation code every eighth bit (Figure 5-3). It also has a 62.5 % duty cycle that doesn't appear anywhere else in the digital network.

Dealing with Inaccuracies

Uncontrolled Timing Differences

Uncontrolled timing differences are the changes in the original timing frequency other than the ones initiated on purpose. They result from a simple thing like changes in the temperature of the cable carrying the timing frequency standard.

Figure 5-4 shows a pulse traveling across two different cables. For comparison's sake, one cable stretches north to Alaska and the other towards Miami Beach. The Miami-bound cable has a higher environmental temperature, and its characteristic resistance increases. The one going north finds that the temperature has dropped below zero. Its resistance drops along with the operating temperature. Raising the resistance slows the pulses, and they appear closer together when they reach their destination. Clock recovery circuits interpret the closer pulses as being a faster clock than the original source. Lower the resistance and the pulses move faster. The distance between the pulses lengthens, and the end equipment recovers a slower clock. Two cables start out with the identical clock, but now develop distinctly different clocks at the ends.

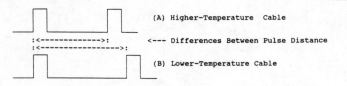

Figure 5-4   Uncontrolled Timing Differences.

Bit-Slips

If you have two Stratum Level-1 clocks in the same network, the difference between them will eventually result in a bit-slip. A bit-slip results from one clocked source being faster or slower than the other. How often a bit-slip occurs depends on the timing difference.

Digitized voice circuits go unscathed from even very high rates of bit-slips. Analog data circuits without built-in error correction may experience an error. Nevertheless, digital data circuits feel even the lowest number of bit-slips. A bit-slip can be either an extra bit inserted in the data stream or the omission of an expected bit.

Bit Stuffing

Reducing the clock differences between telephone company offices is a controlled timing difference. Telephone multiplexers purposely adds bits into the composite stream to adjust for time differences. Bit stuffing is a better name for this process. Stuff bits always appear in the aggregate data stream. If the transmitting end senses a need for a stuff bit, it notifies the other end to use one of the bits.

Plesiochronous Operation

Plesiochronous operation is a pretentious name for connecting two distinct digital networks with separate clocks. In Greek, *plesio* means close and *chronos* means time. Close-time operation merely means using two very close timing sources.

If the two networks are interconnected at a Stratum Level-2 point, the worst case scenario for the number of bit-slips during the day remains small. It is so small that one can think of it as being almost slip-free. You could see the difference with an oscilloscope monitoring the two networks. Connect the two digital networks at a Level-3 point and the drift between the two networks becomes noticeable.

Synchronous Networks

T-1 services refer to the digital networks as isochronous or asynchronous in nature. The following definitions remain valid over the years even if people adapt the names to mean other things.

AXIOM: Isochronous — Serial binary transmission where the digital terminal equipment recovers timing from the received pulses.

AXIOM: Synchronous — Serial binary transmission where the digital communications equipment recovers clock from the received pulses *and* supplies clock to the terminal equipment.

AXIOM: Asynchronous — Serial binary transmission that includes a start and stop bit to identify the data's position. Asynchronous operation refers to data transmission without constraints to a timed event.

Synchronous networks use the telephone company timing system to frequency lock the end-to-end network. The end-user would isochronously lock their equipment to this same source.

DATAPHONE Digital Service

DATAPHONE Digital Service (DDS) was the first synchronous digital network to use accurate nodal clocks to time end-user's access lines. DDS Hub Office equipment transmitted towards the end-user with a Level-3 clock source. If the DDS extended from the Hub Office to an end-office, the end-user would feed off a Level-4 clock.

Data Service Units (DSU) provided the synchronous timing by recovering clock from received pulses on the local loop. While the timing may have originated from a Level-3 source, its stability is missing when it reaches the DSU's clock lead. Phase-Lock-Loop (PLL) circuits in the DSU deliver a clock stream that averages the mean frequency sent but contains a large amount of jitter. End-users planning on using the DSU's clock for a reference source should think twice.

Synchronous DS-3 Transmission — SYNTRAN

When you look at the digital hierarchy in Chapter Three, the Digital Signal Level-3 (DS-3) system uses two multiplexing stages. First the T-1 lines combine into a DS-2 level signal. Next the DS-2 signals combine to make the final DS-3 signal.

DS-3 transmission lines between telephone company offices require the same two stages of demultiplexing to get back to a usable signal. To get to a usable signal, the demultiplexing must return to a T-1 rate. This is the point where the Digital Cross-Connect System can switch DS-0 signals between T-1 lines.

Building a higher-level cross-connect system isn't possible with the present structure. Bit interleaving several layers of digital signals removes any indication of the basic time-slots.

Bell Communications Research has issued technical advisories proposing a synchronous DS-3 system. This kind of digital network permits a DS-3 level Digital Cross-Connect System to break apart the DS-0 time-slots. It also provides the following.

1. Reformatting the Pulse Code Modulated information with robbed-bit signaling into dedicated out-of-band signaling.
2. Convert from line recovered timing to a system clock.
3. Provide real-time monitoring of the DS-3 signal.
4. Provide a DS-3 data link for maintenance and control.

Synchronous Optic Network (SONET)

SONET provides a new outlook on the digital hierarchy and includes additional maintenance controls. It has an electrical signal called the Synchronous Transport Signal–Level 1 (STS-1). The optical counterpart is the Optical Carrier–Level 1 (OC-1) and is a direct conversion of the electric signal.

The difference between SYNTRAN and SONET is that SONET assumes that the entire network is synchronous. SYNTRAN expects to still see remnants of the older types of T-1 services. Some T-1 lines will still need bit-stuffing to account for timing differences. Therefore, SYNTRAN must work equally well with isochronous and synchronous services.

Arriving at a completely synchronous network also depends on the local telephone companies installing accurate clocks in all their offices. Up to this point, the local telephone companies could get away with Level-4 clock sources. Basing a network on a Level-4 source would lead to a high bit-slip rate and poor service.

6

Frames, Formats, and Patterns

Frames, Formats, and Patterns

Framing patterns and frame format play an important role in digital transmission. We purposely make a distinction between frame patterns and format. When T-1 services became available to end-users, there was a general confusion that patterns and format meant the same thing. Unfortunately, the confusion has continued. It becomes convenient to obscure the real facts about equipment by concluding that patterns and format are the same.

Framing patterns are overhead that keep the receiving equipment in synchronization with the transmitting end. Framing format describes the information bit structure. This structure is either bit-interleaved, byte-interleaved, or block oriented.

Bit-Interleaved Format

Bit-interleaving or merging action is somewhat like ordering from a Chinese menu. One bit from Channel-A, one bit from Channel- B, et cetera, et cetera. Multiplexers that have all equal speed data channels take a bit from each channel and arrange the bits in consecutive order (Figure 6-1).

After the multiplexer scans the last channel for a bit, it starts over again with the first channel. The format's simplicity requires very little logic to recognize which bit belongs to which channel. While the format is simple, it still requires a framing pattern to tell the equipment where the channels begin.

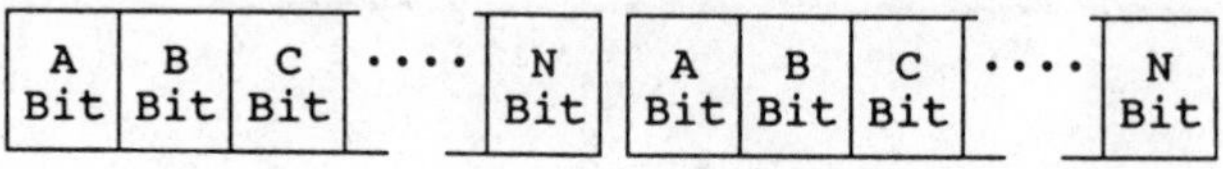

A Bit	B Bit	C Bit	• • • •	N Bit	A Bit	B Bit	C Bit	• • • •	N Bit

Figure 6-1   Bit-Interleaved Format with Equal Data Rates.

Introducing different channel data rates produces a very distinctive frame format. It is so distinctive that both the transmit and receive units need hardware or software instructions. In Figure 6-2, Channel-A and Channel-B run faster than the C Channel. Channel-A in this case is also faster than the B Channel and requires additional bit interleaving.

Another problem with bit-interleaving formats is that they are all different. A bit-interleaved multiplexer from Company ABC will not communicate with Company XYZ's bit-interleaved multiplexer. Proprietary frame patterns and frame formats exist for each manufacturer. There just aren't any standards for bit-oriented formats.

Software instructions require overhead or extra training time to instruct remote equipment. There isn't an easy way to locate bits from an individual channel in an aggregate or bit-interleaved line.

Low-level encryption is a hidden advantage to bit-interleaving. It would take a large amount of computer time to analyze and reconstruct the message from a scrambled bit format. Nevertheless, one should not rely on bit-interleaving as a means of encrypting messages. At best, it will prevent the unsophisticated interloper from picking up information from a piece of test equipment.

Byte-Interleaved Format

Byte-interleaving combines bytes or characters. The early days of digital commercial multiplexing used the term character-interleaving. Then a character had the asynchronous start and stop bit to locate the data information. Multiplexers stripped the start and stop bits as they entered the box. Exiting the remote end, the start and stop bits reappeared.

In the mid 1960s, terminals came in many varieties. They came in 7-, 8- or 9-bit characters. Being asynchronous, they also had a variety of stop bit sizes. Worst of all, a 5–10% terminal overspeed

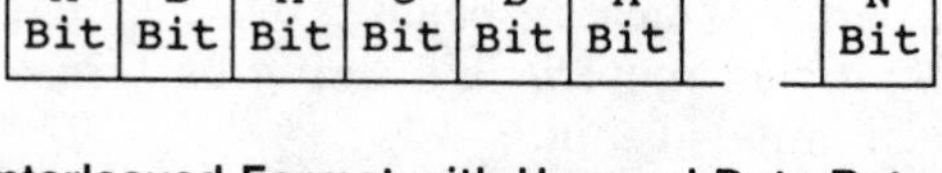

A Bit	B Bit	A Bit	C Bit	B Bit	A Bit	• • • •	N Bit

Figure 6-2   Bit-Interleaved Format with Unequal Data Rates.

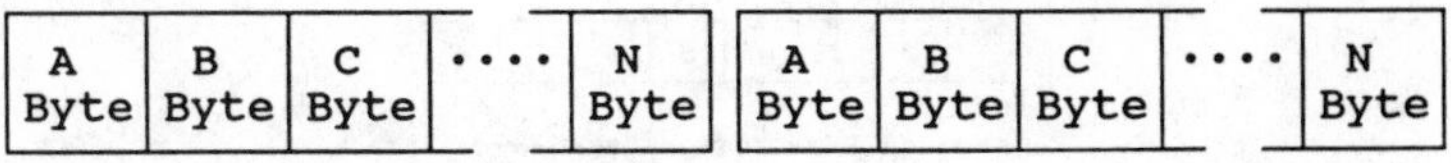

A Byte	B Byte	C Byte	····	N Byte	A Byte	B Byte	C Byte	····	N Byte

Figure 6-3 Byte Interleaving.

was common. This wouldn't phase the modems of the day, but played havoc with digital multiplexers.

Circuit design accounted for overspeed. Terminals faster than 5% overspeed usually led to troubles. Also, multiplexers treated character speed similar to terminal overspeed. One terminal used a 7-bit character transmitting at a 300-bps rate. To the multiplexer, the terminal appeared as 33.3 characters per second. What it really expected from a 300-bps channel was only 30 characters per second. Asking multiplexer manufacturers how their equipment handled that particular terminal usually elicited cold sweat and ashen faces.

Mixed data rate byte-interleaving faces the same structural problems as mixed speed bit-interleaving. Extra bytes appear in the basic frame format (Figure 6-3) to compensate for the higher operating speed. Pseudo-encryption properties from the distribution of bytes lessen when compared to bit-interleaving.

Block-Oriented Frame Formats

Block-oriented units have frame formats that differ from the accepted digital standard. Aydin-Monitor, Inc. blocks 40 samples from one channel in an 192 bit frame. Digi-Voice, Inc. digitally compresses 21 voice channels into a 512 bit frame. Verilink, Inc. uses a 768-bit frame for clear channel transmission (see Chapter Fourteen).

T-1 equipment that relies on nonstandard frame block structures can lead to trouble. Locating the beginning of the block format sometimes depends on its position in respect to the frame pattern (193rd-bit position). When the framing pattern changes its relationship, the units fall out of synchronization. AT&T calls the reliance on a framing pattern position Superframe Integrity. Explaining what that is requires an understanding of information contained in later chapters. Chapter Fifteen, Telephone Networking Transmission Constraints, details the problems expected from superframe integrity.

Framing Patterns

Two framing patterns meet telephone company tariff restrictions. They are the D4 and the Extended Superframe Format. The term

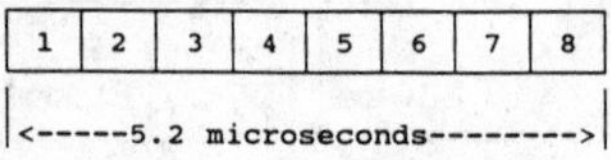

| 1 | 2 | 3 | 4 | 5 | 6 | 7 | 8 |

`|<-----5.2 microseconds-------->|`

Figure 6-4   Basic Building Block.

Extended Superframe Format is another misleading statement. As it is a framing pattern and not a format.

AXIOM — Format is a contiguous sequence of bits or bytes formed serially in a periodic structure.

AXIOM — A frame is one period of the format structure identified by a start (beginning) and stop (end) framing pattern bit. The stop bit of one frame is the start bit of the next frame.

AXIOM — Patterns are a sequence of bits that appear at the start-stop bit positions of the frame a bit at a time. In the case of D4 and ESF patterns, every 193rd bit position belongs to a framing pattern bit. The European frame pattern appears as an eight-bit byte in the first time-slot.

This brings us back to our original premise there is a framing pattern and a framing format. There should be a clear cut differentiation between the two. It is too late to change the name Extended Superframe Format to Extended Superframe Pattern. Nevertheless, one can think the acronym ESF really means Extended Super Frame and forget about the word format.

Terms Common to Standard Framed Formats

Some of the original writings about digital transmission called the smallest frame structure a Main Frame. A group of main frames was a superframe. Main Frame terminology wandered into obscurity since few people knew the original papers exist. Out of tradition, we will use Main Frame to designate the basic frame format.

Main Frame

Twenty-four basic building blocks (Figure 6-4) is a Main Frame (Figure 6-5) according to the North American Standard. Each basic building block is an 8-bit byte. When the basic building block transmits 8000 times per second, we refer to the resultant 64,000-bps unit as a time slot.

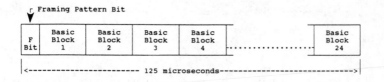

Figure 6-5   Main Frame.

Superframe

A Superframe consists of either 12 or 24 Main Frames, depending on the framing pattern used. A Superframe with a D4 Framing Pattern has only 12 Main Frames before the framing pattern repeats. As the name Extended Superframe implies, the resultant superframe is bigger than the D4 Superframe.

Extended Superframe

Extended Superframe has 24 Main Frames before the framing pattern starts over again. A semantic difference between a D4 Framing Pattern and an Extended Superframe Pattern is that a D4 pattern repeats and ESF starts over again. Only 6 out of 24 bits actually repeat in an Extended Superframe pattern. The other 18 bits vary from superframe to superframe.

D4 Framing Pattern

The D4 Framing Pattern derives its name from the framing pattern used with the D4 Digital Channel Bank. The D2, D3, and D5 Channel Banks all have the same pattern. Since there are more D4 Banks in existence, its association to the framing pattern took precedence.

A D4 Framing Pattern has the bit sequence 100011011100. Some writings place the order of ones and zeroes with a different start and stop position. The sequence stays the same. Also, some have placed the framing bits at the end of the frame. It is easier to understand the functions of the framing bits if we use the bit sequence shown in Figure 6-6.

Trying to remember the D4 Framing Pattern, at first blush, seems beyond normal human retention. On second look, you really only need to remember the first three bits (100). The next three bits are a logic inversion of the first three (011). Now you know the first six bits in the pattern's sequence. To complete the pattern, you need only to logically invert the first string of six bits to get the second six bits.

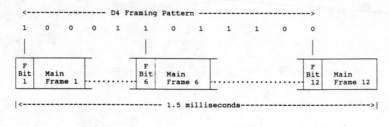

F Bit = Framing Pattern Bit

Figure 6-6   D4 Superframe and Framing Pattern.

A D4 Framing Pattern performs two basic synchronizations. One is for synchronization of the equipment at both ends of the facility. The second designates the Main Frame locations for signaling and signaling supervision. This is important when using in-band signaling or robbed-bit Signaling. Robbed-bit signaling only occurs in the sixth and twelfth Main Frame. Chapter 8 on signaling discusses robbed-bit signaling in detail.

Breaking the D4 Framing Pattern (100011011100) into the two synchronizing patterns, we begin to see the logic of the pattern. Looking at only the odd bits, one sees a new pattern of 101010 called a dotting pattern. Even bit positions made another new pattern (001110) to synchronize position. Again it is easy to look like a memory whiz when writing out that pattern. The first three digits are backward from the (100) you remembered for the entire D4 Pattern. The last three are another logic inversion.

Extended Superframe Patterns

Extended Superframe (ESF) originated after two things happened. First, the end-user knew more about the service than the telephone company. Telephone testing personnel hated the idea that the end-user had a better handle on the service. End-users hated the fact that the telephone had so little in the way to test the service. When one considers that the tariff price for the service includes maintenance, the end-user had every right to feel shortchanged.

The second change was an advance in equipment design that permitted shorter synchronization codes. Quicker response time to framing patterns allowed the reduction of 12 bits of combined synchronization to only six bits.

Testing the service in a real-time situation was the main driving force. Operations personnel had only rudimentary test equipment that wasn't capable of monitoring the service. At best, it could test

Frame Synchronization (F_t)	Signaling Synchronization (F_s)
1	0
0	0
1	1
0	1
1	1
0	0

Table 6-1   D4 Frame and Signaling Synchronization Codes.

for binary-return-to-zero code violations and frame pattern errors. Locating troubles to a particular facility section required weeks of testing effort.

An end-user would complain about a high error rate on the T1 service. Normal testing procedures required the telephone company to ask for a complete release of the service by the end-user. If the errors were really bad, the end-user would release the service right away. Had the error rate just slowed the data retrieval down, there was a good chance for a delay in testing.

Intermittent troubles will drive the best test personnel right up the wall. You wish something would burn out so you could locate the problem and fix it. Remember the last time you took your car to the local garage because it was making a strange sound? Just as you got to the garage, the noise stopped.

ESF's shorter synchronization codes allowed extending the superframe's length to 24 Main Frames (Figure 6-7) before starting over again. Equipment synchronization patterns are still only six framing bits in length before that repeat.

Cyclic Redundancy Code Polynomial-6, or CRC-6 for short, uses another six framing bits. To complete the 24 framing bits, a data link uses the remaining 12 framing bits. Out of the 8000 framing pattern bits, 2000 bps go to synchronization and another 2000 to the CRC. The data link is 4000 bps.

Cyclic Redundancy Codes (CRC)

Cyclic Redundancy Codes (CRC) are simple parity checks of blocks of data. They are simple because the components used to make this complex determination are almost rudimentary. It basically divides a binary number string by a known binary number to arrive at a quotient and a remainder. The remainder is the CRC that rides along with the data.

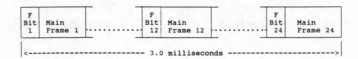

Figure 6-7   Extended Superframe Pattern.

Synchronous or high-level data link control (SDLC — HDLC) used with data communications transmission use CRCs for error detection. You will often see the term CRC-16 for frame check patterns. This means the cyclic redundancy code uses the algebraic polynomial $(x^{16} + x^{12} + x^5 + 1)$. The 16 in CRC-16 indicates the highest degree in the formula. In this case the highest degree is the x raised to the 16th power. If math wasn't a favorite subject for you, CRC-16 says the probability of catching large errors is 1 in 65,536.

Nevertheless, the CRC that checks the data in the 24 Main Frames is an algebraic polynomial $(x^6 + x^5 + 1)$. CRC-6 will catch all small errors but has only a 1 in 64 chance of catching large errors. Using a CRC-6 method gives a 98.4% confidence factor that the formula detects errors. A CRC-16 method gives a 99.999% confidence factor.

$$CRC-6 \ = \ 1 \ - \ (\ 2^{-6} \ ) \ \times \ 100\% \ = \ 98.4\%$$
$$CRC-16 \ = \ 1 \ - \ (\ 2^{-16} \ ) \ \times \ 100\% \ = \ 99.999\%$$

It's ironic that 4608 information bits use a CRC-6 error checking code, while small packet messages on the data link have a CRC-16. Here the main data stream has a 98.4% confidence factor, and small sporadic data messages have a 99.999% factor.

Greater is the irony that the CRC-6 code just detects errors. These errors only become historic data. The CRC-16 code in the data link can initiate a message resend for near error-free transmission.

The designers never had any inclination of how much data would traverse the data link. If they had, the CRC and the Data Channel would reverse sizes.

Superframe Data Link

The superframe's data link bits occupy every odd-bit position in the framing pattern. It uses the standard X.25 Packet protocol to send data between end-user premise and telephone company office equipment. The key concept here is *between equipment*, and that it was not considered a secondary channel for end-user data.

Originally, AT&T ESF designers felt the 4000-bps data link belonged solely to the telephone company. They proposed control signals, maintenance reports, and other telephone-oriented information. Not knowing how much data would traverse the data link left them guarding the 4000 bps with their life. One of the problems on hand was a general lack of understanding of X.25 packet protocol and data throughput.

Since the conception of ESF and its data link, vendors have been fighting for a portion of the capacity. They are perfectly justified in sharing the data link. Packet addresses can separate the telephone company from the vendor. Complex equipment could send commands across the facility to operate switches or change software configurations.

Combining the telephone company's use and the equipment's needs would still leave enough data throughput for channel signaling. Revisions to AT&T's Technical Reference PUB 54016 will reflect the desires of the Exchange Carriers Association to allow vendors and end-users entry to the data link.

Superframe Robbed-Bit Signaling

Robbed-bit signaling (covered in Chapter Eight) appears in every sixth Main Frame (Table 6-2). Some literature refers to superframe robbed-bit signaling as the A, B, C, and D signaling bit (Table 6-3). We have limited the signaling to just an A and B designation, since nobody can think of more than four possible combinations. During the past 25 years, very few signaling needs approached four signaling states. Actually, two combinations provide over 95% of the signaling needs.

Unframed Formats

Frame formats without framing patterns comprise the bulk of local transmission either by fiber-optic cable or microwave systems. Again we get into the gray area of formats and patterns. When the format doesn't have an approved standard framing pattern, it is an unframed format. The units actually transmit with their own framing pattern. This pattern may be just start-of-text and end-of-text words to indicate the frame position.

The only group that the telephone companies allow to transmit unframed formats is the U.S. Government. This is a special case where high-level encryption doesn't permit framing patterns that could indicate sequences of bits.

Framing patterns become a necessity for the telephone companies to test the services. They are also a requirement to interface with

Frame Bit	Frame Sync	CRC	Data Link	Robbed-Bit
1			D	
2		C1		
3			D	
4	0			
5			D	
6		C2		A
7			D	
8	0			
9			D	
10		C3		
11			D	
12	1			B
13			D	
14		C4		
15			D	
16	0			
17			D	
18		C5		A
19			D	
20	1			
21			D	
22		C6		
23			D	
24	1			B

A & B = Signaling States
    C = Cyclic Redundancy Code Bit
    D = Data Bit

Table 6-2 ESF Pattern Positions.

Combinations	A	B	A	B	C	D
1	0	0	0	0	0	0
2	0	1	0	0	0	1
3	1	0	0	0	1	0
4	1	1	0	0	1	1
5			0	1	0	0
6			0	1	0	1
7			0	1	1	0
8			0	1	1	1
9			1	0	0	0
10			1	0	0	1
11			1	0	1	0
12			1	0	1	1
13			1	1	0	0
14			1	1	0	1
15			1	1	1	0
16			1	1	1	1

Table 6-3   AB vs. ABCD Signaling Combinations.

telephone company services. Privately owned T-1 facilities without plans to interface with the telephone company can use unframed formats.

An advantage to unframed formats is an 8000-bps increase in available information bits. While this seems great for the bottom line figure, the disadvantages may outweigh the savings. The telephone company has driven the market and design for test equipment. Both the telephone company and the test sets depend on a framing pattern to do their thing.

Testing unframed formats requires taking the facility out of service and putting a framed format in its place. This means two units of test equipment: one to generate a signal and the other to measure the results. Framed formats provide in-service testing, whereas unframed do not. 8000 bits per second of overhead may well be worth the money to make in-service tests.

Digital Channel Bank Format

Telephone company digital channel banks all use 24 time slots to divide a 1.544-Mbps data stream. Some digital channel banks have 24 channels, some 48, and others even 96 channels. They are compatible with each other on a 24-channel basis.

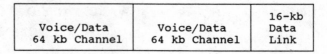

Voice/Data 64 kb Channel	Voice/Data 64 kb Channel	16-kb Data Link

Figure 6-8   ISDN Basic Channel.

Initially, designers thought crosstalk between channels presented concern. As the digital channel bank (D-Bank) evolved, the concern diminished. An incompatibility remains with equipment in use today. Older D-Banks mixed channel positions. D3, D4, and D5 channel banks are in sequential order (Table 6-4).

Private Branch Exchanges that emulate a D2 channel bank present an administrative nightmare when interfaced with newer equipment. Channel 1 on a D2 digital channel bank shares the same time slot that a D4 digital channel bank calls Channel 3. Only time slots 5, 14, and 24 have similar channel number assignments. The prospects of interfacing a D1D channel bank are very slim.

ISDN Basic Channel Format

Integrated Service Digital Network (ISDN) has two configurations. One is the Basic Channel (Figure 6-8) that is also known as the H_0 Channel. Another term is the (2B + D) channel, which clearly states it has two channels for voice or data (B) and data link (D). The general public like (2B + D), telephone companies like Basic, and CCITT literature likes H_0 channel.

ISDN Primary Access Format

Integrated Services Digital Network's Primary Access is the CCITT H_{11} Channel. Again we have the same problem of what to call the thing. Most users know it as (23B + 1D) or just as a T1 line. The telephone companies tout it as a Primary Access, and CCITT as H_{11}.

23B refers to 23 time slots used for both voice or data. The 1D is one time slot used for call processing of the other 23 time slots. One can imagine the B stands for Both (voice and data) and the D means the Data link.

ISDN signaling control goes way beyond simple A and B robbed-bit signaling. It is a complete call processing system that includes the following general categories. A and B signaling at best did on-hook, off-hook, and dial pulses.

Time Slots	Channel Number Assignment		
	D1D	D2	D3 – D5
1	1	12	1
2	13	13	2
3	2	1	3
4	14	17	4
5	3	5	5
6	15	21	6
7	4	9	7
8	16	15	8
9	5	3	9
10	17	19	10
11	6	7	11
12	18	23	12
13	7	11	13
14	19	14	14
15	8	2	15
16	20	18	16
17	9	6	17
18	21	22	18
19	10	10	19
20	22	16	20
21	11	4	21
22	23	20	22
23	12	8	23
24	24	24	24

Table 6-4   Digital Channel Number Assignments.

1. Call origination
2. Called number
3. Forwarding calling number
4. Call set-up acknowledgment
5. Call completion

Summary

Frames, formats, and patterns have three distinctive definitions. Interchanging the terms leads to confusion as to their true meanings. Deliberate misleading to cover deficiencies in systems is not beyond some vendors. To assure definition agreement, meeting and seminar leaders should spend the first part of their session defining terms and acronyms.

Extended Superframe pattern helps telephone companies locate troubles in real time. It provides an historical record of events that happened, and when the telephone networks install a bigger base of ESF monitors, the sectionalization time to locate troubles could be reduced from weeks to minutes.

The ESF's data link has a great potential for other than telephone company use. It has a 4000-bps data packet link that could traverse complex networks and arrive at the proper destination.

7

Coding Methods

The methods of changing analog signals into digital representations come in many flavors. Research and development into coding methods produces many new ways each year. The implementation rate for these new methods is extremely low. It is even more surprising why people spend time and money on data compression while unlimited bandwidth prices continue to drop.

Coding analog signals is an evil necessary to digital transmission. Instead of filling pages with theoretical or minor coding methods, we deal with the five methods that comprise 98% of the market. Pulse Code Modulation accounts for 90–95% of the market since it is the mainstay of the telephone companies. Continuously Variable Slope Delta-modulation gained favor with the multiplexer manufacturers between 1981 and 1986. During 1986, Adaptive Differential Pulse Code Modulation became a standard for 32 kilo-bit voice transmission. Variable Quantizing Level, a proprietary coding method by Aydin-Monitor, presents a coding variation. Lastly, Digital Speech Interpolation discusses another method to concentrate voice channels.

Other coding schemes also change analog signals into digital representations. Some of the schemes are very imaginative but have limited use. Fast or wideband packet voice multiplexers deal with transmission of the digital signals and use the coding methods covered in the book.

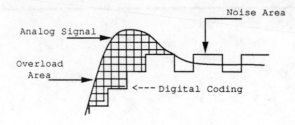

Figure 7-1 Overload Area and Quantizing Noise.

Telling the Difference Between Coding Methods

How manufacturers implement a coding scheme makes a world of difference. Knowing how to tell what the difference is puts one in a commanding position.

> AXIOM — The North American Pulse Code Modulation 64-kb coding is the standard for quality. All other coding methods reduce the level of quality by varying degrees.

Overload Condition

Two major analog waveform properties play havoc with digital encoding: one is the very rapid rise or fall of the analog signal, second is the very flat analog waveform (Figure 7-1).

Very rapid or steep slope changes produce an overload condition. Words like cattle, crisp, and jack will lose their clarity or crispness with an overloaded encoder. Overload really is saying the digital encoding method cannot quickly react to the changes in the analog signal. Reconstruction of the analog signal at the receive end will soften the very harsh sounds. The word cattle may have started off sounding like KaT'l(sic), and ended up sounding like caddle(sic).

Quantizing Noise Area

Flat or nearly flat analog signals do not appear to change. Most coding methods depend on change or the difference between samples. When the signal doesn't change, the reconstructed analog signal at the receive location usually has added noise. This noise is quantizing or granular noise and sounds like frying.

Listening for Overload and Noise

Too many people analyze the speech quality of equipment without knowing what to listen for. Phrases like "How do you hear me?" do not stress the coding method used. People that make a living at voice coding use phrases that include soft sounds as well as harsh sounds. They repeat a phrase like "Asian cattle stay away from the hungry jackals" on the transmit end. Listeners at the receive end then determine the difference between the phrase over a PCM Standard and the new coding method. The experts will record the phrase in both male and a higher-pitched female voice. Higher-pitched voices will stress any overload condition present. Low-pitched male voices will sound acceptable on almost every coding method.

AXIOM — Listener's quality determination is purely subjective. What may be silk purse to one person may be a sow's ear to someone else. One person's opinion should not be the deciding force for any organization.

Toll Quality

As buyers get into the selection of equipment, they are bombarded by vendors' claims. Vendors will state they have Toll Quality or near toll quality. Objective measurement of true toll quality minimum requirements is available. Bell System Technical Reference, PUB43801, November 1982, was one of the last technical references issued before divestiture. Its voice frequency characteristics are still valid.

Frequency Response

The loss measurement of the circuit is made in respect to a 0 dBm0 input of a 1004 Hz tone [dBm0 refers to a decibel unit (db) of power that equals a milliwatt (0.001 watts) of tone]. A 4-wire circuit's receive loss between 300 and 3000 Hz is no greater than plus or minus 0.15 db. Loss at 200 Hz is not greater than 1 db, and the loss at 3400 Hz isn't more than 1.5 db.

Signal to Distortion

The ratio of signal to distortion measurement should not be below 33 db. As the ratio decreases below 30 db, the noise component may be to great for successful data transmission.

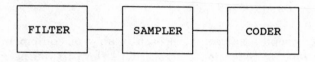

Figure 7-2   Basic Parts to Commercial Coders.

Idle Channel Noise

Idle channel noise should not exceed +23 dBrnc0 (objective is +20 dbrnc0). The unit (dbrn) refers to the ratio of noise to a reference noise level of a picowatt of power (-90 dbm). A dbrnc0 states the noise power uses a C-Message weighting filter at a zero test level point. The C-Message filter closely approximates transmission through the old 500-type Bell System telephone set. Unless you are reading a noise-measuring set, the use of dbrnc0 is meaningless until it's converted to dbm units. Adding the +23 dbrnc0 of noise to the -90 dbm equals -67 dbm of noise. This can now form a ratio with signal power that is already in dbms.

Intermodulation Power

An intermodulation power level lower than -50 dm for the second harmonic and less than -54 dm for the third harmonic.

Peak to Average Ratio

Peak to Average Ratio (P/AR) should have a minimum reading of 94. The old Bell System developed P/AR to provide a simple test of circuits. It never replaced the long-term individual impairment tests. If you receive a reading lower than 94 (no units), the circuit or channel has problems that require individual tests.

Basic Coding Methods

Commercial encoding methods use the same basic parts (Figure 7-2). What they do with the results will set them apart.

Pulse Amplitude Modulation

The encoding or transmitting side of the equipment has a band-limiting filter to reduce the high frequency components of the analog

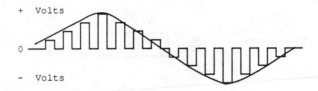

Figure 7-3   Pulse Amplitude Modulation Samples.

signal. Next, it has a Pulse Amplitude Modulation (PAM) section that takes samples of the analog wave (Figure 7-3). PAM is somewhat misleading as to what the section is all about. What it is trying to get across is that there are a stream of pulses whose amplitude varies. The pulse amplitude varies according to the amplitude of the analog signal at the time of the sample.

Decoding the digital code to reconstruct an analog signal also has similar basic parts. One section changes the digital code into variable amplitude pulses. The second section is a shaping filter (Figure 7-4) that softens the extreme excursions of the pulse's amplitudes.

Assigning Digital Codes

Another thing that is common to all commercial coding methods is the assigning a digital code that closely represents the PAM sample. Assigning an infinite number of digital code words for every possible analog amplitude isn't smart or economical. Quantifying the sample applies a logical digital code to a very small range of analog amplitudes. Errors in quantification are small when the range or steps taken is very small. Figure 7-5 shows that the digital code or quantizing level selected for the pulse's amplitude is (1001).

Quantizing

When the digital pulse's amplitude is at the decision line, the quantizer must assign one or the other digital code. Figure 7-6 makes the same quantizing judgment and sends the digital code (1001) to the

Figure 7-4: Shaping filter Action.

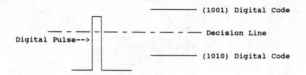

Figure 7-5   Quantizing or Digital Code Selection.

other end. Reconstruction at the receive end will produce a pulse with an amplitude equal to the digital code sent. The difference between the pulse coded at the transmit end and the pulse reconstructed at the receive end is *quantizing error.*

Pulse Code Modulation (PCM)

Today, there are only two standard Pulse Code Modulation (PCM) methods used in the world. The North American standard uses the Mu- Law 255 method and the CCITT uses the A-Law method. What sounds highly technical is really just defining the companding or step size. They both use the same basic coding schemes and use an 8-bit byte to contain the PCM code word. What separates them is the number of companding segments. Mu-Law has 15 companding segments of 7 positive and 7 negative segments. The 15th segment considers the 2 segments located at the center (zero point) as one unit. A-Law PCM uses a 13-segment compander, which changes the digital coding slightly.

Companding

Companding is another term that is somewhat misleading. It is a noise reduction throwback used on the earlier analog N-Carrier system. Ironically, the system was so quiet afterward that they installed

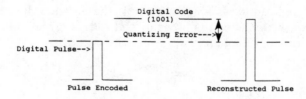

Figure 7-6   Quantizing Error.

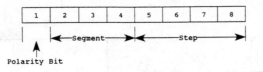

Figure 7-7   PCM Code Word.

neon bulbs on the channel cards to generate a perceived noise level. The N-Carrier squeezed or compressed analog levels at the transmit end. At the receive end, they would expand the levels back to their original level. Combining the words COMpressor and exPANDER arrived at the new word compander.

PCM companding refers to the action of using very small steps between digital code words for very-low-volume signals. Conversely, very large steps occur with high-volume signals. The overall effect is to reduce quantizing errors in the lower volume levels and reduce noise.

Preset steps between digital code words sets PCM off from the other major coding methods. It can use preset steps because its bandwidth of 64 kb provides enough code words for faithful reproduction. Arriving at the total code words brings us back to the magical number of 255 associated with the term mu-Law 255.

Polarity Bit

Figure 7-3 shows the amplitude sampling pulses from the PAM section. First, we note the pulses have a very basic principle of positive and negative polarity. PCM 8-bit code words denote the polarity of the pulse in the first bit's position. A binary one indicates positive polarity and a zero shows negative polarity (Figure 7-7).

Segment Bits

The next portion of the PCM signal describes the segment. Segments, numbered 1 through 8 (Figure 7-8), designate their relative position away from a zero-level signal. Within each segment there are 16 steps or digital code words.

Referring back to the PCM companding action, Segment 8 will span the greatest distance for high-level signals. Since Segment 8 has the same number of coding steps as Segment 1, the step size in the former will be much larger.

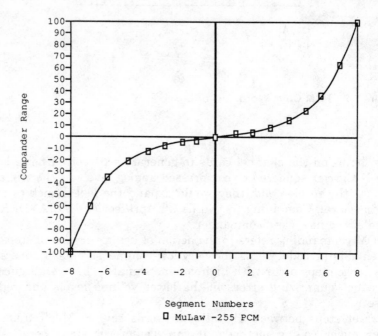

Figure 7-8   Compander Segments.

Step Bits

Polarity occupied the first bit's location in the PCM coded word. Eight segments occupy the next 3 bit locations in the word 000-111. Finishing the code word are the 4 bits needed to indicate the 16 steps within the segment 0000-1111 (Figure 7-9).

Some literature describes the PCM digital signal as a binary 8- bit word. It is not a linear binary representation but instead is a code word for three different parts. If we take the three different parts, we see there could be 256 distinct code words.

```
2 Polarity × 8 Segments × 16 Steps = 256 Codes
```

Chapter Fourteen on Telephone Network Transmission Impairments details ones-density requirements. It basically says the network cannot function properly without sending a certain amount of binary ones. One possible code word could be all zeroes. If we

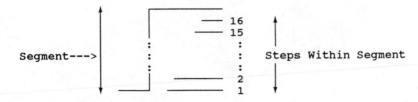

Figure 7-9   Segments and Steps.

eliminated the all-zeroes code word to meet the ones-density requirements, there would only be 255 code words available: hence the
reference to 255 in "Mu-Law 255 Pulse Code Modulation."

As an added ones-density precaution, segment and step coding
uses the greatest amount of ones digits at an idle condition. Coding
with binary ones digits starts at the middle or zero polarity and
decreases towards a binary zero at the extremes.

PCM Sampling

Sampling rate in the PAM section sets PCM apart from the other
coding methods. PCM uses a sampling rate of 8000 times per second.
This more than meets Nyquist's sampling theory of sampling twice
the highest frequency sent. Since 3400 Hz is the highest frequency
sent, 7000 samples per second could satisfy Nyquist's theory.

When PCM was introduced, the telephone networks were oriented
to multiples of 4000 Hz. Every clocking system keys to either a
64,000 Hz or a 4000 Hz frequency supply. Instead of introducing a
new clock set at 7000 events per second, they increased the sample
rate to 8000.

Basic Building Block

PCM's basic transmission block is 64,000 bps. Eight bits form a code
word for each sample. Since there are 8000 samples per second, the
resultant bit rate becomes 64,000.

```
8 bits/sample x 8000 samples/second = 64,000 bits/second
```

Consider what would have happened if the original PCM coding
method used 7000 samples per second. 7000 samples coded by an 8-
bit code word would produce a 56,000 bps basic digital building
block.

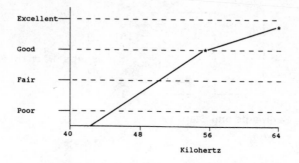

Figure 7-10   Listener Response to Pulse Code Modulation at Different Rates.

PCM Advantages

1. PCM is a coding standard that has the highest quality and meets accepted transmission requirements.
2. Many companies provide the North American Mu-Law 255 PCM Standard. Multiplexer units are compatible with a wide range of equipment.
3. Multiple sources of supply are very available.
4. PCM is compatible with telephone company central office equipment. Voice services are compatible with ISDN switches.
5. Communications evolution requires an open network approach and adherence to strict standards.

PCM Disadvantages

1. PCM requires 64 kpbs of bandwidth for a voice circuit. It is not economical to run low-speed analog data greater than 64 kpbs.
2. Perceived quality (Figure 7-10) of transmission deteriorates quickly with transmission rates below 64 kpbs.

Adaptive Differential Pulse Code Modulation (ADPCM)

ADPCM is a transcoder (Figure 7-11) because it requires a Pulse Code Modulation signal before it can output any signal. It doesn't digitally code an analog signal, but instead changes an 8-bit digital code into a 4-bit code word. Creative minds named the new 4-bit word a NIBBLE to differentiate it from the 8-bit byte.

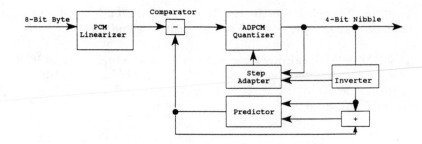

Figure 7-11   ANSI/CCITT Approved ADPCM Transcoder.

Transcoding from PCM to ADPCM Operation

1. As the 8-bit byte Pulse Code Modulation (PCM) signal enters the transcoder, it changes the coded word into a 20-bit linear digital signal.
2. The next section is a comparator, because it compares the new signal entering the unit to one that the device is predicting it will see. The difference between the two feeds to the ADPCM Quantizer.
3. The ADPCM Quantizer is a 7-step quantizer, and its output is in 4-bit nibbles. Bit number 1 indicates the polarity of the signal, and the next 3 bits define the step. If there was no difference between the signals, the ADPCM resultant signal would be 1111. The most positive direction would be 0111 and the most negative would be 1000. Ones density rules prevent sending an all-zero signal.
4. At this point the 4-bit nibble takes three paths. One is to the ADPCM output of the unit and the others are to an Inverter and the Step Adapter. The Inverter changes the ADPCM 4-bit nibble back to a 16-bit linear signal. Information feeds from the Inverter to two other sections. One is the Predictor and the other is the Step Adapter.
5. The Step Adapter locks the size of the Quantizer steps when the unit receives tones or steady power such as data signals. Unlocking the quantizer allows the unit to vary the size of the quantizing steps to account for rapid changes in the signal.
6. Lastly, the Predictor is the crystal ball that guesses what the next signal will look like. It is basically a digital filter.

There are many versions of ADPCM on the market. Each one can only talk to another clone of itself. Even the standard ANSI and CCITT version can be optioned in many ways. The basic telephone company ADPCM unit has four bundles of 11 voice channels and 1 signaling channel. Nevertheless, it can combine both voice and data channels and also provide individual channel signaling.

AXIOM — ADPCM describes a generic transcoding process. It does not guarantee that Brand A's ADPCM will be compatible with Brand B's ADPCM. They should agree to the ANSI and CCITT Standard.

ADPCM and the 202 Type Modem

ADPCM transcoding methods originally had a problem with the 202-type modem in a character mode of operation. As a memory refresher, the 202-type modem uses a Frequency Shift Key (FSK) modulation scheme. It uses two single frequencies (1200 Hz and 2200 Hz) to indicate either a one or a zero. The 202 modem has the simplest design on the market.

When using a 202-type modem in a conversational mode, there are delays between characters. The older ADPCM transcoders tend to mutilate the first characters sent after this delay.

This happened because of several things. One, the 202-type modem's two single frequencies were separated by 1000 Hz. During the delay time between characters, the modem sends an idle or steady mark indication. Detection of the single tone by the Step Adapter locked the quantizing steps. As soon as the first space bit appeared, there were alternations between frequencies.

The Predictor would be way off-base as to what it thought the signal should be. Also, the Quantizer was in a locked condition and could not rapidly change the step size to adjust for the vast difference. When reconstructing the signal at the receive end, the character would be nothing close to the original one transmitted.

Continuous data transmission from a 202-type modem passed good data. Other FSK modems like a 103 type did not exhibit any problem when used in a conversational mode. Their frequencies are very close and the unit could react quickly. Faster speed modems did not have any problem because they used scrambling techniques. Phase Shift Keying and Quadrature Amplitude Modulation presented no vast frequency differences, and the power level was steady.

A fix made dramatic improvements to the problem by changing an algorithm in one of the integrated circuits. This fix adjusts the sensitivity of the Step Adapter so it could adapt more quickly to a drastic change. As with any design modification, you run the risk of producing other problems. The only drawback is a less than 1 db decrease in its overall Signal Noise Ratio (SNR).

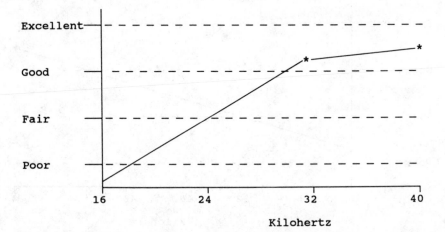

Figure 7-12   Listener Response to Adaptive Differential PCM.

Basic Transmission Rate of ADPCM

ADPCM transcoders have a basic transmission rate of 32,000 bps. If the ADPCM channel uses robbed-bit signaling, the effective quality equals an ADPCM signal transmitting around 28,000 bps. Chapter Eight on signaling details robbed-bit signaling.

ADPCM Advantages

1. Subjectively close to the toll quality of regular PCM transmission.
2. ANSI and CCITT Standard ADPCM. Open network architecture between countries available.
3. Compatible with telephone company services.

ADPCM Disadvantages

1. Telephone companies support only 4800 bps analog data over ADPCM. Being very conservative, they support 4800 bps over several analog to digital transcodings. They could support 9600-bps analog data over one transcoding. Modems over 9600-bps cannot work over ADPCM.
2. Robbed-bit signaling reduces the effective quality (Figure 7-12) below 32,000 bps. Analog data reduces to 2400 bps and below.

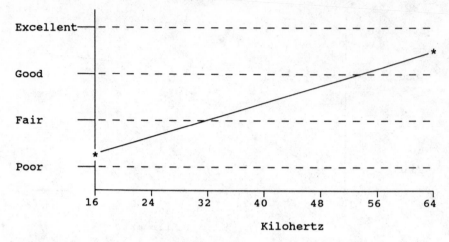

Figure 7-13   Listener Response to Continuously Variable Slope
Delta-Modulation at Different Rates.

Continuous Variable Slope Delta (CVSD) Modulation

Continuous Variable Slope Delta (CVSD) Modulation is another
name for Adaptive Delta Modulation. As the term delta modulation
may indicate, coding looks at only changes or differences in samples
of the analog signal. The term adaptive gives the clue that the quantizing step size varies.

CVSD use surged between 1981 and 1986. One reason was the
relative ease in building an integrated circuit for manufacturers. The
second reason was the hesitation of standards groups to endorse an
ADPCM Standard.

Its format adapts readily to bit-interleaved multiplexers. When the
great T-1 revolution started, the prominent end-user-oriented multiplexers were all bit-interleaved. This was a normal operation for
lower-speed synchronous multiplexers since the late 1960s. It was a
natural evolution to just increase the operating speed to 1,544,000
bps instead of format changes.

CVSD Sampling

Sampling for CVSD differs from PCM. Nyquist's theory isn't in
jeopardy because the sampling rate is usually 32,000 bps. It can
operate at higher or lower rates by varying the clock input to the integrated circuit. Lower operating rates result in poorer quality
(Figure 7-13).

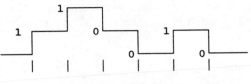

32,000-bps Samples

Figure 7-14   CVSD Coding.

Since the normal sampling rate is 32,000 bps, the coding is simplistic. Upward or positive direction analog signals encode as ones bits, and downward directions code as zeroes bits (Figure 7-14). It looks for the change instead of the magnitude of the signal.

Regular delta-modulation cannot follow rapid analog changes. Overload conditions occur and the quality of the voice reproduction is poor. Adapting or changing the step size to cover greater distances became necessary (Figure 7-15). A rapid change in the analog signal will cause long strings of ones or zeroes.

Knowing this basic principle, one only has to count the ones and zeroes to determine when to adjust the amount of change being measured. CVSD counts four ones or zeroes and then increases the step size.

CVSD Advantages

1. Economic alternative for manufacturers of bit-interleaved multiplexers. Available CVSD integrated circuits came from several sources to drive the price down.
2. Bit-oriented structure of CVSD was a natural extension of the bit-interleaved multiplexer format.

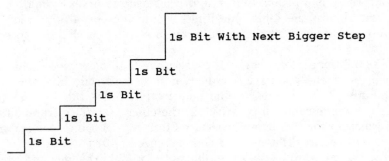

Figure 7-15   Changing CVSD Step Size.

3. Understanding CVSD voice conversations during severe error conditions is much better than PCM conversations.

CVSD Disadvantages

1. Quality decreases on a linear basis from good around 48 kbps to poor at 16 kpbs. Using CVSD below 32 kbps, to achieve greater bit compression, pays a heavy penalty of dissatisfied users.
2. Poor reaction to extreme overload conditions. May not be satisfactory for interfacing with customers or executive use.
3. Prone to quantizing or granular noise. May not be satisfactory for analog data modems over 2400 bps. Many manufacturers claim at least 4800-bps modem speeds, but these may be minimal levels.

Variable Quantizing Level Encoding

Variable Quantizing Level (VQL) is Aydin-Monitor, Inc.'s adaptation of the NEC, Inc Nearly Instantaneous Companding (NIC) scheme. VQL starts out with the normal PCM approach of sampling the analog signal. Instead of sampling 8000 times per second in the PAM section, they sample 6666 2/3 times per second. With a reduction in the sampling process, the upper end of the frequency bandwidth reduces to something around 3000 Hz.

Analysis of 40 samples from a particular channel takes place. A maximum amplitude (MA) signal of the 40 samples selects the step size of a secondary quantizing process. This value then codes into a 6-bit word. One of the more important parts of the VQL system is the setting of secondary quantizing levels. The greater the signal, the greater the size of 11 linear quantizing steps. Digital representation of an 11-step quantizer requires a 4-bit code. Just as with encoding PCM, there is a polarity bit assigned for each sample. By adding the polarity bit to the 4-bit code, there would now be a 5-bit code per sample. Using a 5-bit code results in an equivalent channel speed of 35,333 bps.

Assumptions are that 40 consecutive samples would have a majority of one polarity. A reduction in overall code bits occurs by combining two samples to one polarity bit. Since the two samples have only one common polarity bit, the effective bits to transmit the information for two samples reduces to 9 bits (4.5 bits per sample). This now reduces the effective channel speed to 32,000 bps.

An 192-bit word or packet builds out of a 12-bit header and the 40 samples for the particular channel. Each header has the 6-bit MA

$$\frac{1.536 \text{ Mb}}{\text{Second}} \times \frac{1 \text{ VQL Word}}{192 \text{ bits}} = \frac{8000 \text{ VQL Words}}{\text{Second}}$$

$$\frac{8000 \text{ VQL Words}}{\text{Second}} \times \frac{40 \text{ Samples}}{\text{VQL Word}} = \frac{320,000 \text{ Samples}}{\text{Second}}$$

$$\frac{320,000 \text{ Samples}}{\text{Second}} \times \frac{1 \text{ Channel}}{6666.7 \text{ Samples}} = 48 \text{ Channels}$$

$$\frac{1,536,000 \text{ bps}}{48 \text{ Channels}} = \frac{32,000 \text{ bps}}{\text{Channel}}$$

Table 7-1   Variable Quantizing Level Calculations.

code, a 2-bit signaling indication for the particular channel, and a 4-bit Forward Error Correcting (FEC) code. FEC protects the MA indication that will set the size of the quantizing level at the other end. The 40 4.5-bit samples complete the frame.

```
Maximum amplitude + Signaling Bits + FEC      + 40 Channels   =
       6 bits)       +      (2 bits)    + (4 bits) + 40 x 4.5 bits =
               12 bits                  +  180 bits           = 192 bits/
                                                                VQL word
```

When looking at the logical sense of this scheme we have to do a little math (Table 7-1) to make it have some meaning.

VQL Advantages

1. Less quantizing noise heard than CVSD.
2. Data compression of the voice signal to 32,000 bps. Aydin-Monitor also offers a Digital Speech Interpolation method that provides a maximum of 96 voice channels on a T1 line.

VQL Disadvantages

1. Proprietary coding method by Aydin-Monitor, Inc. No other manufacturer uses this method.

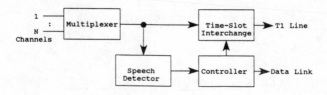

Figure 7-16   Digital Speech Interpolation.

2. Analog data limited to 9600 bps on a point-to-point basis. Extensions of the analog service off the coder may introduce impairments that preclude transmitting at 9600 bps.

Digital Speech Interpolation (DSI)

Digital speech interpolation (DSI) grew out of the analog Time Assignment Speech Interpolation (TASI) system. TASI relied on pauses between bursts of speech to assign more channels into a given high-speed line. By looking for active voice patterns, the TASI equipment could switch a larger number of circuits in and out of the aggregate high-speed facility.

The high cost of underseas cables to Europe prompted the telephone companies to devise ways to cheaply add more circuits. During World War II, the telephone companies split some voice channels in half and crammed two conversations over one circuit. Both methods had their drawbacks. Split channels cut down on the overall quality of the voice. TASI suffered from clipping of the voice.

DSI assigns various time slots to active talkers. A speech detector monitors the multiplexer's output (Figure 7-16) and swaps active time slots into inactive spaces. Time-slot assignment information travels on a dedicated time slot to the other end to unravel the time slots.

Besides switching time slots around, a DSI system can also gracefully degrade its channels by dropping bits out of each channel. Channel degradation can start with just a few channels and progress through all the inputs.

Digital Speech Interpolation Advantages

1. Bottom line economics improves by sharing the transmission cost with more channels.
2. Unless the voice capacity is grossly underestimated, the quality of the voice channels is quite adequate for business internal communications.

Digital Speech Interpolation Disadvantages

1. Half-duplex operation of analog data circuits will not perform properly over DSI type circuits. Full-duplex operation of analog data circuits will reduce available time slots for voice assignment.

2. Quality of the voice circuits may degrade to an unacceptable point during heavy traffic periods. Not recommended for external customer contact.

Summary

There are a variety of strange coding methods on the marketplace. They comprise a very small portion of available equipment and were left out of this writing. Some are very ingenious, and the designers deserve credit for original thought. While they may look attractive when judged on economics alone, they are lower in voice and analog data quality than PCM and ADPCM.

Most designers feel all data will be hardwired directly to digital data channels. Contrary to marketing and engineering digital direction, analog modems are getting faster and cheaper. They are not going away. Coding methods should account for analog data running at least 9600 bps. Higher-speed dial-up modems are already available as plug-in boards to personal computers.

Picking the right coding method for your organization is a large task. Too often the choice doesn't go past the bottom line, and people overlook other features. Quality, low failure rates, and adapting to a changing communications world should rate along with economics. Convincing people with a bottom line mentality takes a greater effort.

8

Signaling Supervision,
Signaling, and Call Processing

Often the three terms signaling supervision, signaling, and call
processing blend into the same meaning. Signaling supervision
provides the simple on-hook or off-hook indications. Signaling
provides either dial pulses or tones to send call information. Call
processing is a way to send messages about the status of the call.
This status covers call origination, acceptance, acknowledgment, and
completion.

Signaling Supervision

On-hook and off-hook are ancient telephone company names for in or
out of service. An on-hook condition says the telephone handset is in
its holder and the circuit is open. Old time telephones had a hook to
hold the earphone. It was a dual purpose component serving as both
a switch and a hook. Consequently, the telephone term of a switch
hook now refers to all on-off buttons under the handset rest.

Off-hook means the removal of the earphone from the hook and
the switch connecting the line for use. Seizure is another telephone
company name for connecting a circuit.

Signaling supervision occurs when initiating a call. A caller
decides to dial another person. The caller lifts his handset off the
telephone base or seizes the line. Seizing the line alerts the switching machine that someone wants to make a call. The switch acknow-

ledges the caller's request and sends dial tone to notify the caller to proceed with the call set-up.

At the end of the conversation, either the called or calling party hangs up or goes on-hook. A disconnect process tells the switch to stop billing for the call and release the equipment used for the call.

For a number of years the telephone company used single-frequency units to control the seizing of trunks between switching machines. They delivered a 2600-Hz tone until the switching machine seized the trunk. Disappearance of tone told the other end that the trunk had a request for service and signaling information would follow.

Another form of signaling supervision is the wink start. Delays between seizing the trunk and sending called numbers presumed the equipment was ready for reception. Instead of assuming the distant switching machine was ready for signaling information, the wink start provided a positive response. After the initial seizure completed, the distant switching machine would flash or wink a pulse to the originating switch. This indicated the distant switch had equipment on line to receive the called numbers.

Signaling

Signaling with dial pulses is just an extension of the signaling supervision. As soon as the signaling supervision establishes a circuit connection, it is in an off-hook state. Toggling a string of on-hooks and off-hooks is the same as sending pulses and no pulses. A string of 10 on-hooks or pulses means the number 10. Longer off-hook periods between strings of pulses separated the numbers dialed.

Using tones to signal may take two different forms. One is the single-frequency signaling unit that provides signaling supervision over the older telephone system. The other method is the familiar use of dual-tone frequencies from the telephone handset. Telephone companies use a different set of dual-tone frequencies between switching machines to convey signaling information. A telephone handset's dual tones use two out of seven different frequencies. Telephone companies use multifrequency (MF) tones, which are two out of five frequencies strictly for telephone business. People on the outside found that they could access the long distance network and make fraudulent calls with a tone generator or the infamous "blue box." After the telephone company discovered they were losing millions of dollars, they changed their network to prevent outside use of multifrequencies.

MF pulses introduced calling-number forwarding to centralized automatic billing machines as well as the called number. It also gave operators greater control of the telephone call processing. This was the start of the phase in message switching that went beyond just signaling.

Call Processing

Call processing provides status about the switched message circuit. At one time this process belonged only between telephone company switches. The promise of ISDN moves the call-processing feature out to the end-user's location. Private Branch Exchanges (PBX) or any of the newer digital end-user premise switches will emulate what the telephone company always did.

Common Channel Interoffice Signaling (CCIS) introduced the first out-of-band signaling. All the intermachine trunks (facilities between switching machines) sent the signaling and call supervision over a separate dedicated circuit. CCIS sent packets of data long before commercial packet transmission became popular.

CCIS's accomplishment was the ability to use a data base besides simple call processing. Accessing central data bases during the call became available due to the speed of the CCIS operation. Call set-up first verifies that the call can complete before signaling. Data bases screen the calling number to check if the caller can make that type of call. Equipment and called number availability pass the test of the data base. Telephone network services permitted end-users to dial one number and have the call complete to a totally different number.

Basic Signaling — A & B Bit Transfer

Transferring signaling between locations takes several methods. A and B signaling bits are a simple designation for the digital stand-ard. Manufacturers of bit-interleaved and block-oriented multiplexers usually bury the signaling bits in their framing patterns. If they offer only E & M Signaling, there is a good chance they offer just two combinations with one binary digit.

Binary digits with A & B bit signaling supervision permits four possible combinations (Table 8-1). What the combinations mean depends on the systems that connect to the multiplexers. The systems are PBXs, telephone end-users, or switching machines.

Loop-Start and Ground-Start Signaling use the full four combinations of ones and zeroes. Supervision goes through a number of steps beyond open and closed circuit. Multiplexers that have only one signaling bit cannot pass the information needed.

A Bit	B Bit	Dial Pulse	E & M
0	0	Loop Open	M-Lead Ground or Open
0	1	—	—
1	0	—	—
1	1	Loop Closure	M-Lead Battery

Table 8-1   A and B Bit-Signaling Supervision.

E & M, Loop, and Ground Start are the common signaling arrangements available. There are others that pertain more to the telephone companies than an end-user base.

Robbed-Bit Signaling

The first PCM coding method used the 8th bit location of every time slot in every frame. This method sacrificed the quality of the voice transmission for signaling. A second method improved the quality of the PCM coding by robbing a bit in the time slots every 6th Main Frame. In the case of the D4 Frame, the 6th and 12th Main Frame carried signaling. A Superframe has signaling in the 6th, 12th, 18th and 24th Main Frames.

Robbed-bit signaling is exactly what it says. It steals or over rides the 8th bit in each time slot in every 6th Main Frame. One finds the A signaling bit in the 6th (18th) frame and the B signaling bit in the 12th (24th) Main Frame.

A standard PCM byte's last 4 bits indicate the step associated with a particular segment. Taking the least significant (Figure 8-1) or 8th bit from the byte causes the least damage. Least damage means the quality of the restored signal closely approximates the original signal. Using only every 6th Main Frame (Figure 8-2) to steal the 8th bit lessens the damage even more.

Some literature and manufacturers refer to the standard PCM as an equivalent 7 5/6 bit byte instead of an 8-bit byte (Table 8-2). They are really talking about robbed-bit signaling using the least significant bit every 6th Main Frame. When not using the robbed-bit signaling option, the multiplexer would use the full 8-bit bytes in every main frame.

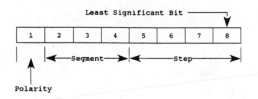

Figure 8-1   PCM Code Word.

When you get into the finer points of PCM coding, you will see a change in the quantizer during robbed-bit signaling. Quantizing steps change from a Mid-Riser to a Mid-Tread to improve the quality of these signaling Main Frames. Thankfully, the manufacturers of PCM integrated circuits have included all the small details.

E & M Signaling

E & M Signaling is the most common signaling used in the telephone network. It is very popular with many manufacturers of multiplexers because of its limited binary states.

Trying to remember what E & M stands for goes back to a simple method drummed into some telephone workers over the years. The receive signaling lead was the E-Lead, since the word receive had an E. And the transmit signaling lead was the M-Lead since the word transmit had the M. Other telephone people used the reference E for ear for receiving and M for mouth and transmitting.

All this was very simple when you were on one end of the circuit. Nevertheless, looking at the circuit in the middle always caused problems. Testing signaling pulses on one side of the office were on the E-Lead and on the other side the pulses were on the M-Lead. At that point, one would go through the little drill of E is receive and M is transmit.

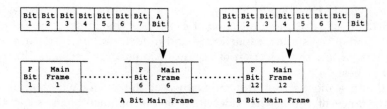

Figure 8-2   Robbed-Bit Location.

$$\frac{8 \text{ Bits}}{\text{Byte}} \times 5 \text{ Bytes} = 40 \text{ Bits}$$

$$\frac{7 \text{ Bits}}{\text{Byte}} \times 1 \text{ Byte} = 7 \text{ Bits}$$

$$\overline{ 47 \text{ Bits}}$$

$$\frac{47 \text{ Bits}}{6 \text{ Bytes}} = \frac{7 \ 5/6 \text{ Bits}}{\text{Byte}}$$

Table 8-2   Robbed-Bit Equivalent PCM Signal.

Loop-Start Signaling

Loop-start signaling is another common method of signaling used for many subscribers. Subscriber loop services are finding their way into long distance switches via T-1 lines. Testing A & B Bit signaling conditions requires some knowledge of what is going on during call set-up.

Foreign Exchange Office (FXO) circuit boards take the place of the normal D-Bank Channel Card. You will see the designation of FXO for the Central Office or switch end of the circuit (Figure 8-3).

The circuit board used in the D-Bank close to the end-user has a Foreign Exchange Station or a FXS card. Just remember FXS stands for station or end-user and FXO means the telephone office.

One item that is common to Loop-Start, Ground-Start, and 2-Wire E & M Signaling is a hybrid network. The 2- to 4-wire hybrid provides transformer coils and return-loss balance components. Transformer coils isolate the 2-wire section from the 4-wire section and transfers energy between the two. Balance components are critical to reduce echo to the circuit.

Echo return is a function of the selection of balance components in the hybrid. How much energy reflects or returns depends on the selection of resistors and capacitors. Since the impedance (a combination of resistance, capacitance and inductance) of the 2- or 4-wire circuit varies, the selection of balance components becomes theoretical at best.

Balance means that the impedance of the 2-wire side equals the impedance of the 4-wire side. Picture the balance beam scale that has too much weight on one side. When balance no longer exists, the heavier side is lower. With electrical circuits, the imbalance reflects

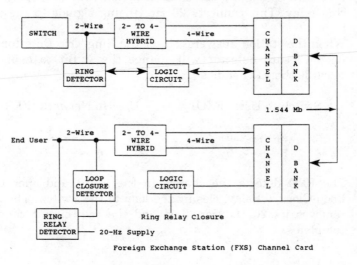

Foreign Exchange Office (FXO) Channel Card

Foreign Exchange Station (FXS) Channel Card

Figure 8-3   Loop Start Signaling.

energy back into the circuit. Reflected energy and propagation delay produce a perceived echo.

Loop-Start Call from the Network

1. Idle condition: No connection from the switch to the user's line, and the user is on-hook.

Switch to User (FXO)	User to Network (FXS)
A----> 0	0 <----A
B----> 1	1 <----B

2. FXO card detects 20 Hz ringing from the Switch. The B Signaling Bit changes to a zero towards the D-Bank at the station end.

Switch to User (FXO)	User to Network (FXS)
A----> 0	0 <----A
B----> 0	1 <----B

3. FXS card recognizes the change in the B-Bit and operates the ring relay. This connects 20 Hz ringing signals to the station loop.

4. When the station answers, either the Ring Trip Detector or the Loop Closure detector will change the A Bit to a one back towards the FXO end.

```
        Switch to User (FXO)           User to Network (FXS)


        A----> 0                       1 <----A
        B----> 0                       1 <----B
```

5. The FXO detects the change in the A Bit and operates the Loop Closure Relay, closing the loop to the Switch. The Switch removes its 20 Hz signaling, and the talk circuit connection completes.

Loop-Start Call to the Network

1. Idle condition: No connection from the switch to the user's line and the user is on-hook.

```
        Switch to User (FXO)           User to Network (FXS)


        A----> 0  .                    0 <----A
        B----> 1                       1 <----B
```

2. User picks up telephone handset: FXS Card Loop Closure Detector recognizes an off-hook by the user. It changes the A Bit from a zero to a one towards the switch end.

```
        Switch to User (FXO)           User to Network (FXS)


        A----> 0                       1 <----A
        B----> 1                       1 <----B
```

3. The FXO card recognizes the change and closes the Line Closure Relay. Dial Tone from the switch connects to the circuit.

4. User hears dial tone and dials desired number. Dial pulses received by the FXS are opens and closes on the station loop. The FXO sees dial pulses as A Bits toggling between ones and zeroes. The Loop Closure Relay in turn pulses to the Switch. After completing pulsing, the talking circuit completes.

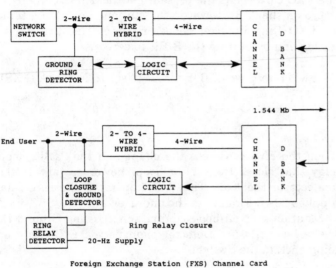

Figure 8-4   Ground Start Signaling.

Ground-Start Signaling

Ground-Start Signaling extended the range of Loop-Start Signaling (Figure 8-4). It is a little more complex than the Loop-Start and the A and B Bits respond differently.

Ground-Start Call from the Network

1. Idle condition: No connection from the switch to the user's line and the user is on-hook.

Switch to User (FXO)	User to Network (FXS)
A----> 1	0 <----A
B----> 1	1 <----B

2. When calling the end-user, the Switch connects to the circuit. A ground condition appears on the Tip Lead (2-wire designates the two leads as Tip and Ring). 20 Hz ringing also connects to the loop from the Switch.

3. The FXO card sends the presence of the Tip Ground by sending a zero on the A Bit towards the station end. At the same time, the FXO Ring Detector senses ringing. This transmits to the station end by putting the B Bit to zero also.

        Switch to User (FXO)   User to Network (FXS)

            A----> 0   0 <----A
            B----> 0   1 <----B

4. When the FXS card sees the change on the A Bit, it operates relay that closes the station loop. Power or talk battery also connects to the loop. The B Bit operates the ring relay that supplies 20-Hz ringing to the end-user.
5. The station goes off-hook, and either the Ring Ground Detector or the Loop Closure Detector changes the A Bit to a ones bit going back to the Switch.

        Switch to User (FXO)   User to Network (FXS)

            A----> 0   1 <----A
            B----> 0   1 <----B

6. The FXO card then senses the change in Bit A and closes the Loop Closure Relay to complete the talking circuit.

Ground-Start Call to the Network

1. Idle condition: No connection from the switch to the user's line, and the user is on-hook.

        Switch to User (FXO)   User to Network (FXS)

            A----> 1   0 <----A
            B----> 1   1 <----B

2. When the station goes off-hook, a ground connects to the Ring Lead of the station loop. The FXS ring ground detector senses the ground and changes the B Bit to a zero. The FXO card sees the change in the B Bit and operates the Ring Relay, placing a ring ground on the Ring Lead to the Switch.

        Switch to User (FXO)   User to Network (FXS)

            A----> 1   0 <----A
            B----> 1   0 <----B

3. When the Switch sees the ring ground, it answers back with a ground on the Tip Lead. The FXO Card detects ground on the Tip Lead and changes the A Bit back towards the end-user to a zero.

```
    Switch to User (FXO)          User to Network (FXS)


         A----> 0                      0 <----A
         B----> 1                      0 <----B
```

4. The FXS senses the change in the A Bit from the Switch and operates the Tip Lead ground relay. This in turn feeds power or talk battery to the station by closing the loop.
5. As the Tip Lead ground relay operates, it converts the detector from ring ground to loop closure. This reverses the A Bit and B Bit condition from the user to network.

```
    Switch to User (FXO)          User to Network (FXS)


         A----> 0                      1 <----A
         B----> 1                      1 <----B
```

6. Sensing the change in the A and B Bits, the FXO card closes the loop to the Switch and releases the ground on the Ring Lead. Dial tone from the Switch connects to the circuit and the end-user dials. Dial pulses transmit to the Switch by toggling the A Bit.

CCITT Signaling System 7

Developing a standard international telephone company signaling system has taken many years. The basis for the CCITT-7 grew out of the AT&T Common Channel Interoffice Signaling (CCIS). The resultant system now allows signaling to traverse several different networks. Like so many other international standards, the United States has its own version of the CCITT-7 protocol.

CCIS sent cryptic notations in very short packets as a replacement to multifrequency pulses. It used separate 2400-bps data lines to transmit 1200 bps of information. Two 2400-bps lines transmitted the full 2400 bits of information. If one line went out, the full 2400 bits of information would transmit over one line. While that should be adequate protection of the signaling lines, there was a complete redundant hot-spare package. What resulted was the installation of four data lines and eight 2400-bps modems to transmit short packet data. Innovative ideas on ways to use CCIS were encouraged and the traffic load on the system increased. Alleviating the strain on the system meant going to 4800-bps modems.

Divestiture of the Bell System played a funny trick on the national telephone system. The AT&T-Long Lines Department was the source of all development money for CCIS. That meant CCIS became the sole property of AT&T and was not common property of the Bell Operating Companies (BOC). All the services that used the AT&T data base and CCIS could no longer be a BOC service offering. One of the biggest money makers was the 800 calling service that AT&T controlled for many years.

Changing to the ANSI version of CCITT-7 protocol brought changes to the AT&T network. Switching transfer equipment changed to handle the new packet format. Data lines were upgraded to 56 kpbs and initially placed on DDS facilities. Other telephone companies faced the problem of installing CCS-7-type equipment to traverse to other telephone networks.

Telephone companies are paranoid about other entities gaining entry into their systems and exploiting their internal services. Network gateway switching transfer points screen calls from other networks and pass signaling information only. Access to internal data bases and service are denied.

Typical of the X.25 Packet Switching type protocol, the packetized data information is transparent to equipment between the end-users. Information as to call originator and destination are the screening decider's. Calls from the ABC telephone company can traverse through Company XYZ's network but would not access XYZ's data base.

CCS7-type signaling lends itself to integrating to other packet oriented signaling. ISDN's D Channel and the data link with Extended Superframe are other X.25 packet types of packet transmission. Producing equipment to bridge the signaling from the various services will lead to the evolution of digital services.

ISDN Signaling

Both the ISDN Basic and Primary Access use out-of-band signaling to carry all signaling information. Signaling only comes in two varieties, as in- or out-of-band. In-band signaling rides in the same channel frequency bandwidth or digital time slot. Out-of-band signaling goes in another frequency bandwidth or digital time slot.

ISDN's Basic Access uses a 16-kpbs channel to send the signaling information. Sixteen kb is an overkill for just two voice/data channel signaling information. Therefore, end-users can send additional X.25 packetized data over the same channel.

Sixty-four kpbs in the time slot of the ISDN's Primary Access provides signaling. Again there are provisions for separate packetized data to exist with the signaling information. The bandwidth is so great that two T-1 lines can share the one signaling time-slot.

Delving into all the call-processing messages and the packet structure of the ISDN signaling is way beyond the scope of this book. Bell Communications Research, Inc.'s Technical Advisory on ISDN Basic Access signaling is approximately 3 inches thick.

One needs only to understand that ISDN's signaling is X.25 packetized data. Very few people can find value in knowing all the numerous ISDN's call-processing messages and structure. One doesn't remember all the telephone numbers in the Yellow Pages, but where the book is to look for a needed number.

Summary

Signal supervision controls the accessing of circuits. Signaling sends calling information between the user and the switching machine. "Switching machine" is a generic term that covers Private Branch Exchanges and telephone company switching machines. Call processing covers a complex set of rules to originate, acknowledge and terminate calls.

Simple E & M Signaling requires only two signaling states (a binary one or zero) to transfer information. Loop- and Ground-Start Signaling need four signaling states to complete their handshaking. Commercial multiplexers often provide only two signaling states and may not function in all end-user's planned networks.

Future trends in signaling and call processing are finally coming together. Nevertheless, it is questionable whether the different telephone companies can handle either intra- or internetwork signaling. There were other technically feasible telephone services that never became public because the maintenance force didn't know how to test it.

9

Telephone Company Network Interfaces

Most telephone company network T-1 interfaces resemble a digital channel bank. They respond to the basic building block or the 64-kpbs time slot. Alarms received and sent are the same. They respond to robbed-bit signaling in different ways, but all transmit the bits in the same fashion. The only T-1 telephone company interface that remains unchanged is the passive Digital Signal Cross-Connect Level 1 (DSX-1) frame.

Telephone company T-1 interfaces for integrated digital services separate the digital data from the digital voice. One would expect mixed data and voice on the end-user's terminal equipment. Nevertheless, mixed data and voice separate at the first telephone company office and ride dedicated all data or voice facilities. While mixed data and voice could technically traverse entire telephone networks, telephone cost accounting will not. As long as there are individual cost accounts for voice message and data services, the services will ride separate facilities.

Separating services at the telephone company office belong to the Digital Cross-Connect System (DCS) and the #5-ESS switching machine. The DCS and the #5-ESS switch produce some of the same results. As a consequence, telephone company personnel have argued long into the night as to which one to install. When it comes to a true ISDN structure, the #5-ESS switch responds to rapid changes in a real-time mode.

Bell Communications Research, Inc. refers to the digital cross- connect device as the Digital Cross-Connect System (DCS). AT&T has called the same unit the Digital Access Cross-Connect System

(DACS). For many years, the Bell Operating Companies and AT&T purchased only the Western Electric Digital Access Cross-Connect System. It had its own proprietary operating system, and no one else could build a compatible unit. Divestiture changed the compatibility issue, and now many manufacturers build DCSs or DACSs.

We use the acronym DCS throughout the rest of this book because it has a truer meaning. It is a digital cross-connect device that electronically connects time slots together. One T-1 port of the DCS is a maintenance port to access the different time slots within the Digital Cross-Connect System. Telephone test personnel are the only ones that have access. Electronic time slot cross-connection is the main task, and access remains limited.

Understanding how the DCS functions leads to an understanding of certain transmission restrictions. Frame formats that rely on the Superframe Pattern to locate framing information depends on "Superframe Integrity" from end to end. Changing the Superframe Pattern in the middle of the circuit will usually result in the equipment's loss of synchronization.

Superframe Integrity remains one of the least understood phenomena by many people. It also remains one of the least publicized issues by the telephone companies. One first has to fully understand the workings of a DCS before the proverbial lightbulb goes on. A technical instructor to marketing types once described his student's sudden awareness as "Seeing God." That's the point of understanding when the eyes glisten and the brain begins to function again.

Digital Cross-Connect System (DCS)

AT&T-Western Electric's Digital Cross-Connect System (DCS) has the largest installed base of all the different manufacturers. It is the model for other manufacturers to emulate or surpass. Surpassing DCS features is not difficult. Typically the old Bell System over designed functions into their equipment.

Newer digital cross-connect devices can easily surpass the software operations of the older Digital Cross-Connect System. When the DCS arrived on the scene, any speed improvement over weeks of manual connection time was a blessing. Working within a 30-minute window or time frame was a miracle. Now that 30-minute window seems like a lifetime.

Before getting into the operations software for the installed DCSs, it is best to describe the physical structure. A basic DCS cross-connect unit can handle up to 32 T-1 lines. Each unit has 4 cross-connect modules that terminate 8 individual lines. A full-blown DCS has 4 basic units that terminate 127 T-1 lines. Figure 9-1 shows the

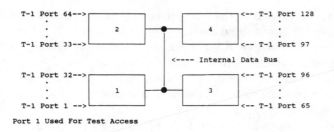

Figure 9-1 Digital Cross-Connect System.

physical layout of the DCS frame with growth from the bottom of the frame towards the top. Subrate Digital Cross-Connect units provide less than 64-kbps digital data rates and replace one or two of the Basic DCS Units.

Simple arithmetic says 4 times 32 equals 128. Maintenance access uses the first T-1 port to test individual 64 kbps time slots. Control software alone was difficult enough without adding maintenance access software to the design woes. Connecting a D4 Digital Channel Bank to the T-1 port made economical sense. Access jacks provide a means to test any one of the 24 time slots; a simple and expedient way to obtain testing capabilities.

Microprocessors control the time slot transfer information between T-1 ports. Packets of data travel over buses to form a Time-Space-Time switch. Ports are in a time domain and the internal switching is a space domain.

Read-Only Memory (ROM) stores the program information for the Digital Cross-connect System. Random Access Memory (RAM) stores part of the program and cross-connection information. Magnetic Bubble Memory provides a nonvolatile memory of cross-connection information. Redundant ROM and RAM information provides even greater safeguards, another example of overdesign to protect against the remote possibility that a telephone office would lose total power. Telephone company offices usually have a string of dc batteries and ac emergency power engines that prevent lose of power.

Each DCS unit detects alarms and sends alarm signals. Alarms and alarm signals have original names like Red, Yellow, and Blue Alarms. These are telephone network alarm conditions that now extend from their networks to end-user's premises. Alarm coverage is an important issue, which we cover at the end of this chapter.

Four cross-connect modules, each containing 8 T-1 ports, make up the basic DCS Unit. Control circuitry reads out the 24 time slots from each T-1 port. It then combines the resultant 192 time slots into a bit stream equivalent to 256 time slots transferred in the same time period. Supposedly, the faster transfer of time slots prevents blockage of cross-connections. This bit stream zips along at less than 500 nanosecond rate.

In the full blown DCS, each basic unit receives the other 256- slot bit streams from the other units. Under program control, the DCS Basic Unit pulls off the information it wants from the bit stream. It then organizes the time slots in a new order to transmit out from its T-1 lines.

Software programs can strip off a time slot or a group of time slots from one T-1 line and broadcast them out to many T-1 lines. Video teleconferences to several locations use this property of the Digital Cross-Connect System. Programming the entire 24 time slots makes the DCS a T-1 switch.

Superframe Pattern Reintroduction

Superframe pattern reintroduction provides the independent action between T-1 lines. Incoming T-1 lines' superframe patterns can be either the D-4 or Extended Superframe (ESF). They also have independent pattern initiation. One T-1 line could have a D-4 pattern and be transmitting the 5th Main Frame. The adjacent T-1 line could have an ESF Pattern in the middle of the 23rd Main Frame. A snapshot of the different T-1 lines, at a given instant, sees wide variations in the format and pattern locations.

An alternative to independence would coordinate the pattern sequence on all outgoing T-1 lines. This would add additional delay and cause major problems during trouble recovery periods. Synchronization is a beautiful thing while running properly. Have one little trouble and watch the retraining process to get back into synchronization.

The example in Figure 9-2 shows the simplest connection through a Digital Cross-Connect System. One may think of transferring all 24 time slots from one T-1 line to another T-1 line as a Digital Signal Level One (DS-1) switch. It transfers the 24 time slots intact without removing or inserting other time slots.

Transferring intact is not quite true. The DCS control circuitry transfers the 24 time slots individually one at a time. Programming has 24 instructions to the cross-connect modules to pick off each time slot from the bit streams. Software updates reduces the instructions to 24 continuous transfers instead of 24 separate transfers.

Transferring One Time Slot

We have seen a complete separation of the T-1 ports by an internal data bus running at less than 500 ns. There is the total inde-

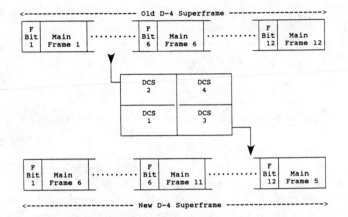

Figure 9-2   DCS Superframe Reintroduction.

pendence of framing patterns between T-1 ports and lines. And the software instructions transfer one time-slot at a time.

In Figure 9-3, incoming T-1 Port #60 has a time slot designated (****) in the Main Frame. At this instant, the incoming T-1 line is in its first Main Frame and Time Slot 3 is designated (****). We used this strange character to prevent misunderstanding about which time slot was under discussion. Since we will next talk about A & B robbed-bit signaling, we also stayed away from using letters.

All 24 time slots from the T-1 Port #60 incorporate into its cross-connection module's 256-slot bit stream. Software instructions tell

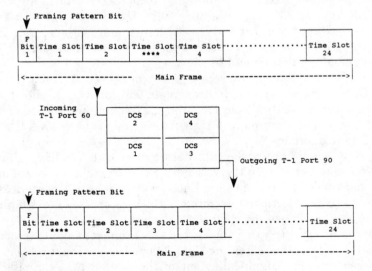

Figure 9-3   DCS Transfer of a Single Time Slot.

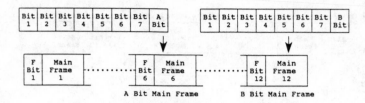

Figure 9-4   A & B Robbed-Bit Signaling Main Frame Locations.

the outgoing T-1 Port #90's cross-connection module that time slot (****) is destined for time slot position 1. Note that the outgoing cross-connect module has no instructions to wait for a particular Main Frame to come by. Instead the module places time slot (****) in the first available number one time slot. Our example shows that the 7th Main Frame was the first available.

Transferring A & B Robbed-Bit Signaling

Transferring A & B robbed-bit signaling is the only instance where the DCS waits for a particular outgoing Main Frame. The A or B signaling bit occupies the least significant bit position of each time slot in every 6th Main Frame. We assume all 24 time slots are voice circuits with in-band signaling in the example. After an explanation about A & B robbed-bit transfer, we will cover what happens when some time slots do not have signaling.

Cross-connect modules monitor the incoming T-1 lines for the D4 or ESF framing pattern. Once in synchronization, the T-1 port knows when to expect the A-Bit and B-Bit Main Frames (Figure 9-4). Since the A and B Bits may indicate specific conditions, their positions must remain true from end to end.

In either the A or B Bit's case, the process of traversing through the DCS is the same. Our first example will follow only the steps to transfer the all A Bits from an incoming T-1 line to an outgoing T-1 line. The second example will transfer only one time slot's A Bit from one line to another.

A Bits locate in only the 6th Main Frame of a T-1 line using the D4 Framing Pattern. In the Extended Superframe, they locate in the 6th and the 18th Main Frame. Each DCS port has software instructions as to the particular framing pattern to expect. For simplicity, our example will use the shorter D4 pattern.

As the 6th Main Frame enters, the cross-connect module copies the A Bits. When the signaling bits started out, they robbed and replaced the least significant digit of the 8-bit byte. Originally, the 8th bit remained unchanged after copying. The telephone companies found a possibility of false framing of T-1 lines that went through multiple DCS installations. Now, the DCS overrides the copied A and B Bits with a ones bit to prevent any false frame recognition. After the cross-connect module copies the A Bits, the bits transfer to the outgoing module on a separate bus. Once at the outgoing module, the A Bits must wait for the next 6th Main Frame to appear. Our example in Figure 9-2 shows the old 11th Main Frame located in the new 6th Main Frame. As far as the distant end knows, it was never anything else but the 6th Main Frame. This change in frame number results strictly from the new framing pattern inserted by the outgoing module. A Bits override the 8th bit of each time slot in the new 6th Main Frame.

When the signaling bit started out, it robbed a bit's location and changed the quantizer to compensate for the missing bit. Now the DCS has taken a heavy handed step and replaced a normal bit with a signaling bit. The distant end compounds the preemption of the normal bit by thinking the 8-bit bytes came from a different quantizer. It is a minor transmission problem with just one DCS in the midstream. Place many DCSs in the path and the minor problem grows into a concern.

Our second example uses the structure found in Figure 9-3: DCS transfer of a single time slot. Now the transfer of the single time slot with A and B Bit signaling follows a similar process. The time slot transfers to the new time-slot location and the A Bit waits for the new 6th Main Frame.

Software instructions tell which time slots do not have A- and B-Bit Signaling. Programming tells the incoming cross-connect module to forget about copying the signaling bits and inserting a ones bit in their place. Outgoing cross-connect modules just watch an unchanged 8-bit byte go out in the new superframe.

DCS Advantages

1. Timing or master clock source available. Normally, point-to-point T-1 services use clocking from end-user equipment shown in Figure 9-5a. When using a DCS, each outgoing T-1 line uses the telephone company's master clock for transmission (Figure 9-5b). Going through a DCS produces a high speed service similar to Digital Data Service (DDS). DDS's high quality rests on the end user seeing one master clock and not many different ones.
2. Terminal equipment must slave-time their transmit clock to the master clock furnished by the Digital Cross-Connect System. Switching from a non-DCS hook-up to a DCS for disaster restoration causes timing problems. Equipment's timing options change from slave to internal for non-DCS facilities.

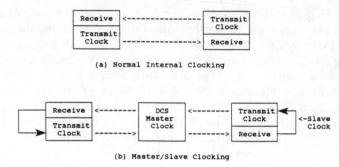

(a) Normal Internal Clocking

(b) Master/Slave Clocking

Figure 9-5   Clocking.

Equipment timing option location and ease is critical to changes in operation.

3. Efficient filling of the time-slot in the T-1 lines. Telephone companies use DCSs to improve utilization percentage of the T-1 lines. This leads to a problem if efficiency rules over good judgment.

4. Telephone companies gain access to the time slots riding over the T-1 lines connected to the Digital Cross-Connect System. Over the years, the telephone companies studied the use of DCS for all T-1 services. This never happened because the cost of DCS provision exceeded the maintenance cost saved.

5. Can serve as a T-1 switch for disaster restoration plans.

6. Can serve as a point to remove excess jitter on the line.

DCS Restrictions

1. Transmission problems likely when several DCSs connect in tandem. Data delay occurs from DCS equipment and adding facility propagation delay. Reproduction of circuits with A and B robbed-bit signaling can suffer. Perceived echo occurs when there are 2- to 4-wire hybrids and facilities over 1850 miles in length. Fiber-optic cable has a longer propagation delay and a factor of 1250 miles for echo control calculations.

2. Terminal equipment requiring the same superframe pattern in respect to its own frame format cannot connect to a DCS.

3. Ones density of video signals is a requirement of the video terminal equipment. DCSs will interject ones bits into a nonvideo digital stream if it senses a long string of zero bits.

4. DCSs send normal telephone company alarms. Terminal equipment should respond to the "Yellow and Blue Alarms."

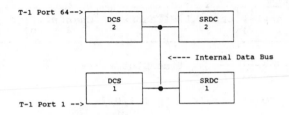

Figure 9-6   Subrate Data Multiplexer.

Things To Ask When Using a DCS Service

If you plan to use telephone company DCSs in your network, you need to know the following items.

1. Actual length of the T-1 lines between the telephone companys and between the DCS and your premise. This information is necessary to determine the need for echo cancellers and data response times. Airline mileage distance does not represent your true mileage. Telephone engineers and operations personnel can tell the real mileage while sales people often only have the billing mileage.
2. Find out what types of facilities are used. Facility mixes of many different types usually have the highest percentage of errors and troubles.

Subrate Digital Cross-Connection (SRDC)

SRDCs provide electronic cross-connections for digital data rates of 2400, 4800, 9600, and 56,000 bps. They have the same format and framing patterns that DDS Subrate Digital Multiplexers have.

A SRDC replaces one DCS unit in the DCS's frame, and no more than two SRCDs can replace DCS units. SRDC access is via the DCS internal data buses and does not connect to the outside world by itself. Each SRDC Unit eliminates 32 T-1 lines by replacing the DCS capability. In Figure 9-6, there are two SRDC units and the maximum number of user T-1 ports reduces to 63. Port #1 still provides maintenance access.

Access to the SRDC section is at the 64,000 bps level only and uses the same frame format and pattern of the SRDM (Figure 9-7). Once inside the SRDC, the basic time-slot demultiplexes and takes on the attributes of a DDS hub office. A SRDC not only cross-connects services but also provides a multipoint digital bridge capability.

The time slots can technically support a mixture of digital data speeds. Nevertheless, economics dictates greater efficiencies with

F 0	Channel 1	F 1	Channel 2	F 1	Channel 3	F 0	Channel 4	F 0	Channel 5

|<--------------   Time Slot   ------------------>|

F = 9600-bps Frame Bits (01100)

Figure 9-7   SRDC Framing Pattern for 9600 bps.

dedicated time slots for the different data rates. Besides reduced efficiencies, administrating mixed data speeds becomes a nightmare for the telephone company.

SRDC Advantages

1. Standard framing format guarantees compatibility from many sources. Intermix of digital services possible. Transferring between different telephone companies is also possible.
2. DDS like services from end to end. Nevertheless, telephone companies will not support DDS performance on the an end-to-end basis. Mixing apples and oranges in error performance yields telephone jelly. One cannot tack it up on the wall to look at.
3. Only rational way to provide digital data throughput and integrate services.

SRDC Disadvantages

1. Cost! A full blown DCS installed cost was approximately $450,000. Equipment advances and competition should drive this figure down. Costs spiral upward because several DCSs are required at one telephone office to provide the subrate function.
2. Standard format is rigid. This results in inefficiencies of not using all the bits in a T-1 line.

DFI and DIF Interfaces

The A in AT&T must stand for Acronym instead of American. Digital Facility Interface (DFI) and Digital Interface Frame (DIF) provide the same basic service. They are T-1 line interfaces to the #5-ESS and #4-ESS switching machines. One is a DFI and the other a DIF. People who work with these acronyms on a daily basis easily mix up DIFs with DFIs.

Basically, a DFI or a DIF provides a single port interface into the switching machine. When the telephone companies used analog switching machines, the T-1 digital services were brought back to analog signals by a D-bank. This meant 24 separate switch access ports for every T-1 line attached.

The thing to remember about DFIs or DIFs is that they respond as if the D-Bank hadn't gone away. They respond to failures and send appropriate alarms. A and B robbed-bit signaling changes to E & M signaling for interoffice signaling.

Digital Signal Cross-Connect Level 1 (DSX-1)

A DSX-1 is a passive cross-connect frame and the first point of presence of the T-1 line in a telephone company office. T-1 lines connect to each other or they connect to telephone office equipment. Each cross-connect frame has jack access for either the telephone office equipment or the T-1 lines. This is the only place the telephone office personnel can access a T-1 line for testing, since telephone engineers considered T-1 lines as facilities instead of end-user services. the test frame is basically primitive in nature.

Other than being the first test point for the telephone company, the T-1 signal found here is the system standard. All references to T-1 signals refer to the DSX-1 signal. End-user premise multiplexers list they have a DSX-1 signal. A DSX-1 signal specifies the electrical interface and nothing about format framing or pattern. Nevertheless, the electrical specification has enough caveats to make a Philadelphia lawyer happy.

DSX-1 Specification

Line Rate

The line rate is 1,544,000 with the following tolerance.

- AT&T = + or - 130 parts per million (equivalent to 200.72 bps). Nevertheless, the signal emanating from an end-user location should adhere to the CCITT standard.
- AT&T measures jitter with a quasi-random signal that has a + or - 50 pulses per second tolerance.
- Bell Communications Research = + or - 200 bits per second.
- CCITT = + or - 50 parts per million (equivalent to 77.2 bps).

Parts per Million

The other specifications correlate fairly well. They do not leave it to your calculator to determine how many parts per million equal a bit per second. One should ask about vendor's claims that their equipment meet DSX-1 signal constraints. Conversion between parts per million and bits per second is a simple calculator function.

$$\text{Bits per second} = \frac{1,544,00 \times \text{Parts per million}}{1,000,000}$$

or

$$\text{Parts per million} = \frac{\text{Bits per second} \times 1,000,000}{1,544,00}$$

Digital Signal Level 2 (DS-2) Service

Digital Service Level 2 (DS-2) is a 6,312,000-bps service that few telephone companies propose or offer. While it seems like a logical step between T-1 lines and a 45 Mb line, it may never be anything more than a passing idea. D4 and D5 Digital Channel Banks are the only equipment that a DS-2 service can interface at a telephone office. End-user premise equipment hasn't addressed the DS-2 service because of a very low market forecast.

Digital Signal Level 3 (DS-3) Service

Digital Signal Level 3 (DS-3) is a 44,736,000-bps service that gains popularity daily. It is a choice because it fits the fiber-optic world so well. AT&T ACCUNET T45 service uses the DS-3 signal and became cost-effective after a need for five to seven T-1 lines.

DS-3 telephone office equipment interfaces with a DSX-3 (Digital Signal Cross-Connect Level 3) frame similar to the T-1 lines. AT&T had limited initial test access to a DS-3. They required the end-user to provide the Extended Superframe pattern on each of the 28 T-1 lines that could combine into a DS-3 signal. This was another case of the "If I can't test it, I can't support it" attitude of maintenance personnel. Maintenance performance hinged on the performance of the parts instead of the whole.

Studio-quality video and hyper-speed, host-to-host transfer use the composite DS3 signal. One should expect to only maintain the framing constraints of the DS-3 signal without breaking it into individual T-1 lines.

Central Office T-1 Multiplexers

Telephone office T-1 multiplexers are usually only the D4 Bank or ANSI-approved ADPCM type. Occasionally, they have strayed away from the standard multiplexer to provide a special assembly to meet an end-user's request.

AT&T offers the M24 Service Function under their ACCUNET T1.5 Service tariff: it was a D4 Bank called the C.O. (Central Office) Multiplexer before divestiture. Most C.O. Multiplexers in service resided in the Bell Operating Company (BOC) office. AT&T changed the D4 Bank's name when the offering moved into their own offices. BOCs still referred to C.O. Multiplexer.

ADPCM multiplexers also became service telephone company offerings. Ironically, they offer the same ADPCM unit that they shy away from using themselves. As a number of people have discovered over the years, analog data did not go away but instead got faster and cheaper. Dial-up modems higher than 4800 bps, could not travel through an ADPCM multiplexer. Long distance message networks found they couldn't use ADPCM the hard way.

T-1 Telephone Company Alarms

Telephone company T-1 alarms come in a variety of colors. Each color describes the location of the alarm and the response taken. Alarms not only alert maintenance personnel, but perform signal conditioning. Conditioning is simply ways to notify voice and data channels that the service is in trouble. Voice circuits would go on-hook and then indicate busy. Data circuits should drop a Clear-To-Send lead to stop data transmission.

Figure 9-8 shows three different telephone offices with a break in the line between Office B and Office C. This could very well be end-user locations at Offices A and C and a telephone company office in between.

Red Alarm

A Red Alarm occurs at Office A where the equipment senses a loss of framing on the T-1 line. Since it is called a Red Alarm, one should expect the visual alarm to be a red lamp. Another name for the Red Alarm is the Carrier Failure Alarm (CFA). A response to the CFA is

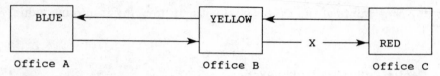

Figure 9-8   Telephone Company Alarms.

the Carrier Group Alarm (CGA). A CFA is the detection of a trouble condition and the CGA is the timed reaction.

Yellow Alarm

A CFA or Red Alarm at Office C initiates a Yellow Alarm toward the B Office. It notifies the other end of the facility that the line from Office B to Office C is in trouble. If the T-1 line between Office C and B uses a D4 Framing Pattern, the Yellow Alarm forces every second bit in each time slot to a zero state.

Using an Extended Superframe (ESF) Framing Pattern will send the Yellow Alarm in the pattern's data link. ESF Yellow Alarms leave the second bit of each time slot alone and send an alarm code of 1111111100000000.

Blue Alarm

Blue Alarms are primarily signal conditioning notifications to equipment not directly involved with the trouble. Our example shows the trouble between Office B and Office C. Office B received the Yellow Alarm as a result of the failure. It in turn sends a Blue Alarm toward Office A to force signal conditioning. A Blue Alarm has two other names — "all ones" and "Facility Alarm Indication Signal" (FAIS). T-1 lines with a D4 framing pattern will force an all-ones signal in each time slot. Robbed-bit signaling will toggle the A Bit to a zero and then lock it to a ones bit for the duration of the failure.

Out-of-Frame Alarms

Out-of-Frame (OOF) Alarms are best known as "oophs" to telephone company personnel. If the receiving equipment loses frame synchronization, an OOF occurs. OOFs became an issue with the ESF format.

Summary

Telephone company interfaces follow North American Standards to the letter. The North American or American National Standard Institute (ANSI) standards usually have minor changes from CCITT international standards.

While following standards reduces flexibility, it offers ways to cross between telephone networks around the world. There are ways intelligent manufactures can use the standards and still remain competitively flexible.

Disaster restoration with a DCS requires thought as to timing, delays, and superframe integrity problems. Most of the problems appear at the least opportune time. One end-user had very expensive equipment ready for shipment when they heard about superframe integrity. Last minute bandaids salvaged what could have turned out to be a monumental mistake.

10

End-User Premise Multiplexers

End-user premise equipment presents the most confusing spectacle known to man. Claims and counterclaims are ready to boggle your mind. Creative marketing minds work overtime when faced with a borderline product. A recent television set advertisement blazoned a 110 cable TV channel capability. Examining the set closely showed you could preset and watch only 12 out of the 110 channels. If your cable service delivered 30 channels to watch, you could still only see the 12 preset channels you selected.

Cutting through the verbiage to find the bare facts comes from knowledge. Sometimes knowledge is just being able to ask the right questions. Recognizing that a person didn't ask the right question is a special talent that few venders possess. Sales presentations lose value to the vendor and the buyer when there isn't an exchange of intelligent questions and truthful answers.

Asynchronous Multiplexer Introduction

End-user premise digital multiplexers have followed the market demand more than leading a communications revolution. In the mid-1960s, the demand for data transmission outweighed Frequency Division Multiplexers' capability. Data was still basically in a low-speed asynchronous world. Higher-speed synchronous data transmission at 4800 bps was fairly new to most users.

Time Division Multiplexer (TDM) introduction addressed the asynchronous data demand first. Usually the first product on the market reaps the rewards and remains the leader. In the case of the first TDM manufacturer, there are a few people that remember the product's name or who designed it. Its main claim to fame is that it started a communications revolution that fostered many new multiplexer ventures.

Character Interleaved

Asynchronous data multiplexers were character- or byte-interleaved similarly to the original telephone voice digital channel banks. Calling the multiplexers character-interleaved described the data communications aspect, while voice multiplexers were byte-interleaved.

Stripping the asynchronous character's start and stop bit as it entered the multiplexer improved the aggregate data stream's efficiency. Computers already used the Universal Asynchronous Receive-Transmit (UART — acronym pronunciation is "you-art") integrated circuit. UARTs also found a home in multiplexers to raise the transmission efficiency over 100%.

Multiplexer Efficiency

Multiplexer output reinserted the start and stop bits to satisfy the receive terminal. Efficiency of the multiplexer is the total number of input channel bits to the aggregate high-speed line.

$$\text{Efficiency (\%)} = \frac{\text{Input Data Information}}{\text{Output Data Stream}} \times 100$$

$$\text{Efficiency} = \frac{9 \text{ Channels} \times 1200 \text{ bps}}{9600 \text{ bps}} \times 100 = 112.5$$

bps = bits per second

Terminal Overspeed and the Multiplexer

Most multiplexer manufacturers learned early that asynchronous terminals had very poor internal timing. It wasn't necessary to worry about timing in a strict frequency domain. Now the terminals connected to time domain devices and the timing problems were quite evident. If you have a 12 ball per minute baseball pitcher (terminal) and a 10 ball per minute catcher (multiplexer), you can expect two dropped balls. In the case of multiplexers, usually the second version handled terminal overspeed better.

Allowing for terminal overspeed used more overhead and reduced the multiplexer's efficiency. Framing and control information also reduced efficiency to a point somewhere between 100 and 120%. One asynchronous multiplexer stripped the start and stop bits and then added a couple of their own bits for internal control. Every other multiplexer could send eight or nine 1200 bps data streams over a 9600 bps line. Because they added additional bits, their multiplexer could send only seven. Creative marketing minds failed this time to find the magic words to sell this borderline product.

Synchronous Multiplexer Introduction

Towards the end of the 1960s, synchronous data became number one on the communications managers' hot list. Great strides in modem design and terminal capabilities started to make inroads on the slower asynchronous data. Speed of transmission and response time became almost as important as seeking the Holy Grail.

Delay Through Multiplexer

One failing of the character-interleaved multiplexer was the one- to two-character delay through the box. Adding another six or seven more milliseconds round-trip delay to the data was close to committing a mortal sin. Reducing the delay through the multiplexer created bit-interleaving. Bit-interleaving caused only one or two bit delays and reduced response time to an acceptable level.

Synchronous Efficiency

Synchronous data introduced inefficient multiplexer transmission. No start and stop bits existed to strip off on one side and replace on the other. Framing patterns and control signals now showed the true multiplexer picture. Overhead easily used 10% of the aggregate high-speed line. Communication's savings still made synchronous multiplexers a viable product. One could overlook the lost bits to overhead if the savings justified the decision. When you look at a 56,000-bps multiplexer, the overhead seems staggering.

```
56,000 bps x (-10%) = 50,400 bps
```

Synchronous multiplexers introduced a new area of timing concern. Loop or slave timing to a single clock became important. Some modems lacked external timing leads to accept the multiplexer's clock. Extending analog data lines from each multiplexer found the timing coming back on itself and causing problems. Larger buffers alleviated the clocking problems.

Transition to the Intelligent Multiplexer

Inexpensive microprocessor chips led to the introduction of the intelligent statistical multiplexer. It was another communications revolution brought on by the same person who helped launch the first end-user premise time division multiplexer. This time the time division multiplexer had a dynamic frame structure that adjusted to the amount of data sent at a particular instant.

Time Division Multiplexers had assigned time slots for each channel. If the channel didn't have any data flowing, the time slot was empty. Statistical multiplexing used the empty time slots for active data from other channels. Efficiencies between 200 and 300% were reached with this technology.

Input data storage size increased to a point where a 10-second open of the high speed aggregate line prevented data loss. High-Speed Data Link Control (HDLC) provided error detection and retransmission (ARQ error control) of the data. Near error-free transmission (1×10^{-12} bit error rate) became available to asynchronous traffic that once depended on terminal operator visual detection.

Since the intelligent multiplexer was software oriented, it was only a matter of time before program options became real-time. Most options until now where accessible to the user in the form of dual-in-line-package (DIP) switches. DIP switch changes required turning the power off and locating the right DIP out of a string of other switches.

Changes in option selection led to real-time reconfiguration of remote multiplexers. Channel data rates and other options were made on the fly without interrupting data on the other channels. Statistics on data errors and transmission use followed in short order.

Introduction of the T-1 Multiplexer

T-1 multiplexing remained native to just the telephone company environment until approximately 1980. Originally, the U.S. Government requested AT&T to furnish T-1 facilities. Not long after, a couple of the fledgling long distance companies took action to have AT&T provide them similar service. A T-1 Service tariff based on preliminary costs found its way into the DATAPHONE Data Service FCC 267 Tariff. When AT&T provided a T-1 service for the general public, the tariff took a major drop that made it cost effective for almost everyone. Another communications revolution began. When this revolution started, one multiplexer worked at a rate higher than 72,000 bps. The manufacturer didn't take long to modify their unit to work at T-1 rates. Other manufacturers rushed into the scene, but they needed various stages of product development. At first T-1 multiplexers were either voice-oriented Digital Channel Banks or upgraded bit-interleaved synchronous multiplexers.

Before long, manufacturers began blending the software control found in the intelligent multiplexer into the T-1 devices. Network control became the next evolution for software control.

Manufacturers of software-oriented T-1 multiplexers began to sense the need to interface telephone companies. Software programming makes bit-interleaved multiplexers look like byte-interleaving, and the units can exist in two worlds. It was easy to add bits together and create multiplexers that were mixed bit- and byte-interleaved.

Splitting off DS-0 time slots at a Digital Cross-Connect System requires extra care from mixed systems. Besides the additional cost for a software controlled multiplexer, there are other concerns. Frame location for the 8-bit bytes rely on the superframe pattern, while the bit-interleaved section relies on its own framing pattern. Superframe patterns and internal framing patterns may play havoc with each other after going through the Digital Cross-Connect System.

Overhead

Overhead exists in all multiplexers. Bits for framing patterns and control signals chew up some of the available transmitted data bits. A T-1 line without any other signals uses 8,000 bps for the framing pattern. Some multiplexer manufacturers handle ones density requirements by adding a ones bit every 8th bit in the frame. This removes 192,000 more bits from the end-user. Incorporating frame block formats, control signals, and data link control could remove another 20,000 bps. This all reduces the efficiency shown in Table 10-1.

Marketplace for Multiplexers

T-1 multiplexers fall into three major markets. We label these low-end, mid-range, and high-end. These are general categories because, like buying automobiles, one can option any economy car into a luxury one in minutes. Many manufacturers offer bare-bones priced equipment that requires additional options just to operate in the simplest configurations. It's like hearing about a $3,000 car only to find that the wheels, seats, and engine are extra.

End-User Rate	Efficiency

```
Basic T-1 Line = 1,544,000 bps                              100%
1,544,000 bps - 8,00 bps Frame Patern = 1,536,000          99.48%
1,536,000 bps - 192,000 bps Ones Density = 1,344,000 bps   87.05%
1,344,000 bps - 20,000 bps Frame/Control = 1,324,000 bps   85.75%
```

Table 10-1   Efficiency with Added Overhead.

Low-End Multiplexers

Low-end multiplexers cover the Digital Channel Banks (D-Banks) or the basic telephone company type unit. The majority of the available end-user premise units originally sold only to an exclusive telephone company market. When the T-1 market opened, they were the only ones compatible with telephone company multiplexer services.

D-Banks are basic communications devices without any frills. They respond to telephone company alarms and signaling conditioning. While basically point-to-point devices, the telephone companies established Drop & Insert or Bypass circuits with analog connections. A Drop & Insert (Figure 10-1) is thinking the main T-1 line is between the A and C Office. Some circuits from Office A drop off at Office B. Office B inserts some circuits back into the main T-1 line towards the C Office. Bypass simply says Office A's circuits to Office C pass through the Office B multiplexer.

A voice circuit from City A to City C is routed through City B's two multiplexers. The digital signal would return to an analog signal for connection on the channel side of the multiplexer.

Instead of calling this bypass, the telephone companies referred to it as tandem connections. Their stipulation for toll quality transmission required no more than eight such conversion or tandem connections. If they used ADPCM multiplexers, the limit of tandem connections is reduced to four.

Low-End Multiplexers Advantages

1. Lowest cost of all T-1 multiplexers.
2. Least amount of components and thereby the longest mean time to failure. Large-scale integrated circuits time-proven for trouble-free operation.
3. Compatible with telephone company services. Compatible with all equipment following the standards. User has many sources to choose from and can strike the best deal between competitive units.

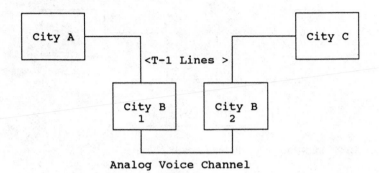

Figure 10-1 Low-End Multiplexers and Bypass.

4. Structure lends itself to ISDN evolution. Service upgrades replace circuit boards in the existing multiplexer frame.

Low-End Multiplexers Disadvantages

1. Limited features. Networking control requires additional or external equipment.
2. Adheres to inflexible standards. Nevertheless, it is basic transportation for the person who doesn't need the bells and whistles.

Mid-Range Multiplexers

Mid-range multiplexers are analogous to looking at the full-size car after finding the economy car didn't quite meet your needs. End-user premise multiplexer manufacturers responded to the T-1 revolution by introducing the mid-range units.

The low end of the mid-range multiplexers were units that addressed the point-to-point market. Manufacturers saw the urgency to enter the T-1 market as quickly as possible. This meant developing fast versions of their existing product line. Developing products is very frustrating. Given a little more time and you could get the best product out the door. Waiting for that extra time may close and lock the door.

It wasn't long before manufacturers introduced units with two or more T-1 outputs. Digital bypass or drop and insert capability ended concern about tandem connections. That same voice circuit from Office A to Office C went through Office B on a digital basis (Figure 10-2).

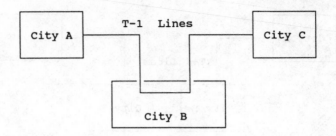

Figure 10-2   Mid-Range Multiplexers with Bypass.

Increased features began to enter the market because the competition was heating up. Just as taught in the Marketing 101 course, adding features also increases value and the ultimate cost of the unit.

Mid-Range Multiplexers Advantages

1. Digital bypass or drop and insert available.
2. Small star configured networks possible.
3. Some networking control features available with software programming.

Mid-Range Multiplexers Disadvantages

1. Prices range from $20,000 to $75,000 per unit.
2. Additional components and custom large-scale integrated circuits have a lower mean time to failure than low-end multiplexers. One can expect longer outages.
3. Noncompatibility with telephone company services and any other manufactured unit unlikely. Single source locks user to proprietary equipment.
4. Evolving to ISDN unlikely.

High-End Multiplexers

At last we have found the top-of-the-line luxury car in the showroom. When we entered the marketplace, there was the old Model T with its choice of colors — as long as it was black. It wasn't long before we noticed units with a variety of colors and a list of options. Towards the other end of the marketplace sits the unit with every option or feature you could crave.

High-end multiplexers address the large communications needs of the Fortune 500 user. After the Bell System break-up, end-users

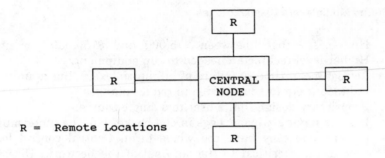

R = Remote Locations

Figure 10-3 High-End Multiplexers in a Star Configuration.

were finding the control of their network also broken. It became apparent to many large communications users that they had to create their own networks. Control meant having a central location with unattended remote control of outlying offices. Two major network configurations used with high-end multiplexers are star (Figure 10-3) and ring (Figure 10-4).

High-End Multiplexers Advantages

1. Complete control of the network. Dynamic remote reconfigurations of the network's individual channels. Historical information about usage becomes available on some units.
2. Software structure allows telephone company service emulation. Normally a bit-interleaved multiplexer that can program the T-1 line to interleave the channels by 8-bit bytes instead of bits. Some units can address a proprietary world as well as standards.

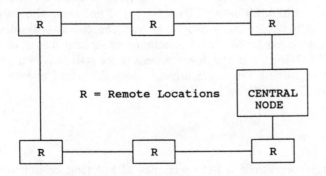

Figure 10-4 High-End Multiplexers in a Ring Configuration.

High-End Multiplexers Disadvantages

1. High cost ranges between $75,000 and $750,000 per unit. Higher-level technician needed to run equipment.
2. Lowest mean time to failure of all multiplexers. Spare units or redundant equipment needed to reduce outages.
3. Proprietary design limits user to a single source.
4. Besides having all your eggs in one basket like the other multiplexers, one may have the whole farm. Central control locations become critical to the survival of the network. Disaster restoration plans become complex.
5. Timing is critical due to the number of T-1 lines entering a single multiplexer from many different locations.

Multiplexer Interfaces

Interface specifications for a variety of products are the subject of Electronic Institute of America standards. AT&T and Bell Communications Research have specified interfaces in their technical references. Nevertheless, multiplexer interfaces are up to the imagination of the designer.

Voice Interfaces

The ideal voice circuit interface is the standard 50-pin connector used by telephone companies. It provides a rapid connection to other equipment. Better yet, it's a blessing when changing defective equipment, and one only loosens a couple of screws to get back into service. Not all multiplexers provide telephone company standard connectors. They vary from wire-wrap pins to soldered terminal blocks.

Voice channel cards either have a fixed 0 dbm output level or provide an adjustable level. Either way, the end-user should plan for jack access between the multiplexer and the collocated voice equipment. Test access is essential to adjust levels and locate equipment troubles. Relying on multiplexer access jacks still leaves a gray area to question during trouble analysis. External jacks should also include signaling lead access.

Data Interfaces

Data interfaces stand a better chance of meeting or approximating standard interfaces. Most manufacturers use integrated circuit driver sets that provide the proper voltages and impedances. How they provide the mechanical data interface remains a mystery. Again, one can expect almost anything.

One interesting interface is the D-Bank Dataport Card interface. It is a 4-wire connection that requires a Data Service Unit (DSU) to turn it into a usable interface. What makes it interesting is that you can place a DSU 650 feet away from the multiplexer.

EIA RS-232C interface voltages can normally span only 50 feet. Greater distances require the use of low-capacitance cables or line driver devices. No matter what arrangement you select, the data interface has tighter distance constraints than the voice circuit.

Signaling Lead Interfaces

Signaling interfaces depend on the signaling used. Some multiplexers can furnish current to ring telephones. One approaches this interface differently than a simple E & M lead connection. Most signaling leads should have jack access adjacent to the transmission jacks.

T-1 Line Interface

Western Electric 551A Channel Service Units (CSU) were the only end-user interface at one time. On the telephone side of the unit, there were screw terminals to connect up to six wires. Four wires provide digital signal transmission in both direction, and two wires for fault detection. The end-user's side of the CSU had a 15-pin connector.

Divestiture played another trick on the end-user. CSUs became the responsibility of the end-user, and the telephone companies stopped at a terminal block. Users soon found themselves in the cable and wire business. While AT&T recommended the 15-pin connector as a point of telephone company interface, the Bell Operating Companies couldn't agree.

Electrically, the end-user interface follows the signal specifications found at the cross-connect frame in the telephone company central office. Pulse variations from the 1,544,000-bps rate adhere to the CCITT standard of plus or minus 77.2 bps.

Premise Digital Cross-Connect Systems

Premise Digital Cross-Connect Systems (DCS) provide greater flexibility at the end-user location. Two varieties of the DCS function exist. One is the stand-alone external device and the other is the integrated unit. Debating the merits of the stand-alone DCS versus the internal function could go on forever. One could provide convincing arguments for either selection.

DCS's value is the ability to efficiently pack various T-1 lines with 64,000 bps time slots. Systems that switch low-speed data circuits are digital switches and are not digital cross-connect systems.

Another DCS value is gaining test access similar to what the telephone companies have with Digital Cross-Connect Systems. One end-user based their network design on the ability of accessing remote time slots back to a central test site. A dedicated maintenance time slot on each T-1 line allowed connection of any terminal to a centralized testing location.

Network Control Concerns

Network control and multiplexer reconfiguration software tools are gaining popularity. Vendors are bending over backwards opening up their proprietary message control in the guise of an open network architecture. The "me-first" approach has worked before in setting a standard. This time several groups are all yelling "me first" at the same time.

Reconfiguring a network during a disaster situation requires great thought about the consequences. The following concerns the reconfiguration of an installed network with control functions:

1. Telecommunications and MIS groups must agree on levels of priority for each circuit. Voice circuits usually have the lowest priority since the Private Branch Exchange usually has automatic routing to other services. Data circuits may have several layers of priority depending on the service use.
2. Disaster restoration plans play "what if" games for facilities as well as building locations.
3. Complex rerouting of priority circuits introduce additional delays to the response time for data. Signal to distortion ratios decrease in value.

End-User Multiplexer Concerns

Transmission

Transmission concerns revolve around what the end-user expects from the network. Quality of voice transmission is subjective and individuals have different tolerance levels. Analog data over voice circuits will never go away. New technology can displace it, but never eliminate its use.

1. Toll quality voice circuits should have an almost flat frequency gain characteristic between 300 and 3400 Hz. Multiplexers that provide a channel frequency spectrum less than this can't be called toll quality.
2. High-speed analog data circuits require full spectrum frequency bandwidths. One should expect a signal to distortion ratio of 35 db from one multiplexer to another. Additional noise on analog extensions can lower the ratio to a point where data transmission stops.
3. Voice transmission evaluations should include high-pitched female voices. Use only test phrases that stress the coding method.

Signaling Concerns

Voice circuits require signaling to control or supervise the connection. Seizing the circuit and signaling is the responsibility of the switching device. Network equipment must pass the information needed by the switching controls faithfully.

1. Loop- and Ground-Start Signaling have four-state signaling. The A and B Signaling Bits each have independent operating states (00, 01, 10, 11).
2. E & M Signaling usually requires only two-state signaling (11, 00). Switching machines often will treat the B Signaling Bit as a don't care bit and switch strictly on the A Bit.
3. Bypassing the local telephone company end-office eliminates assumed or expected functions. Private Branch Exchanges look for the telephone company's dialtone when going off-net.

Distance from Multiplexer to Voice and Data Equipment

Data circuits have critical cabling distances. Voice equipment can stand longer cabling runs from the multiplexer. Multiplexer location usually depends on the controlling communications group in a company.

1. Data circuits using RS-232C electrical specifications have a 50-foot limit to the terminal equipment. Distances greater than 50 feet require special cabling or line driver equipment.
2. Synchronous data circuits have the following cabling needs.

Frame/Signal Ground	Data Terminal Ready
Send Data	Data Set Ready
Receive Data	Transmit Clock

Clear-to-Send   Receive Clock
Request-to-Send   External Clock

3. Voice circuits have the following cabling needs.

Transmit Tip Lead (T1 — telephone company reference)
Transmit Ring Lead (R1)
Receive Tip Lead (T)
Receive Ring Lead (R)
E Signaling Lead
M Signaling Lead

Alarms — Telephone Company-Generated

Telephone company services generate and respond to Yellow and Blue Alarms. End-user premise multiplexers may react differently to these alarms and the user should know what to expect.

Failures

Facility failures drop terminal equipment out of synchronization. Equipment connected in tandem to the first units also falls out of synchronization. This becomes a ripple effect like dropping a stone in the water.

Our example (Figure 10-5) shows a facility failure between Terminal A Units. Terminal A Units fall out of synchronization. The B terminals then sense a failure has occurred. Finally, the C terminals get the last word and enter an alarm condition. Getting back into synchronization is another ripple effect. What started as a 2-second outage between the A terminals turns into a 10-second outage for the C terminals.

Interface Cables

Equipment manufacturers have different ideas about interface connections. Simple male or female gender connector considerations have delayed installations for hours as technicians fabricate cables on site. Proposed tests or installations should have prior agreement as to the connectors and who provides the cables.

Figure 10-5 Ripple Effect of Failures.

Trouble Handling by the Telephone Companies

T-1 facility troubles are usually just another trouble to the telephone company. Their trouble clearance practice has always been on a first-in-first-out basis. Nevertheless, a T-1 trouble affects many end-user services and should have a higher priority than a single voice in trouble. Local agreements with the telephone companies can often obtain priority handling.

11

Other Premise Digital Terminal Equipment

Premise Switches

Premise switches come in many sizes and colors. There are Private Branch Exchanges (PBX) that integrate voice and data services. Another premise switch is the data switch primarily used as a matrix switch in the computer room. Now it is getting difficult to tell the differences between multiplexers and PBXs. While data multiplexer manufacturers move towards the role the PBX played for years, the PBXs take on switching data.

Major PBX vendors now offer T-1 interfaces with their units. Some include the T-1 Channel Service Unit as an integral part of the interface, and others require separate devices. The advantage of the single T-1 interface is the reduction of access ports and separate multiplexers to combine the voice or data circuits. Premise switches used in private networks can use any format. Nevertheless, premise switches connected to telephone company services have the following requirements.

1. The premise switch's T-1 data stream must use 24 8-bit byte formatting.
2. The T-1 line must have either D4 or Extended Superframe framing patterns.
3. Analog to digital conversion must use the North American Mu-Law 255 Pulse Code Modulation coding process.
4. The premise switch must loop or slave time to the T-1 recovered receive clock if connected to a telephone company

service. Multiple ports should provide buffering for clock and phase differences.

5. Signaling information must use A and B robbed-bit transfer if connected to telephone company services. Private networks can use in-band tones.

6. Loop- and ground-start signaling features at the premise location require special channel cards.

7. Premise switch should respond to Yellow and Blue Alarms from the telephone network. It should also issue a Yellow Alarm when recognizing an incoming failure.

8. Install a Channel Service Unit (CSU) or function if the T-1 service uses metallic wire facilities. CSUs should have a self-powered option in case the local telephone company doesn't furnish line power.

Switched 56-kb Digital Service

Switched 56,000-bps digital service makes sense for end-users with small daily data demands. Nevertheless, the greatest demand for "switched 56" is restoring failed 56,000-bps DDS circuits. A similar demand is access to commercial disaster restoration companies.

Rounding out the market for switched 56 is access to computer-aided design and manufacture computer mainframes. Available circuit boards for personal computers provide the high-speed interface. While standards exist for low-speed computer data ports, nobody has tackled how a 56,000-bps port handles telephone ringing current.

Customer Switched Digital Capability

Customer or Public Switched Digital Capability (CSDC or PSDC) barely survived the Bell System's divestiture. Unfortunately, it was another service in the introduction mill to fall in the crack. If one had to select one service or product to sacrifice, CSDC would have the most votes.

There was an argument about the marketing need statement describing switched 56-kb digital service. AT&T originally described switched 56-kb digital service combined with a regular voice circuit. The rationale rested on using the existing 2-wire telephone network. This was a good start at developing the first integrated voice and data terminal.

While the integrated terminal goal had merit, it also had a very high price tag for the local telephone companies. Costly switching equipment at the local switch (Figure 11-1) separated the voice calls from the digital data calls. As a result, telephone companies opted for restricting the CSDC to switching only digital data.

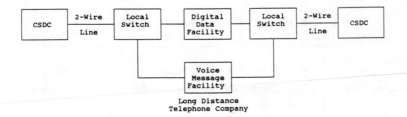

Figure 11-1   Original Customer Switched Digital Capability.

Datapath

The basic CSDC network uses 2-wire facilities between the end-user and the local telephone office. Four-wire facilities transport the 56 kbps between the local telephone companies and the long distance carriers. While the service could transfer to existing digital data systems, the service remains integrated with the regular message network or on dedicated CSDC facilities.

AT&T–Western Electric produced the #1A-ESS switch for telephone companies' end-offices. A metropolitan area with many #1A-ESS switches could draw upon one modified switch to provide CSDC service in a general area.

Northern Telecom introduced their own version of a 2-wire digital data-only CSDC unit. Their concept was different from AT&T and a new debate started. Bell Communications Research Technical Reference TR-TSY-000277 resolved the issues and described Datapath as the accepted method.

Datapath Frame

Datapath is a switched 56-kb service using Time Compression Multiplexing (TCM). Compressing the time it takes to transmit a given amount of data led to its formal name. Nevertheless, TCM's popular name is the descriptive term ping-pong. Transmitting time compresses, but alternating data frames looks more like a ping-pong ball.

End-user starts out as 56-kbps per second data. A control bit adds to the 7 data bits to build the basic 8-bit block transmitting at 64,000 bps. Eight basic building blocks and 8 signaling or operation bits add to raise the basic frame to 72 bits in length. A start bit and stop bit

1 Bit	8 Signal Bits	64 End-User Bits	1 Bit

```
|<------------ 74-bit Frame -------------->|
```

Figure 11-2 Two-Wire Customer Switched Digital Capability Frame.

similar to asynchronous transmission completes the frame for a total 74 bits (Figure 11-2).

Transmitting data simultaneously in both directions or full-duplex transmission is easy for 4-wire facilities. Full-duplex transmission over 2-wire facilities uses several methods. Analog data employs different frequencies in the two directions. The ISDN Basic Access uses echo cancelers and hybrids to transmit simultaneously both ways. CSDC elected to speed up the transmission time and alternate directions during built-in transmission delay periods (Figure 11-3).

Transmitting the basic 74 bit frame at 1,000 frames per second yields a 74,000 bps transmission rate. Double this rate for blank transmission time in one direction and we have a 148,000 bps speed. The next step in arriving at the final transmission rate adds a 0.075 millisecond delay before each direction starts transmission (Table 11-1). Turnaround time, transmission in both directions, and blank periods add up to a 160,000 transmission rate.

Datapath Advantages

1. Low access charges between the end-user and the telephone company's end office. Minimal distance between results in lower access charges in comparison to 4-wire dedicated DDS services.

```
|<---- Delay ----->|<- 74-bit Burst ->|  --------->

             --->| |<--- 0.075 milliseconds

      <----------|<- 74-bit Burst ->|<---- Delay ----->|

                 |<---------- 1 millisecond ---------->|
```

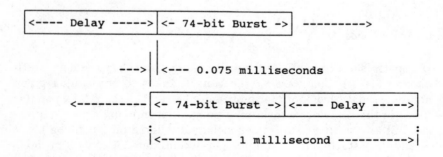

Figure 11-3 Two-Wire Ping-Pong Frames.

Data Bits Transmitted at 160,000 bps

$$74 \text{ Bits} \quad \times \quad \frac{1}{160,000 \text{ Bps}} \quad = \quad 0.4625 \text{ Milliseconds (ms)}$$

One-Way Frame = Data Bits Plus Minimum Rest Time

2×0.4625 ms = 0.925 ms

One-Way Frame Plus Turnaround Time

```
  0.925 ms  — One-Way Frame
+ 0.075 ms  — Turnaround Time
  1.000 ms    for a Single One-Way Frame
```

Table 11-1   Calculations for Ping-Pong Frame.

2. Lower long distance rates because many users share the same facilities.

Datapath Disadvantages

1. Higher terminal equipment costs to provide ping-pong transmission.
2. Limited distance between end-user and telephone office because of the high transmission rate. Transmitting at the Nyquist Frequency of 80,000 Hz limits the transmission distance to 3.4 miles.

AT&T-Accunet Switched 56-kb Service

AT&T's ACCUNET Switched 56-kb Service started during the confusion about CSDC. Getting the service into the marketplace required an equipment kludge. Instead of accessing the telephone network by time compression multiplexing, the access lines used 56-

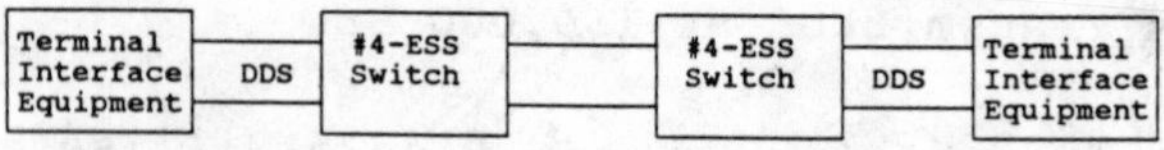

```
┌─────────┐       ┌───────┐       ┌───────┐       ┌─────────┐
│Terminal │       │#4-ESS │       │#4-ESS │       │Terminal │
│Interface│ DDS   │Switch │       │Switch │ DDS   │Interface│
│Equipment│       │       │       │       │       │Equipment│
└─────────┘       └───────┘       └───────┘       └─────────┘
```

Figure 11-4   Initial AT&T Switched 56-kb Service.

kbps DDS circuits. Once getting to the AT&T office, they had to bridge DDS and the #4-ESS Switch (Figure 11-4).

Four-Wire Access

Designing a new end-user terminal interface equipment (TIE) became the next order of business. Since access used existing 56,000 bps DDS services, the TIE revolved around the Data Service Unit (DSU).

The DSU provided the standard interface for the end-user terminal equipment. Terminating the DDS circuit at AT&T's office presented different problems. The #4-ESS Switch's interface is at a T-1 rate. Bridging the gap between a T-1 interface and a 56,000-bps DDS circuit was part of the kludge.

56-kbps DDS access lines terminated in Channel Service Units in the AT&T office (Figure 11-5). This in turn connected to a Dataport office channel unit (OCU) in a D4 Digital Channel Bank. The T-1 output from the D4 Bank connected directly to the T-1 interface of the Digital Interface Frame (DIF) of the #4-ESS Switch.

Switching Information

CSDC's original dialing concept had the end-user establishing voice contact between locations before going to a data state. The end-user premise equipment allowed local dial arrangements (tones or dial-pulses) to call the remote end. After completing a voice connection from end-to-end, each end would throw a switch to "go to data." Changing from the switched mode to a dedicated access line did away with the local dialing arrangements.

Since DDS access lines didn't permit dialing tones, some form of signaling had to transfer information about calling destination. Sig-

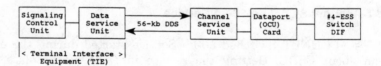

Figure 11-5   Four-Wire Dedicated Access of Switched 56 KB.

naling became another part of the kludge. A #4-ESS Switch uses only two states of signaling, and luckily the DSU has two states of operation. By turning the Request-to-Send (RTS) lead on and off (data mode and idle mode condition), the DSU transfers signaling states or pulses to the switch. Turning the RTS lead on and off in rapid succession produces dial pulses to the other end.

Getting from dial pulses to A and B robbed-bit signaling was another problem. The #4-ESS Switch understands only A and B robbed-bit signaling or Common Channel Signaling Systems. As a result, the Dataport office channel unit required modification to change data and control mode information into A and B signaling bits.

Four-Wire Access Advantages

1. Only available access to areas without local telephone company 2-wire offerings.

Four-Wire Access Disadvantage

1. 56,000-bps DDS access costly when compared to 2-wire local access.
2. Kludge arrangements don't meet AT&T's usual way of doing business. Testing to the end-user is difficult.

Integrated AT&T Accunet Switched 56-kb Service

End-user equipment for integrated switched 56-kbps digital service has different signaling responsibilities. Direct 4-wire access used the change from data to control mode as a way to send signaling information. This information changes to A and B robbed-bit signaling at the telephone company modified DATAPORT unit. Integrating switched 56 kb pushes the conversion to A and B robbed-bit signaling out to the end-user's location.

Going from a direct access to an integrated access will change the end-user equipment. A natural approach would use a PBX to channel the 56,000-bps service into the right time-slot of the T-1 line. During the sixth and twelfth Main Frame of the T-1 signal, A and B Bit signaling bits occupy the 8-bit location in the basic block. All other Main Frames would send control or data mode indications in the 8th-bit position. A ones bit indicates data being sent, and a zero designates a control signal.

Primary	Secondary	Line Rate
2400 bps	133 1/3 bps	3200 bps
4800 bps	266 2/3 bps	6400 bps
9600 bps	533 1/3 bps	12800 bps
56000 bps	2666 2/3 bps	72000 bps

Table 11-2 DDS Secondary Channel Rates.

Integrated Switched 56-kb Service Advantages

1. Cost-effective to share the T-1 facility with other services compared to dedicated DDS access.
2. Service available through a PBX or similar premise switch that can send signaling and control information needed to complete connections.

Integrated Switched 56-kb Service Disadvantage

1. Ties up a single time-slot on the T-1 line. Not a cost effective way if the switched 56-kb service has limited use.

Data Service Units with DDS Secondary Channel

Manufacturers have viewed the secondary channel in two major ways. One use for the secondary channel is network management control. The other use is second data transmission circuit with 56,000-bps service.

The original concept for the second in-band circuit was implementing network control. Nevertheless, four different odd data speeds resulted instead of a typical 110–150 bps used for network management. Designers face a job to bit-stuff and downshift between usable rates and the speeds shown in Table 11-2.

Figure 11-6 shows two issues for 56,00-bps DDS and a secondary channel. One is the odd data rate of 2666.7 bps for the secondary channel. Since there isn't a clear definition for the secondary channel, manufacturers have taken different approaches. The other issue is the higher 72,000-bps line rate. First the local telephone companies must upgrade their equipment to furnish the secondary channel capability. Once you have cleared this battle, the next problem is the distance between the end-user and the telephone company. Since

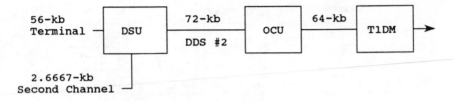

Figure 11-6   56-kb DDS Secondary Channel.

there aren't any 72,000-bps repeaters, the end-user location must be within three or four miles of the local end-office.

Channel Service Units

Channel Service Units were known as Network Communications Terminating Equipment (NCTE) during the transition of the Bell System divestiture process. The telephone companies and the end-user premise equipment manufacturers argued about who should provide the unit. Some telephone companies claimed it was still part of the network and they had to install the unit. Other telephone companies claimed their facilities stopped just before the channel service unit. End-users found themselves furnishing a CSU on one end and the telephone company not allowing them to at the other end.

Finally, it was declared premise equipment, and provisioning was the end-user's responsibility. While the CSU function is the interface between the terminal equipment and the digital facilities, there are differences in CSUs.

DDS Channel Service Units

Digital data systems' CSU function integrates into the facility side of the Data Service Unit (DSU). Ironically, the CSU function separated from the DSU back in 1975 to purposely label the CSU as the line's termination. Between 1975 and 1981, the Bell System installed only a few stand-alone CSUs. Divestiture came along, and the CSU had reason for separation. Two years later, the DSU and the CSU were back together again.

Figure 11-7 shows the main purposes of the DDS channel service unit. This is to provide a loopback, build out the electrical distance, and electrically seal the circuit closed. There is also one section that shapes the incoming signal into a new bipolar signal. The one thing that separates the DDS CSU from a T-1 CSU is its lack of concern for ones-density. A DDS CSU's ones-density is a function of the DDS Data Service Unit, while the T-1 CSU assumes the duty.

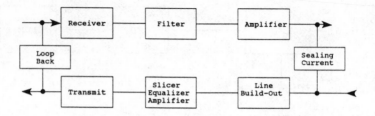

Figure 11-7   DDS Channel Service Unit.

We say the CSU assumes the duty, because the original technical reference on the subject never specified that the CSU maintain ones-density. The reference implied the task was the responsibility of the end-user, and CSU manufacturers inferred it meant it was the CSU's work.

T-1 Channel Service Units

Several major changes to T-1 Channel Service Units occurred during 1986. When the telephone companies adopted the Extended Super-frame (ESF) pattern, the CSU's role expanded to include event registers. At the same time, the telephone companies also agreed to replace ones-density control with Bipolar Eight Zero Suppression.

Older vintage CSUs had little in the way of receive circuitry. Newer versions with ESF capability have an additional role to monitor the receive data stream for errored second events. Records of error events during 15-minute and 24-hour periods provide the telephone companies and the end-user with vital information. Test equipment can remotely interrogate the registers of the CSUs and provide historical data during the past day. Printouts of this data produce the best evidence of problems to the T-1 line.

Ones-density compensation remains the greatest problem to the North American digital network. People involved in the initial selection of ones-density control at the 64,000-bps level openly admit their mistake. This mistake compounded itself when basic digital services went to the T-1 rate. Older CSUs considered any lack of ones bits as a rarity and dealt with them ruthlessly.

A monitor in Figure 11-8 sensed a drop below a 12.5% ones-density in 24 bits or 15 consecutive zeroes. The monitor keys a pattern generator to indiscriminately insert ones bits into the data stream. This is fine if indeed the string of zeroes was a omission on the part of the user or terminal equipment. It was a different story when the signal purposely included strings of zeroes to transmit a video picture.

Providing Bipolar Eight Zero Substitution eliminates numerous transmission problems. End-users could transmit 64,000 bps clear

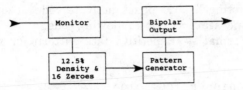

Figure 11-8   Alternate Mark Inversion Channel Service Unit.

channel. Video signals could include long strings of zeroes, and CSUs wouldn't insert ones bits where they shouldn't.

The monitor (Figure 11-9) in the CSU checks for a string of eight zeroes in the T-1 data stream. Once sensing the string, it initiates the B8ZS violation code. T-1 facilities are just starting to see B8Zs used in the telephone company network.

B8ZS solves so many end-user problems, they should plan its use in their own facilities. They should also push for B8ZS provisioning on all leased lines. Until that happens, the CSU should still have an option for AMI or B8ZS transmission. Minimum requirements for a T-1 Channel Service Unit are as follows:

1. Channel service units should have the option of self power for installations without telephone company power on the T-1 line.
2. For optimum T-1 line maintenance, the channel service unit should have Extend Superframe registers. It should also respond to telephone company's operation codes specified in AT&T's Technical Reference PUB 54016.
3. The CSU should react to the following code to activate a loop-back towards the T-1 line.

Frame Format — Repetitive 00001 pattern for more than five seconds.

00001000010000100001 ------>

Frame Pattern — Don't care or arbitrary ones or zeroes in the 193rd bit position during the sending of the loopback code.

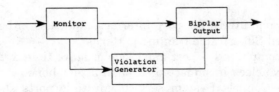

Figure 11-9   Bipolar Eight Zero Substitution Channel Service Unit.

4. After reacting to a loopback activate code, it should return to normal operation with the following code.
Frame Format — Repetitive 001 pattern for more than five seconds.

```
001001001001001001001-----> 
```

Frame Pattern — Don't care or arbitrary ones or zeroes in the 193rd bit position during the sending of the loopback code.
5. The CSU should provide a method for the end-user to initiate the loopback activate and deactivate codes. End-users should have the capability to loopback the remote location. Loopback activation should light a red light on the CSU to indicate a loopback condition.
6. The CSU should have B8ZS ones-density control as an option. As soon as the facilities can handle B8ZS, the option should activate and eliminate the need for an all-ones signal.
7. When the terminal equipment is not transmitting, the CSU should generate an all-ones data signal. Alarm Indication Signal (AIS), "keep alive," or Blue Alarms are forms of the all-ones signal.

Host-to-Host Interfaces

Host-to-host connections at a T-1 rate aren't new. Extending these connections beyond a local area are coming into their own. Initial installations of T-1 facilities between hosts found problems when interfacing a telephone company Digital Cross-Connect System. Framing patterns essential to the telephone companies were missing. Besides host-to-host connections, Computer Aided Design and Manufacture (CAD/CAM) units also operated at T-1 and higher rates. Most host-to-host or CAD/CAM terminal applications are confined in a campus environment. When the T-1 line uses a telephone companies facility, consider the following requirements.

Host-to-Host Requirements

1. The computer's T-1 port interface must use either D4 or Extended Superframe framing patterns.
2. The computer T-1 port must loop or slave time to the recovered receive clock if connected through a telephone company Digital Cross-Connect System service. Multiple ports should provide buffering for clock and phase differences.

3. The computer should respond to Yellow Alarms from the telephone network if connected through a Digital Cross-Connect System. It should also issue a Yellow Alarm when recognizing an incoming failure.
4. Install a Channel Service Unit (CSU) or function if the T-1 service uses metallic wire facilities. CSUs should have a self-powered option in case the local telephone company doesn't furnish line power.

T-1 Line Encryption

Encryption has one basic characteristic that presents problems when T-1 lines connected to telephone company equipment. To be truly secretive about data transmission, they encrypt framing patterns to prevent anyone knowing where the frames start and their size.

The telephone office equipment requires the T-1 framing pattern along with the end-user's data. No framing pattern means an alarm condition and no connection. Encrypting the framing pattern is the same as no framing pattern to a Digital Cross-Connect System.

There is a way to get around this problem. Several companies offer a device that adds the standard framing patterns to the end-user's data after encryption. It is a separate unit and doesn't compromise the secrecy of the encrypter. The one stipulation of the device is the encrpyted data runs at 1,536,000 bps.

One last concern is the possible wide swing of isochronous bit rates associated with some encrypters. The isochronous maximum variance must agree to standard T-1 tolerances.

12

Equipment Selection

Product or equipment selection starts with a clear definition of the required attributes. Judging products on how closely they meet the defined criteria comes next. Extensive documentation completes the process to substantiate the decisions made. Those are the three main steps used in the selection process. Nevertheless, they can be summed up in just one statement: Make intelligent and honest product selections as if you expected a lawsuit from one of the losers.

The old Bell System product selection process showed that outside manufacturers had a chance at the telephone market. Decision packages were very thorough and were reviewed for any flaws in thinking. Reasonable searches for available equipment reduced complaints that the Bell System just bought products from their own manufacturing arm.

Before the selection process started, telephone equipment usually came only from Western Electric. Picking Western Electric resulted from not looking past their nose for other comparable equipment. Some people were astounded that other manufacturers existed.

The Bell System's selection process went beyond just making a reasonable search for comparable products. It introduced quality standards and life cycle methods as well. This chapter assumes you have established the need for a particular type of product already.

Determining Product Attributes

Determining a product's attributes requires an open mind. Placing personal interests into the selection process leads to failure of the final litmus test. Could your decision stand up in a law court if the losers were to sue?

Companies get around this issue by appointing large committees to make the decision. Committee decisions often lead to confusion, delays, and vendor frustrations. Placing the selection process into the hands of a few good people eliminates these problems. A committee can agree on the basic needs while a small selection group justifies the final decision. This is where the finished product is a signed document by the product selectors. Documented reasons why different manufacturers were chosen or eliminated helps maintain open minds. A reasonable search of available manufacturers is the first step.

Reasonable Search

What constitutes a reasonable search of products? While the word reasonable seems boundless, it can find limits when time limits cut off further searching. Selecting products for emergency situations limits the reasonable search time to hours.

Looking for all the T-1 product manufacturers in the world is beyond reason. There are over 50 different products available and another dozen on their way. A reasonable search in this case may take only a few days to find a dozen candidates. Searching for manufacturers of public switched 56-kbps digital units takes longer than T-1 multiplexers. The end result is a list of manufacturers and a description of how you assembled the list.

Depending on the time allotted for the product study, the following product search methods are in order of preference.

1. Trade shows have a cross-section of prominent vendors.

    Prominent data communications equipment trade shows:

    a. Interface
    b. Telecommunications Association (TCA) in San Diego, CA
    c. Communications Network (ComNet)

    Prominent voice communications equipment trade shows:

    a. International Communications Association
    b. ComNet
    c. Interface

2. Trade magazines and newspapers: *Data Communications, Communications Week, Network World,* and *TPT* provide new product information.

3. Consultants: Knowledgeable consultants already know almost all vendors. Hiring uninformed consultants results in additional costs for their learning process. CAUTION — A consultant may have financial associations with specific manufacturers and provide biased recommendations. Check on associations before contracting their services.

4. Reference services: Reference services paint with broad brush strokes when listing products. Their reports are like economic studies that obsolesce before the ink dries.

Required/Desirable/Nice,But Attributes

Descriptions of physical attributes of a product fall into three categories. One category is the required features that meet all the basic needs. The second category has the features that make the unit desirable but are not essential to its operation. Lastly comes items that are nice to have but are on the bottom of the priority list.

Basic needs are easy to list. The T-1 multiplexer must transmit so many voice and data circuits. It must meet a certain level of voice coding quality. All the things you cannot do without make up this list. Safety specifications are essentials items and fall into the required category.

Desirable items are subjective and draw upon the openness of the selector's mind. They are also the extra cost items that can destroy the basic economics that started the project. Going into our friendly car showroom, we have told the salesperson that we need a car to get to work. We have reached the spot between basic transportation and minor pleasures. Side view mirrors, radio, and an automatic transmission are desirable but not essential to basic transportation.

Developing the last category of "nice, but" usually covers a small child's fantasy in the candy store, better yet, the grown-up child back in our car showroom. Rational thinking disappears when presented with a choice of genuine cordovan leather instead of the crushed velvet. Responses from vendors about this category serve as tiebreakers if several products meet the other two categories.

The one thing you do not want to do is revise your product attributes in the middle of the selection process. Making revisions in midstream forces the whole process back to square one.

Set Minimum Acceptable Levels

Your real minimum acceptance level stops at the required basic category. Nevertheless, there is a point in the desirable category that becomes essential for operation in the future. Compatibility to future telephone company services could play a big part in a few years. These issues are like attributes and are firm items that don't change during selection.

Boiler Plate Specifications

Boiler plate specifications are really minimum acceptable industry manufacturing standards. They follow the accepted practice for circuit board manufacture and power wiring conventions. The unfortunate part for neophytes getting into quality control is the lack of a composite reference.

Experiencing the worst possible manufacturing methods teaches you what to look for in all other products. You quickly learn that the solder plating on the circuit board should shine instead of being a dull gray color. Components should lie flat on the board and have their leads bent and crimped properly. Solder capillary action draws up through the plated-through holes to make a positive contact. Hand-soldering shouldn't leave excess rosin flux that leaves a brown residue.

Component parts in any product should be consistent. One manufacturer varied the types of capacitors used with their power supplies. While it is an excepted practice to use different manufactured components, it is a mistake to vary the types or the values. The top quality manufacturer uses extra inspection stops to assure consistency.

Acceptable industry manufacturing standards is a motherhood statement that belongs in the required category. Standard references become your crutch to ensure compatibility.

Standards

Three major standards organizations (ANSI, EIA, and IEEE) issue specifications for North American interfaces and connectivity. Besides these normal standard organizations, the telephone companies issue technical references. These either agree with the major standards or set quasi-standards when no other exist.

AT&T, Bell Communications Research, and GTE all issue Technical References. Bell Communications Research by far are the most prolific writers of technical advisories and references. Technical advisories precede references and serve to notify the communications industry of their plans.

The following Technical References cover digital services. Both AT&T and Bell Communications Research issue free catalogs each year to keep up with changes. Bell Communications Research issues monthly reports about advisories and references in their monthly *DIGEST of Technical Information.*

AT&T Technical References

AT&T Customer Information Center
P.O. Box 19901
Indianapolis, IN 46219

800-432-6600

PUB 10000 — Catalog of Communications Technical Publications (Obtain each year to uncover the latest issues)

PUB 10020 — Writer's Guide for Product and/or Procedural Documentation

PUB 41458 — Special Access Connections to the AT&T Communications Public Switched Network

PUB 41459 — Integrated Services Digital Network (ISDN) Primary Rate Interface

PUB 41460 — Special Access Data Channel Interface

PUB 43202 — AT&T Analog Voice

PUB 43801 — Digital Channel Bank

PUB 53250 — Quality Program Evaluation

PUB 54010 — X.25 Interface Specifications

PUB 54014 — ACCUNET T45 Service

PUB 54015 — Customer Controlled Reconfiguration (CCR)

PUB 54016 — Requirements for Interfacing Digital Terminal Equipment to Services Employing the Extended Superframe

PUB 54017 — Automatic Protection (T-1 automatic switch at the telephone company office)

PUB 54070 — M44 Multiplexing (ADPCM multiplexers)

PUB 54075 — 56 kb/s Subrate Data Multiplexing

PUB 60110 — Digital Synchronization Network Plan

PUB 61330 — ACCUNET Switched 56 Service to Public Switched Digital

PUB 62120 — Digital Data System with Secondary Channel

PUB 62310 — Digital Data System Channel Interface

PUB 62411 — ACCUNET T 1.5 Service Description and Interface Specifications (T-1 specifications)

Bell Communications Research Technical References

Bell Communications Research
Information Operations Center
60 New England Avenue
Piscataway, NJ 08854-4196

201-981-5600

CAT 10000 — Catalog of Technical Information

TR-TSY-000021 — Synchronous DS3 Format

TR-TSY-000170 — Digital Cross Connect System Requirements

TR-TSY-000210 — Low Bit Rate Voice (ADPCM multiplexers)

TR-TSY-000367 — ISDN Basic Access

PUB 62508 — High Capacity Digital Access Service Transmission Parameter Limits and Interface Combinations

DIGEST of Technical Information (Subscription — monthly issues list all the latest technical advisories and references)

Bell Operating Companies

Ameritech Services, Inc.
Information Release Organization
3040 West Salt Creek Lane 3-27
Arlington Heights, IL 60005

AM-TR-NPL-000001 Public Packet Services Technical Interface

AM-TR-NPL-000002 Technical Interface Specifications for X.25 Service

AM-TR-NPL-000004 Northern Telecom Digital Multiplex Switch

AM-TR-NPL-000005 Datapath Network Interface

AM-TR-NPL-000007 Digital Service Interface Specifications

AM-TR-NPL-000008 Data Over Voice Multiplexer Interface (X.25 Service)

Bell Atlantic Network Services, Inc.
Manager — Information Exchange
1310 N. Court House Road 5th Floor
Arlington, VA 22201

TR 72009 Bell Atlantic Data/Voice Multiplexer Service Specifications

IP 72020 Writer's Guide for Vendor Documentation

BellSouth Services
Documentation Operations
9th Floor
2121 8th Avenue
North Birmingham, AL 35203

IP 73151 Vendor Writer's Guide

TR 73501 Lightgate Exchange Access Service Channel Interface

NYNEX Enterprises
Information Management
441 9th Ave., 7th Floor
New York, NY 10001

NTR-74250 Infopath[SM] Packet Switching Service X.25 Interface

Pacific Bell
Information Exchange Administrator
2600 Camino Ramon
Room 1E200
San Ramon, CA 94583

PUB L-780056-PB/NB Advanced Digital Network

Southwestern Bell Telephone Co.
Information Release Manager
500 North Broadway, Room 1300
St. Louis, MO 63102

US West Inc.
Manager — Information Release
1999 Broadway, Room 510
Denver, CO 80202

Publisher's Data Center, Inc.
P.O. Box C9104
G.P.O.
Brooklyn, NY 11202
(An outlet for technical references)

GTE–Communication Systems Corporation

GTE–Communication Systems Corporation
Publications Manager
Department 431.1 — Tube Station C-1
400 North Wolf Road
Northlake, IL 60614

CH-600 Basic Telephone Course

CH-700 Engineering Considerations for Microwave Communications

CH-710 Readings in Pulse Code Modulation

FCC Part 68 — Registration Criteria

Breaking the Bell System's control of equipment connected directly to their network brought about FCC, Part 68. This is a comprehensive collection of manufacturing standards compiled by AT&T–Bell Laboratories and the Federal Communications Commission.

A better name for FCC Part 68 is "Shake and Bake." Shake and bake is a literal definition of the tests made against the FCC Registration criteria. There are drop and vibration tests for the shake part. Bake tests include raising the temperature and humidity levels. In between the shake and bake are a battery of electrical tests to ensure the safety of the product.

Drop tests use a weight-to-height ratio to determine how far to drop the equipment. It is reasonable to think that the equipment will experience falls during and after installation. Lightweight equipment should not fall apart if dropped a few inches. Even the most secure-looking device may destruct under the lightest stress conditions. Drop tests include dropping the unit on all flat surfaces and on each corner. Tests include drops with and without shipping packages.

Shake tests place the equipment on a vibration table to check for loose components. Again, it is reasonable to think the equipment's trip to the installation site may be in the back of a truck and subject to vibration.

Bake tests put the device in temperature and humidity chambers. Both the temperature and the humidity vary over a wide range. Telephone equipment often experiences a hostile environment. Hostile environments included the frugal end-user that turned the heat off when leaving work in the wintertime. Whenever the temperature dropped below 40°, the terminal stopped working. The telephone company soon learned to call the user to turn the heat back on when a subscriber service reported a trouble condition.

Electrical tests provide a measure of safety for the end-user. One test is a 20,000 volt discharge to all sides of the equipment. An end-user may walk across a carpet and build a static electrical charge on the body. Reaching out to touch the equipment may produce that electrical discharge and that familiar zap sound.

Another electrical test is saved to the last because it is a known destructive test. It places a variable electric voltage on all the interface leads to the unit. Next, they raise the voltage to 400 volts to simulate the interface leads coming in contact with high voltage in the building's cable runs.

While being destructive to the interface components, it should not catch on fire. If it does catch on fire, the end-user shouldn't face the problem of toxic fumes.

Passing the FCC Part 68 Registration tests is costly and time consuming for the manufacturer. It is well worth the consumer's time and effort to have all equipment meet these standards. Besides protecting your own health, it will also meet fire-code standards around the country.

Writing Specifications

Writing a Request for Proposal (RFP) is the next step after compiling a list of products and standards. A description of your communication needs should preface the actual requirements. Your description of your needs and goals include enough detail for the RFP responder to offer an intelligent reply.

This is a good place to determine your basic and desirable needs. List all your communication's basic needs and standards in the first section of your requirements. Desirable features and the "nice, but" items are in the next two sections. Each section includes a clarification on the position or value you place on each one. There are times when available products do not meet your basic needs. Taking the best features from several products leads to two different results. One, the entrepreneur vendor may quickly change their equipment to meet the RFP. Two, you assign weighted values to the basic needs. Like buying that car, you absolutely need tires and an engine. You may assign a value of 10 points to that basic need. Windshield wipers are a basic need but you only need them on rainy days. Rainy days occur only 20% of the time and have a 2-point weighting.

Eliminating the Obvious

Eliminating the obvious vendors from the competition is relatively easy. They are the ones that have responded with a no-response or don't answer your proposal. When they do respond, there are glaring deficiencies in meeting your basic needs. Glaring deficiencies are either actual fact, or the RFP lacked clarity for a good response.

Before putting the vendor in the nonresponsive file, verbally check the vendor to see if their answer was for your specific question. People often supply the wrong answer for the right question. They also can furnish the right answer for the wrong question.

All oral and written contacts with vendors becomes part of your final document. Document all oral contacts with vendors and include the following items.

1. The date and time that you had contact with the vendor.
2. The vendor contact's name.
3. A brief statement about the conversation.

For your own protection, document verbatim any comments of intent from either side. Nevertheless, nothing replaces a formal written statement of intent.

Reducing the Winners to a Precious Few

You have cleared away the wheat from the chaff and a clear-cut winner hasn't emerged from the wheat. Now the character of the product selectors shows through. This is the time for that police officer who would give his own mother a ticket for speeding. You have to physically and mentally distance yourself from the vendor's and manufacturer's personnel. One cannot remain impartial after buying stock in the company or spending a night on the town with the vendor. Business lunches or dinners are on the outer limits for accepting gifts.

Product selection can get down to the fine points. Getting the right information and making life-cycle studies help you reach the correct decision. Vendor presentations help one understand the value of the equipment and can clear up questions. Life-cycle studies cover the maintenance cost over the life of the product. A product with a lower initial cost may cost more to maintain over time.

Vendor Presentations

Vendors are usually eager to make presentations about their equipment to end-users when a sale may result. Their time and your time is a complete waste without preplanning.

1. Audience for presenters: Making a marketing intense presentation to a group of engineers leads to frustration on both sides. An engineer wants to know how it works and not that it comes in six decorator colors. The best vendor presentations include a person for sales hype and a technician for the engineer's questions.

2. Presenter's qualifications: Factory representatives are well meaning but lack the knowledge of the actual manufacturer. Your final decision may rest on the information gathered at the presentation.

3. Review of presentation: Understand exactly what the presentation covers before scheduling a time. Clarify exactly what you expect from the presentation and the time allotted.

4. Size of audience: Don't surprise the presenter by changing the size of the audience at the last minute. Presenters plan their delivery to meet the audience demands. Changing an intimate conversation planned for several people to an audience of 30 people has an unsettling result. Conversely, planning for a large audience and then finding only a few people is another presentation pain.

5. Presentation control: A presentation's value increases if run as a well-controlled meeting. Gate-keeping during the session keeps the presentation from wandering away from the intent.

6. Open items: Sometimes questions arise to which the presenters do not have answers. Write these questions and the questioner's name on an easel or note pad. The vendor should furnish an answer in an agreed-upon reasonable time. Having the questioner's name helps get the answer back to the right person.

Clarify Perceived Shortcomings with Vendor

Perception is another name for assumption. One assumes the vendor meant her product was or wasn't compatible with a particular standard. The manufacturer seemed to purposely duck a point in your RFP by omission or evasion.

Unless you and the vendor are master communicators, there are chances for perceived shortcomings. A major reason to write at an eighth- grade reading level is understanding. Showing everyone your vocabulary skills and lengthy sentence structure leads to misunderstanding. Misunderstanding leads to perceived shortcomings.

Life-Cycle Studies

Life cycle studies look at the total picture of a product. Making only initial cost evaluations is nearsighted. Maintenance costs over the life of the product include maintenance time, failure time, spare units, and power requirements.

1. Mean Time to Repair (MTTR): How long does it take to repair a unit? How far away are replacement parts? Are spare circuit boards necessary to keep the unit running?
2. Mean Time to Failure (MTTF): After a product passes an infant mortality period, one can expect a 63% average failure of the unit or its components during the MTTF hours. A normal year has 8,760 hours. If you had 100 units, each with a MTTF of 8,760 hours, you could expect 63 units to fail in the first year. Each component has a theoretical MTTF. Quality inspections and burn-in testing raise the actual number of hours.
3. Power and Cooling: Power and air-conditioning to lower the heat produced by the power cost money. It usually works out to be a minor difference between products but could be a fine point to make your final decision.
4. Floor Space: Land and building space for the equipment costs loaded money. The load includes power, heating, cooling and maintenance services. While a few square feet of building space seems insignificant, it can become costly in a computer room in New York City.

Quality

Quality of a manufacturer's product starts at the top person in the company and is a state of mind. If this state of mind doesn't exist at all levels in a company, the chances are the product has quality control problems.

Involvement in quality is more than a sign on the wall. It permeates every phase of the manufacturing process, and visiting the manufacturers plant is the only way to ascertain quality.

1. Quality manuals: Quality manuals detail every phase of the manufacturing process. They should include graphic pictures showing acceptable and unacceptable limits. After the manufacturer completes a quality manual, they should be readily accessible to the workers. Having one manual in the front office demonstrates quality lip service. Employees should know exactly where the manuals are and how to use them.

2. Component inspections: Component quality has three general classifications. Top quality parts are the most expensive because the original manufacturer made a 100% inspection before selling. Users of the components have a choice to pay more for quality parts, inspect incoming parts on their own, or do nothing. Some manufacturers wait for bad components to show up in the final test of the finished product.

3. Product inspections: Product quality inspections vary from inspection stations interlaced throughout the entire manufacturing chain to nothing. Quality control pinpoints what phase of manufacturing introduces problems. Inspections along the way sectionalize trouble spots and helps eliminate the faults.

4. Product handling: Circuit boards require special handling throughout manufacture and installation. Racks should separate the boards so they do not touch. If they are piled on top of each other, chances are some damage will result. Besides being a sign of carelessness, some damage may show when it is critical to your business.

5. Employee attitude: Employees' attitudes makes the difference in quality control. Their attitude toward quality and their company sticks out like a neon sign. Plant tours at the employees' lunch time serve a purpose for the manufacturer: You can't determine the real size of their capability and you can't ask embarrassing questions. If a plant tour is part of your schedule, do it when the workers are present.

6. Return products for repair: Even the highest quality plants have some products returned for repair. Finding actual numbers of units returned is similar to asking the true age of a person over 30. Review their trouble repair process instead. There should be quality control records to pinpoint particular component failure. Your main interest is how they get around to repair your equipment and what they do with a known component failure problem. Car manufacturers recall their lemons, and so should telecommunications manufacturers.

Technical Support and Operating Documents

Technical Support

Technical support varies from company to company. You never really know how well they provide support until an emergency arises. If you do not have previous experience with the manufacturer, request user contacts to talk to.

The old Bell System had a data technical force that provided assistance around the clock. It had the ability to tap the minds of some of the brightest people to solve difficult problems. DATEC (DAta TEChincal) grew out of end-user frustration with long outages from strange and difficult problems.

When you have problems, you also want quick resolution. Trouble identification is difficult over the phone, but becomes easier if given more facts other than "it's broke." Before calling the technical support, compile a chronological event list.

Training Availability

Training your personnel on the new equipment is another cost item. Manufacturers can spread their cost of constructing a training program over a larger segment. This doesn't automatically make them the best source for your training needs. If they have an established training course, review their manuals or monitor a training session for compatibility with your company's needs.

Operating Documents

Nothing is worse than buying a product and finding poorly written operating instructions. One instruction manual spent two pages on the power cord and how to insert the plug into an electrical outlet. It then covered the calibration process with a single sentence.

Telephone companies turn out operating instructions about everything in sight. They all follow the same format at the eighth-grade reading level of understanding. Technicians usually write at a reading level far above the reader's capability. Letting the marketing department write the instructions leads to redundant use of trade names. One such manual had 23 trade names on one page. Trying to read "Take the blank cord and place it into the blank connector of the blank circuit board" detracts from the understanding.

Operating manuals remain long after trained people move on to other jobs. They may be your last refuge during a crisis period. As such, you do not have time to interpret the manual.

Other Selection Concerns

Single Source Supplies

Deciding on a vendor that makes proprietary equipment locks you to that group for years. It becomes a long-term commitment to the manufacturer's technology not crossing over to standard services. Changing in mid-stream to other technology is costly.

At one time, the telephone company was a single source for telecommunications. One was locked into the telephone company's pricing. If you didn't like the latest tariff increase, just wait to see what happens next year.

Divestiture of AT&T brought multiple sources to choose from. Multiple sources for equipment leaves you an out when the unforeseen happens. Standard compatible equipment may not provide all the bells and whistles, but it is a life preserver when everything else sinks into the sea.

Buy-out Possibilities

Selecting a product is like marriage. Some marriages are made in heaven and others in hell. If you are lucky, the company you selected is right there when you need them. Finding out that the original manufacturer of the equipment sold by your vendor now belongs to the manufacturer's competitor leaves a support void.

Predicting corporate buy-outs rapidly changes one's financial picture. Crystal ball magic isn't everyone's forte, but common sense is available. Vendors selling someone else's equipment always face quick divorce proceedings.

Testing for Final Compatibility

One last step verifies your product decision. Does the equipment really work as well as they say it will? Was it ever used for the same purpose before? Testing before purchasing reduces the risks in selection.

Laboratory Testing versus Real-Life Testing

Performing tests in a laboratory or on a test bench is better than nothing. You can verify about 80% of the conditions seen in real life. Connecting equipment to the actual network is the final proof.

Manufacturers base their claims of analog data performance on tests in their lab. They can't reproduce the same conditions you experience in your network. That 9600-bps modem looks good on the bench but falls apart on your network.

Telephone Company Testing

AT&T tests telecommunications equipment for compatibility with their services. They make these tests either at the request of the manufacturer or if they have some internal need. Consequently, the testing information has limited distribution within the company. Vendors that successfully completed compatibility testing refer to the test in their advertising.

Other telephone companies offer similar testing arrangements for a fee. They provide the end-user or the manufacturer with a testing facility for hire.

Stress Testing Considerations

Testing the equipment before the buy decision gives valuable information. Determining which tests to run usually rests with the imagination of the tester. Usually the only choice is testing telecommunications equipment against published standards. The following stress tests really tell the worth of the equipment.

1. Test the equipment under a full load. It takes longer to fully load the unit with voice and data circuits, but this prevents problems later on when your network grows. Some equipment looks great under a light load: Load the device down and discover the internal buses or buffers can't handle the bits of data.
2. Stress the voice-coding method with a wide voice pitch range. High-pitched female voices stress the coding better than anything. Repeat phrases with soft and harsh sounds.
3. Data test may look great under a quasi-random word generator but cause problems with a repetitive pattern. One piece of telephone office equipment charged a capacitor with a string of ones bits and discharged back during an occasional zero bit. The problem existed for years before the repetitive pattern discovered the situation. Use a repetitive pattern of many ones bits with occasional zero bits to generate false framing. Alternate inverse ones bit dominant patterns with zero bit dominant patterns to stress jitter characteristics.
4. Simulate worst operating conditions. Stress the unit by raising the temperature of the surrounding area and operating an electric drill nearby. Meet but do not exceed the manufacturer's claimed operating temperature.

Documenting the Results

Final documentation of your work serves a twofold purpose. One, the information will keep you from explaining your actions to lawyers. Second, it shows the quality of your decision process. Each product selection package should include the following.

1. Need Statement: Why make the product selection in the first place.
2. Product Requirements: Enter the requirements used in the Request for Proposal. If you used weight factors with the requirements, list the rationale in your assignments.
3. List of Manufacturers: This is the original list of manufacturers found during your reasonable search.
4. Nonresponsive Manufacturers: List the reasons the manufacturers were not responsive to your requirements.
5. Support Documentation: Include all documents, notes, and meeting minutes.

13

Facilities

Getting from one place to another requires a transport system of some sort. When it comes to transporting telecommunications, the task falls to something called "facilities." This word doesn't really jump out and produce a clear picture of a transport system. Looking up the definition of the word in the dictionary leaves one still unenlightened.

Facilities, according to time-honored telephone company practices, refers to cables, microwave radio, and associated equipment. It can be hardware or software. It can mean almost anything between the end-user and the telephone company switch. The telephone companies have a clear view of telecommunications. There are customers, telephone switches, and facilities.

This chapter deals with the main facility types available. These categories fall into four major areas of cable, fiber, microwave radio, and satellite. Each has its own characteristics, which the end-user should understand.

Cable

The generic term cable covers two main subcategories. One is the metallic wire that one finds on end-user premises with the connections to the local telephone office. The second grouping is a coaxial cable that may appear on the premises as well as at interconnecting telephone offices.

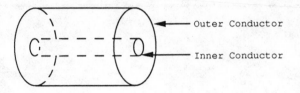

Figure 13-1   Coaxial Cable.

The nature of high-frequency transmission became the basic reason for coaxial cables in the first place. At low frequencies, the electrons evenly distribute throughout the entire diameter of a wire. As the frequency increases, the electrons transferring energy move towards the perimeter of the wire. Coaxial cables use the "skin effect" principle (i.e., the center portion of the wire has no value) in their construction.

Coaxial Cable

Coaxial cables are better suited to transmitting a high range of frequencies. The Bell System installed coaxial cable with an outer conductor that had a 3/8 inch diameter of overlapping copper strips. An inner 10-gauge wire locates at the center axis of the outer conductor. Insulating disks every inch kept the outer conductor equidistant from the inner. The overlapping outer conductor permits bending, and the disks keep the inner conductor in the middle (Figure 13-1). While this size seems overkill for coaxial design, the cable also carried electrical power to many repeaters along the way.

Smaller size (3/16 and 1/4 inch) coaxial cables are prevalent with video and other electronic equipment. Instead of using copper strips for the outer conductor, the smaller cable uses a flexible fine wire interlocking mesh. While the coaxial cable has some flexibility, it must take gradual bends to change directions. Running coaxial cable in tight or small building cable ducts presents problems.

Coaxial cable's niche in the telecommunications world lies between 1,000,000 and 1,000,000,000 Hz (1 MHz and 1 GHz). Equipment that has frequencies below 1 MHz would normally use twisted-pair wire. Frequencies greater than 1 GHz limit the use of coaxial cable due to the reaction to small differences in the cable's manufacture.

Splicing coaxial cables together is an easy process with previously installed threaded connections. The hard task is putting the connector on the end of the cable. Both the outer and inner conductors should have a secure or soldered linkage to the connector, Connectors need more than hand tightening to assure a tight fit.

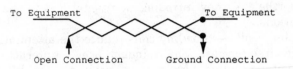

Open Connection   Ground Connection

Figure 13-2   Unbalanced Twisted-Pair.

Twisted-Pair Metallic Cable

In the world of the telephone company, twisted metallic wire pairs still remain a large part of the local network. While they are installing large quantities of local fiber cables, it will take a long time to replace the wire cable facilities.

Normal connections with twisted-pair wire require the least amount of expertise. Telephone companies changed their connection methods years ago. At one time, technicians solder-connected the wires or used screw terminals. They then changed to wire-wrap and push-on connections to speed installation time. While both methods reduced connection time, they led to poor connections if it corroded.

Usually twisted-pair provides a complete loop connection between locations. The general concept has energy traveling towards the remote end on one wire and returning on the other. Energy requires a potential difference (positive and negative voltage) to move — otherwise it would stand still. Sending energy down one wire requires the use of an earth ground as a potential reference. Since all outside noise interference uses the same ground potential, twisted-pair wires pick up junk signals close enough to induce a voltage.

Twisted metallic pairs can emulate a coaxial cable (Figure 13-2) and provide a shield to noise. One of the wires remains unattached at one end and connects to an electrical ground on the other end. All noise and radiation products effectively remain shielded from entering or leaving the working wire. The drawback is that two metallic pairs produce the same load-carrying capacity that the single unshielded twisted-pair did.

Two major transmission considerations occur with the telephone company's twisted-pair wires.

1. Bridge Taps — Bridge taps are stub-wires attached along the cable during installation. They allow greater flexibility to bridge or make connections off the main cable anywhere along the route. As the customer requests service, cable assignments can quickly take place without opening the cable sheath.

Nevertheless, they introduce additional loss to the overall calculations.

2. Loading Coils — Loading coils reduce the attenuation of upper voice frequencies. Their inductance counteracts the stray capacitance found between the twisted-pairs. While ideal for voice circuits, they introduce a high loss to signals over 4,000 Hz. This frequency cut-off is too low for most digital data services, and technicians must remove the load coils. When the telephone companies unload a cable, they physically detach the inductance load coils every 6000 feet or less.

Advantages of Cable

1. The shielded electrical structure of coaxial cables lessens chances for radiation of signals. If someone attempted to tap into a telephone company coaxial, the system would alarm and shut down. An intruder would also get a large charge from the electrical current on the line.
2. Connecting coaxial and twisted-paired wires doesn't require highly trained technicians. Available fixed length coaxial cables provide screw-together connectors. Custom-made coaxial cables require some technical ability.
3. It is economically sound practice to use existing twisted-pair in-house wiring instead of installing other methods.

Disadvantages of Cable

1. Coaxial cable doesn't bend around sharp corners. Right-angle connectors (additional cost) permit sharp bends at terminals or other locations. Each connector adds a slight amount of loss to the signal.
2. Twisted-pair metallic cable radiates signals, especially at frequencies over 1,000,000 Hz.
3. Twisted-pair metallic cables present the following transmission problems:

   a. Wire-wrapped connections lead to corroding and an electric open.
   b. Acts like an antenna and picks up stray radiated signals. Twisted-pair wire should never run next to power cords or equipment.

Fiber-Optic

Fiber-optic cable is the way of the future since it provides so many advantages to expanding integrated digital services. We like to include both terms of fiber and optic, since they each have equal influence. Just as one thinks the combined equipment's capacity has peaked, fiber designers introduce a new method; optic people, undaunted by fiber's progress, make another major breakthrough.

When a new cast of designers shows up, one can expect a new set of terminology to follow. Wire and coaxial designers worried about signal attenuation. Fiber people worry about a link budget instead. The following terms appear in fiber-optic references.

1. Core and Cladding — Both the core and the cladding use similar material in manufacture. Their main difference is the a refraction index that indicates the amount of light bending. The core has a higher level of refraction in comparison to the cladding and results in almost total internal reflection. Light hitting the boundary at an angle greater than the critical angle (Figure 13-3) will totally reflect. Angles less than the critical angle will allow part of the light power to penetrate the cladding. Cladding's refraction index remains constant, but core indexes can vary for graded or step light dispersion.
2. Launched Signal Power — The maximum light power delivered at the transmit end of the fiber.
3. Link Budget — The difference between the launched power and the receiver's sensitivity. It's like a personal budget where one knows how much they can spend without going bust. You know your limit and make design trade-offs to stay within the bounds.
4. Numerical Aperture — Numerical aperture (NA) indicates the coupling efficiency of the light source to the fiber. Launched power at greater angles than the NA rapidly attenuates (Figure 13-3) when the light hitting (critical angle) the cladding doesn't totally reflect. The NA is the sine function of the following expression. Smaller numerical aperture angles provide higher bandwidths.
5. Wavelength Division Multiplexers — A wavelength division multiplexer is really a just a coupling device that connects up to three different light sources into one fiber. Each light source has its own wavelength. The unit is small enough to fit into your hand and befits the old cliche that good things come in small packages.
6. Single Mode — Single mode fiber cables use a step index (constant refraction properties in the core). Single mode fiber

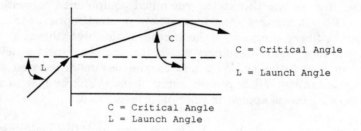

$$\text{Network Aperture} = \sin(L) = \sqrt{n^2_1 - n^2_2}$$

Where n_1 = Core Refraction Index
n_2 = Cladding Refraction Index

C = Critical Angle
L = Launch Angle

C = Critical Angle
L = Launch Angle

Figure 13-3   Launch and Critical Angle.

cables use a core size around 10 μm (μm = millionths of a meter). Single mode propagation is possible when meeting the following parameters.

$$(3.1456) \times \sqrt{n^2_1 - n^2_2} \times \frac{\text{Radius}}{\text{Wavelength}} = < 2.405$$

7. Multimode — Multimode fibers use step or graded index, which lets the light rays or modes travel a zig-zag path. Graded index varies the refractive properties from a maximum deviation between n_1 and n_2 at the center to a minimum at the edges. Originally developed for the short haul or local area networks. They show a greater tolerance to component imperfections and mechanical connections.

8. Short-wave — Short waves are around 850 nm range. For those who think only in inches, the wavelength is 0.000034 inches long.

9. Long-wave — Long waves are in the 1300 and 1500 nm range. (0.000051 – 0.000059 inches long)

10. Light-Emitting Diodes — LEDs are the most commonly used light-transmitting devices because of economics. There are two classifications of LEDs — surface emitting and edge emitting. Edge emitters provide a smaller concentration of light for the smaller core sizes.

11. Injection Laser Diodes — Commonly referred to simply as Lasers, they emit a very narrow beam in comparison to LEDs and couple light energy into small numerical aperture fibers.

12. PIN Detectors — Best receiver for the lower range of optic frequencies (long wave) lower than 1050 nm. PIN stands for positive-intrinsic-negative in the design of the junction photodiode. Intrinsic simply means an area in the material without the contaminants used to make the P and N section. Another term for contaminants is doping and the intrinsic is undoped.

13. Avalanche Photodiode (APD) Detectors — Both the PIN and APD detectors start out being made from the same type of material — germanium (Ge) and indium gallium arsenide (IaGaAs). As the term avalanche suggests, the electron chain reaction set off by reverse voltage biasing generates gains of 10 for Ge and 20 to 30 for IaGaAs. PIN detectors have only a unity gain.

Fiber Cable Sizes

Fiber-optic cable comes in several major core and cladding diameters. Multimode fiber cables have four main variations of sizes. The following are the four main fiber sizes used with multimode transmission. Numerical specifications refer to the core size (first number) and the fiber's outside diameter (second number).

50/125 Cable This size cable was the first major telecommunications fiber, and remains one of the best selling multimode. Since its core size is only 50 μm, tolerances are more critical.

Nominal Numerical Aperture = 0.200

62.5/125 Cable This cable size was a compromise between the 50 micron fiber and the 85 micron one designed for local area networks. Its primary purpose was reaching the telephone company subscribers. Signs point to this size fiber becoming a standard size in the Unites States.

Nominal Numerical Aperture = 0.275

85/125 Cable The 85/125 micron cable meets the needs of the local area network equipment and international applications. It basically meets the needs for the environment of LAN where connections have a wide tolerance level.

Nominal Numerical Aperture = 0.260

100/140 Cable 100/140 micron fiber meets the needs for computer rooms and very short runs with many connectors. It has the lowest bandwidth capability of the multimode fibers, which makes it un-suitable for high data rates.

Nominal Numerical Aperture = 0.290

Advantages of Fibers

1. Reduced fiber size compared to comparable load carrying metallic cables makes fiber highly desirable. Fiber installs easi-ly in old metallic cable ducts and reduces right-of-way costs.
2. Inexpensive upgrade in circuit capacity possible with wavelength division multiplexers.
3. Reduced effect from transmission impairments provide a better error performance in comparison to metallic cables. Neverthe-less, fiber is not totally free of impairments that introduce er-rors.
4. Since it uses light for transmission, fiber doesn't radiate electromagnetic waves. Normal eavesdropping equipment can-not pick up information. (See Disadvantages of Eavesdropping).
5. Fiber systems have an error performance design worst case factor of 10^{-9} Bit Error Rate. The quality is high enough to review the use of High Level Data Link Controls. Normal frame check sequences may be an overkill.

Disadvantages of Fibers

1. Need higher level of technical competence for fiber connections. Fiber cables vary from sloppy to very stringent tolerances. Nevertheless, the skills needed for low-loss connections are above the untrained technician. Fusion (high temperature) con-nections require great expertise and costly equipment. Mechanical connections vary in their complexity.
2. Contrary to previous thoughts, people can tap the cable for un-authorized entry. Light from the core will escape when some-one scrapes away the cladding from the core. Only a slight drop in the overall level will indicate presence of cable tapping.
3. Greater care needed to prevent stress to the cable since glass doesn't stretch like copper. Cable manufacturers point out the tensile strength of fiber is 50,000 pounds per square inch. Nevertheless, the cross-section area of a fiber is a small frac-tion of a square inch, and the tensile strength need to break the fiber is less. Moisture reduces the stress level for glass and will cause breaks sooner than under dry loads.
4. Bends in the fiber cable add to the loss by reducing the critical angle (see Figure 13-3). Connectors also add to the total loss.

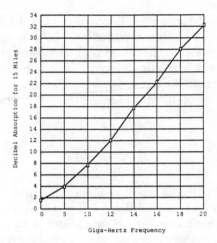

Giga-Hertz Frequency

Figure 13-4 Transmit Power Rain Absorption Loss.

Microwave (4,6,11,18,23 GHz)

Microwave radio systems were introduced to telecommunications in 1949 as the primary carrier for network television. Microwave systems grew over the years, and the service demand between locations quickly outgrew available frequencies. As each band of available radio frequencies reached saturation, the Federal Communications Commission approved new and higher bands.

The transmission of microwave radio is line-of-sight as if one was shining a huge flashlight at some distant point. While the majority of the light remains in the center, there is light that disperses to the sides. Dispersed radio waves cause interference with other receivers and allow reception by intruders.

Impairments Affecting Microwave Radio

Moisture presents a signal absorption factor that decreases the received signal. Microwave radio systems in the 18 and 23 GHz range will suffer the most. If the transmit and receive antennas are at their outer designed limits, the signal will drop too low with high moisture content. Automatic gain circuits will amplify the signal to a point. After that the signal will degrade rapidly. Figure 13-4 shows the absorption factors for a heavy rain.

The other major impairment to microwave radio is fading. Atmospheric conditions change during the year and refract radio signals. Normally the receive antenna sees only the direct line-of-sight transmission. Refracted radio signals out of phase with the direct signal will lower the power or produce fading to the received signal. When the refracted signals are in phase with the direct transmission, they add power and are "up-fades." Expect heavy fading of the transmission path from April through October. The hours between 2 and 10 a.m. suffer the most during fading and error rate increase during this period.

Analog Radio

Analog microwave radio uses frequency modulated (FM) signals or single side-band analog modulation. For a long time, the microwave radio systems didn't have linear amplifiers with high output power. Available amplifiers produced noise and distortion at their maximum power level. FM signals got around the amplitude distortion problem introduced by nonlinear amplifiers.

Single side-band transmission raised the number of voice channels permitted over the same bandwidth. During the modulation process, an upper and lower side-band product of the two frequencies results. Instead of transmitting both side-bands, the transmitter sends only one side-band or half the spectrum. If you only send half the signal, one could theoretically send twice the original number of channels in the same spectrum. Real-life irregularities and added guard bands allow something less than twice the number.

Digital Radio

Digital microwave radio uses transmission methods similar to modems. They use the Phase Shift Keying (PSK) and Quadrature Amplitude Modulation (QAM) found with data transmission. Data bit combinations (00,01,10,11) form symbols for a 4-phase signal. Three-bit combinations form an 8-phase signal, and 4-bit symbols produce 16 level. In the case of a 16-level baud rate, the phase representations also include amplitude modulation factors.

Popular digital microwave transmission speeds are 45 and 90 Mbps. As the signal levels increase, the timing recovery and other transmission impairments cause greater concern.

Microwave Radio Frequencies

4 GHz While there is a lower band of frequencies available for microwave, the 4 GHz band became the most popular. Telephone companies expanded their network with this band for years until they became saturated in the urban areas. Interference from other systems prompted new antenna design to reduce the transmission radio beam's width and lower the signal's dispersion. Additional interference came from satellite's down-link transmission from the space-to-earth direction. Line- of-sight transmission extends to a 30–35 mile range.

6 GHz Overcrowded transmission corridors in the main microwave routes led to the next band of frequencies. This band of frequencies also had interference from satellite transmission with the up-link signal from the earth-to-space direction. The telephone companies went to this band to increase the circuit-carrying capacity of microwave radio. At the same time, improvements greatly increased the capacity of the older systems, and this band found favor. Effective range of transmission is in a 25–30 mile range.

11 GHz Telephone companies originally used this band for short-haul microwave radio transmissions. Long distance carriers shied away from its use since that frequency introduces additional transmission impairments from rain and snow. The satellite (K_U) band down-link transmission from the space-to-earth direction also use portions of this spectrum. The line-of-sight transmission reduces to around a 20 mile range.

18 GHz This band is another short-haul transmission method. The telephone companies used this band for the Digital Signal Level-3 and 4 (44.736 and 274.176 Mb). The commercial rate usually seen is the DS-3 rate for 672 voice channels. The line of sight transmission reduces even further to the 10–15 mile range.

23 GHz This frequency band finds a home in the private very short-haul networks. Since its transmission distance is within a 5–10 mile range, it suits local transmission between end-user locations. It also suits urban areas already saturated with the lower microwave radio frequencies. Typical circuit-carrying capacity is 96 voice circuits.

Advantages of Microwave

1. Quickest way to implement a private transmission path between two line-of-sight locations.
2. Ideal for short-haul transmission between end-user buildings.

Disadvantages of Microwave

1. Microwave radio transmission decreases during rain, snow and heavy fog.

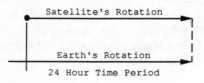

Figure 13-5   Geostationary Satellite.

2. Fading.
3. Saturation of microwave frequencies in urban areas prevents unlimited implementation.
4. Construction of high-rise buildings between transmitting sites will stop the radio signals. Getting around the obstruction requires new radio towers or other means to by-pass the building.
5. Site planning and transmission engineering necessary before applying for a radio license. Line-of-sight transmission as well as interference tests are an added expense.
6. Personnel operating the radio system require Federal Communications Commission licenses to maintain the equipment.
7. Eavesdroppers can easily intercept information sent.

Satellite

One of the best descriptions of satellite is that it is just another microwave system. The difference between the two is that the satellite repeater happens to be high in the sky. They both use similar transmission frequencies and equipment. While similar in nature, there are several major differences. One variation is that satellite receivers require very low-noise amplifiers to recover a good signal. Other considerations revolve around the many trade- offs of power and the size of antennas.

Geostationary vs. Elliptical Orbits

Satellites revolve around the world in two ways. One method is the geostationary, which really isn't stationary. It's moving just fast enough to look as if fixed to a point on Earth. Figure 13-5 shows the satellite's position at a point 22,300 miles above the equator. Needless to say, the satellite must be traveling at a faster rate for it to appear stationary.

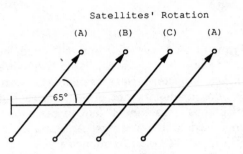

Satellites' Rotation

Earth's Rotation
24 Hour Time Period

Figure 13-6 Elliptical Orbit.

Elliptical orbits overcome poor reception of signals at locations in
the far northern or southern portions of Earth. Instead of a geostationary position, three different satellites travel at a 65 degree angle
to the equator (Figure 13-6). Being an elliptical orbit, the path takes
the satellite as close as 300 miles and as far away as 24,900 miles.
Russia's Molniya Series satellites' perigee (300 miles) nears the
Southern Hemisphere and apogee (24,900 miles) is over the Northern Hemisphere.

As one satellite moves out of the receiver's range, a collocated
receiver antenna dish locks onto the next satellite. This leads to expensive tracking antennas and synchronization during hand-offs between satellites.

FDMA

Frequency Division Multiple Access (FDMA) provides end-users with
a fixed frequency bandwidth channel out of a larger spectrum. Two-
way transmission requires two channels (one channel for each direction of transmission). Video broadcast transmission ideally fits the
use of one FDMA channel.

TDMA

Time Division Multiple Access (TDMA) provides a time-shared access
to one of the satellite's transponders. (A transponder is an amplifier
that receives on one frequency and transmits at another). Each
shared broadcast contains overhead for frame information and also
provides guard time between blocks of data.

VSAT

Very Small Aperture Transmission (VSAT) has obtained mixed reviews. This type of satellite offering looks desirable to businesses with many widely distributed locations. Data transmission around 9,600 and 56,000 bps provides trade-offs not possible with higher-speed transmission. Small dishes (less than 6 feet in diameter) are possible and are easily mounted atop buildings. Antenna size also depends on using the Ku Band (12/14 GHz) frequencies.

This service is like a lot of other satellite services with its trade-offs. When you opt for the very small antenna, you need Forward Error Correction for a reasonable error performance. Heavy moisture (rain, snow, fog) may put you out of business at particular locations. This means one must also provide a dial-backup service at the sites.

Satellite Trade-Offs

Fiber-optic cable installations have a lot of trade-offs, but nothing compares to the decisions one makes for satellite. For every decision there is another question raised. If one opts for small antenna dishes, the satellite's power must increase. Use too much power, and the life of satellite goes down. Use a large antenna dish and the building codes get sticky. End-users need all the help available to make sound decision about satellite installations.

C-Band Frequencies

C-Band frequencies use a 6 GHz (5.925–6.425 GHz) bandwidth for up-link transmission from Earth to the satellite. Down-link transmission from the satellite to Earth uses a 4 GHz (3.7–4.2 GHz) bandwidth. Two things hamper future growth with C-Band transmission. Satellite (C-Band) orbital location congestion and terrestrial interference from microwave routes limit expansion.

Ku-Band Frequencies

Ku-Bands use a 14 GHz (14.0–14.5 GHz) up-link and a 12 GHz (11.7–12.2 GHz) down-link. This band of frequencies allows new services into C-Band-saturated areas and the use of smaller antenna dishes. While they appear advantageous, they have their negative side. Just like microwave radio frequencies, they react to transmission impairments more quickly than the C-Band.

Advantages of Satellite

1. Ideally suited to broadcasting a signal to many receive stations.
2. By-passes local telephone companies and all escalating tariffs.

Disadvantages of Satellite

1. Not suited to heavy rain, snow, or fog areas. It has the same characteristics of signal absorption as microwave radio, shown in Figure 13-4. Rain will also depolarize horizontally and vertically polarized signals.
2. Requires forward error correction equipment to obtain good error performance. This type of equipment will reduce the overall bandwidth available for end-user data communications.
3. Echo cancelers needed for voice circuits. Double hop satellite circuits require adjustment in talking habits and changes in echo canceler delay settings. Front End Processors need extended polling time changes to account for the additional delay.
4. Site engineering required before committing to installation. Costs for site preparation add to the final installation figures.
5. Local zoning restrictions add another stumbling block to implementation.
6. Urban areas require special considerations for shielding against interference.
7. Satellite dishes on top of buildings add weight and wind loading factors to the construction.
8. Twice a year the receive antenna experiences sun-transit outage. Every March and October, the sun is in direct line with the receiver. For about six days running around noon each day, thermal noise is large enough to wipe out transmission for several minutes.
9. Encryption needed to prevent unauthorized reception of signals.

Facility Provider Selection

Selecting which facility provider has the best deal presents more choices than just bottom-line figures. There is no dispute that upper management understands dollar figures and finds it difficult to comprehend intangibles. Nevertheless, intangibles can often offset all but the most super bargain rates. No matter how great the perceived savings, you should still have a full understanding of what you're getting.

Shortest Facility Distance

Transmission impairments and delay are cumulative with distance. It makes sense that a shorter facility distance provides fewer transmission problems. If you have a choice between two or more facility providers, select the one that assures the shortest distance.

Providers are reluctant to furnish such information, since swapping facility assignments is another telephone company practice. If they can't guarantee facility assignments, they can determine availability and likely routes.

Telephone companies with a few main routes have limited ability to provide short direct runs. If the total distance is 10 times what it should be, then you can expect 10 times the troubles, too. High-priority data transmission stresses the need for the shortest-distance facility.

Mixture of Facility Types

Mixing facility types also leads to transmission problems. Jitter and clock recovery are but a couple of the concerns. When the facility provider checks on the distance of the route, have them find the facility types and other equipment used.

Maintenance and Protection

Facility providers also know what level of protection exists for the different routes. Telephone companies do not provide protection channels for every facility route. When they do provide a switching protection channel, it will back up various levels of working channels. One protection channel backing up 20 working lines is better than none, but gives you something less than a warm feeling. You get even a colder feeling when you realize the protection channel is also the maintenance spare. If the telephone company is working on another system, the protection channel isn't available for automatic restoration.

14

Digital Transmission Impairments

Digital transmission extends the basic principles of electronic technology to facilities. The most stringent principle for electronic logic circuits is the clocking pulses that open and close logic gates at the right time. Produce several clocks, or interject a varying clock pulse, and havoc will rule.

Chapter Five discussed timing sources in the telephone companies' digital networks. We can't overemphasize the concern about reducing clock sources to the barest minimum. For successful digital transmission, there should actually be only one clock source and some buffering to handle phase differences between received pulses.

While digital transmission impairments revolve around time domain factors, frequency transmission impairments affect them. Frequency modulation products vary the digital pulses to produce a thing called jitter. Jitter is like seeing your child on a swing. If the swing goes back and forth within reasonable bounds, you have no worries. Let that child swing back and forth beyond those bounds, and you exceed your concern tolerance level. Equipment also has a tolerance level to jitter. Go beyond this level and the equipment also becomes irrational.

While analog services can transmit almost any kind of data pattern, digital systems must include a specific density of ones bits to maintain system performance. Digital systems also dislike repetitive patterns that result in jitter or false frame synchronization.

Lastly, a major difference between analog and digital transmission is the error performance. Analog services have random errors, and digital services have spurts or bursts of errors. Since the error characteristics are different, they use a different error-measurement unit. High-speed analog services use a block error rate and digital

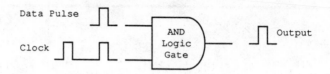

Figure 14-1   Normal Clock Operation.

transmission uses an error-free seconds rate. A correlation between the two error units lies within a simple formula shown later in this chapter.

Timing Problems

Timing has always been a factor for data transmission. Analog modems use an end-user master clock source and slave-time the remote modems. Digital services use either a telephone company or premise master clock. Both services require slave or loop timing throughout the network by recovering timing control from the incoming data. The main difference between analog and digital timing needs lie in the range of the two networks. Analog networks contain a number of individual timed facilities. Digital networks have only one timed source.

In a time domain system, the timing clock is the traffic cop that keeps things moving. Binary integrated circuits require this traffic clock to open and close logic gates at the precise time a bit shows up. Close the gate just as the next bit arrives and the bit smashes against the wall. Opening the gate when a bit isn't around yields zero results.

Too Many Sources

Clocking is one place where you can get too much of a good thing. No matter how accurate two or more clock sources are, there is a difference between them. Cyclic errors indicate more than one clock in the system. While all errors are bad, timing problems stand out by there repetitive display.

Accurate control of the clocking is one important thing. The other clocking concern is the phase relationship. Two circuits may have the same clock source but be 180 degrees out of phase with each other. Figure 14-1 shows the normal operation of a logic AND gate. If the clock pulse appears at the precise moment a data pulse shows up, the AND gate will output a pulse.

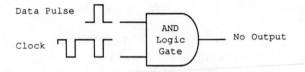

Figure 14-2   Out-of-Phase Clock Pulses.

Figure 14-2 shows the same AND gate, but with out of phase clocking pulses. Since the clocking pulses don't arrive at the same instant the data pulse appears, the gate doesn't open.

Low-Speed Timing

Some T-1 multiplexers can frequency lock their internal clock to one of the low-speed digital ports. It takes a low-speed DDS service clock from the DSU interface and synchronizes the internal clock.

Clock sources normally divide very-high-frequency clock sources down to a usable rate. Dividing the clock source in half also halves the inaccuracies. Taking a low-speed source and raising it to a usable rate multiplies the inaccuracies. Since the recovered DSU's clock is flopping back and forth, multiplying the inaccuracies makes it a dubious source. One example below starts with a worst-case DDS data service unit clock of plus 0.05% speed. Taking this worst-case clock frequency, we then multiply the source to a frequency also divisible by the final rate. The multiplied error frequency is 27,792 bps. Now we divide the clock error by the 36 to develop our final T-1 clock. What results is a clock 10 times the allowable T-1 clock variance. While the DDS data service unit's clock probably won't stray that far, one must consider what happens if it does.

Worst-Case DDS Frequency Tolerance

```
9600 bps × + 0.05% Accuracy = 9604.8 bps
```

Multiplication of Errored Clock to Higher Rate

```
4.8 bps × 5790 Clock Multiplier = 27,792 bps error
```

Dividing Clock and Error to Reach T-1 Rate

$$\frac{27,792 \text{ bps}}{36 \text{ Clock Divider}} = 772 \text{ bps error at T-1 rate}$$

Mixing Services

Telephone companies use all kinds of facilities to furnish their services. Long distance circuits sometime stretch the imagination of the telephone engineer. Lack of available circuits between two points may force the engineer to use round about routing. One created telephone circuit from the East Coast to the Southwest used every conceivable cable and radio facility. Instead of being around 1200 miles long, it traversed over 2600 miles and went through the same city twice.

Microwave radio systems start off from master frequency clock sources, but change frequency sources at each repeater. Connect two different microwave radio systems together and you add to the timing woes.

If your transmission facility is one type or manufacture, you diminish timing problems. Mixing services leads to slightly different nodal clock sources.

Jitter

Technical descriptions of jitter often use the words perturb and perturbation to describe the deviation of the digital signal from its norm. Nevertheless, the dictionary's first definition for perturb as "disturbing the mind" describes such writings better. As perturbing as jitter seems, it becomes tangible when translated from the technical jargon. Technocrats still debate the allowable jitter tolerances at various portions of the digital network. Jitter, as one can guess, generates along the network without any way to eliminate the cause. One either tolerates the jitter or creates a new, jitterless signal.

Cause of Jitter

Jitter results from the phase deviation of a time domain signal. While digital transmission is a time domain signal and analog transmission is in the frequency domain, the two environs interact (Figure 14-3).

Frequency values change the phase or the location of the transmitted signal. Varying the phase of the transmitted signal changes the time one expects to receive the pulses. How much the transmitted signal varies depends on the amplitude of the jitter function.

Jitter originates from three primary sources. Terminal equipment introduces a small amount of jitter to the transmitted signal. Regenerators on the access lines inject jitter from their clock recovery systems. And digital hierarchy multiplexers add stuff bits to

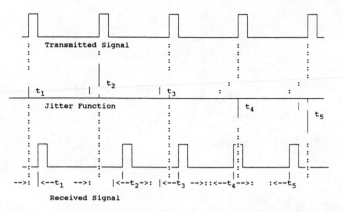

Figure 14-3: Interaction of Frequency Domain and Time Domain.

compensate for clock differences. To the technocrat, jitter has many sources, and they use different names to describe them.

Timing Jitter

Timing jitter is the time deviation between the output pulses and equally spaced time locations (Figure 14-4). This kind of jitter results in information crossing over into other channels, distortion of the recovered analog signal, and possible bit slips.

Alignment Jitter

Alignment jitter is the deviation between the recovered timing pulse positions and the incoming pulses (Figure 14-5). This reduces the margin against making errors.

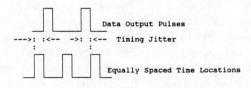

Figure 14-4 Timing Jitter.

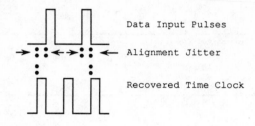

Figure 14-5   Alignment Error.

Systematic Jitter

Systematic jitter stems from the output of regenerators. It follows the incoming signal and adds to its deviation from the norm. Accumulation of jitter along the access line is exponential instead of linear. A few regenerators introduce the major portion of the end product. After a few more regenerators, the rise in the accumulated jitter levels off.

Random Jitter

Random jitter explains all the other components that do not track with the incoming signal. As a result, they may add or subtract from the incoming jitter.

Wait Time or Residual Jitter

Digital hierarchy multiplexers join many T-1 lines into one data stream. Each T-1 line has a slightly different pulse timing train. Merging the different patterns together starts by adding stuff bits to the T-1 line to reach a common higher rate clock. Multiplexing 28 T-1 lines accounts for 43.232 Mb out of the total 44.736 Mbps. Framing patterns and bit stuffing use the difference of 1.504 Mbps.

Stuff bits occur at fixed locations in the digital multiplexer. The receive multiplexer recognizes the stuff-bit locations and blocks the bit. A gap in the pulses result from the blocked stuff bit. While Phase Lock Loop circuits lessen the space between consecutive pulses, a residual jitter remains to the output.

Wait time jitter develops between recognizing the need for a stuff bit and the time a stuff bit enters the multiplexer's frame format.

Wander

Wander is another name for low frequency jitter. Jitter resulting from frequencies below 10 Hz slowly drifts or wanders back and forth across the expected zero point. Clock recovery systems using Phase Lock Loop circuits usually do not effectively respond to this low frequency.

How Measured — Test Equipment

Jitter is a time-dimension impairment that results from amplitude and frequency. Expressing units of jitter leads to the peak-to-peak value of time slots or unit intervals. A Unit Interval (UI) is the reciprocal of the jitter function's frequency under measurement.

Telephone companies design their networks to be under the stated jitter levels. Excessive jitter is possible if stressful data patterns traverse the facilities. The telephone company will test the facility with a particular quasi-random 1,048,575 bit sequence and won't support testing with other patterns.

While one can measure jitter on the facility, the easier approach is to check the terminal equipment's tolerance. Jitter synthesizers adjust over a range of frequencies and amplitudes. Various levels and frequencies determine the terminal's tolerance to jitter.

Dejitterizers

Dejitterizers provide buffering between the incoming data stream and the output. Clock recovered from the incoming signal writes the binary bits into a large buffer. A new clock source reads the binary bits out of the other end of the buffer. The pulses get a fresh start, but the buffer introduces additional delay.

European digital networks use digitizers between their networks to reduce the accumulation of jitter. Since their individual networks are comparatively small, they never had a great concern to limit jitter by design selection. Each country's digital network has its own jitter and doesn't pass it on to other systems.

Scramblers

Scramblers reduce possible jitter from building repetitive data patterns. Quasi-random binary patterns combine with the data stream and change a repetitive pattern into a random signal. Other scrambling methods change the original data pattern by bit inversion and bit-interleaving with other data streams.

Digital Services Error Characteristics

Analog services have random errors that seem to dribble throughout the data transmission. Noise and other impairments skew the frequency domain around inside the modem to produce errored data.

Digital services have distinctive error characteristics. They have bursts or spurts of errors and then long periods of good data. The usual cause for error bursts is automatic switching of facilities to protection services and human error. Frequency skewing in a time domain produces occasional bit slips that usually evade end-user detection.

Burstiness

Burstiness is the peculiarity of sending groups of contiguous errors with long periods of good data in between. Error bursts happen when facilities switch to protection lines because of failure, microwave radio fading, planned maintenance, and human errors. Facility failures and human error occurrences remain unpredictable. Routine maintenance and the radio-fading season have only a slightly better chance of knowing when they will happen.

Microwave radio fading occurs from atmospheric changes from April through October of each year. Also, fading takes place between 2 and 10 a.m. in the morning. It's safe to bet that a microwave radio's error rate will be higher between those hours and those months than any other time.

Errored Seconds

Errored seconds are exactly what they say they are — a second with one or more bit errors. The Extended Superframe (ESF) records errored seconds when an error event occurs. In this case an ESF error event occurs when the cyclic redundancy check (CRC-6) doesn't agree and an Out of Frame (OOF) alarm initiates.

Severely Errored Second

A severely errored second has 320 or more bits in error during the particular second. Ten consecutive severely errored seconds equals one failed signal state. The Extended Superframe registers count a Failed Second for each second a failed signal state exists.

Very Severe Error Burst — Continuous Severely Errored Seconds

A Very Severe Error Burst (VSB) or Continuous Severely Errored Seconds (CSEC) describe longer error bursts. (VSB) described error bursts worse than one bit out of 100 bits for more than 2 1/2 seconds. How one measures a 2 1/2 second burst of errors for a bit error rate of 10^{-2} is one of life's mysteries. Two-and-a-half-second error bursts always were the telephone companies' limit before their own equipment alarmed. AT&T highlighted this limit as a Very Severe Burst to help multiplexer manufactures become aware of a telephone company known problem. The latest thinking is to replace the (VSB) term with the (CSEC) unit. One (CSEC) equals 3 or more Severely Errored Seconds.

Extended Superframe (ESF) Error Registers

ESF error registers store ESF error events, Errored Seconds, Failed, and loop-back states. Registers store information concerning the previous 15 minutes and the previous 24 hours.

Errored-second vs. Bit-Error Rate

Comparing error performance is similar to the old apple and oranges debate. At first, we knew about a bit-error performance of one bit out of 100,000 (1×10^{-5}). Then synchronous data introduced the one block out of 100 1000-bit blocks in error (1×10^{-2}). Along the way, AT&T-Bell Laboratories suggested one character out of 10,000 characters as an error performance for their multiplexer. And digital services produced the error-free seconds performance standard.

How many apples equal an orange, or is it the other way around? Trying to compare one error performance with the other is frustrating. The technocrat stands behind equations that approximate but don't equal each other. A bit error in 100,000 didn't equal one block in 100 blocks because coding schemes skewed the results. It is similar to finding that a new can of ceiling white paint is slightly whiter than the older can. The difference between the two white paints shows only when a strong light shines and you know what you are looking at.

$$P_{(EFS)} = (1 - P_{(RE)})^{BIT\ RATE}$$

$$P_{(EFS)}\ (Percentage) = (1 - P_{(RE)})^{B} \times 100$$

$$P_{(EFS)}\ (\%) = (1 - \frac{1\ Bit}{10,000,000})^{56\ kbps} \times 100$$

$$P_{(EFS)}\ (\%) = (1 - 10^{-7})^{56,000} \times 100$$

$$P_{(EFS)}\ (\%) = (0.999999)^{56,000} \times 100$$

$$P_{(EFS)}\ (\%) = 99.44\% \quad \text{which rounds off to the supported}$$
$$99.5\%\ EFS$$

P = Probability of Error-Free Seconds or Random Errors
EFS = Error-Free Seconds
RE = Random Errors
kbps = kilobits per second

Table 14-1   Calculating Error-Free Seconds.

Ironically, digital services use bit-error test sets to test errored-second performance. So many bit-errors in a 15-minute test period equals so many errored seconds. Error-free second comparisons between digital services is another apples and oranges debate. Fifty-six kbps digital data service has a 99.5% error-free second performance. T-1 lines use a 95% error-free second performance. At first glance, one would pick 99.5% over 95% performance. Nevertheless, the 95% error-free performance has a higher bit-error figure than the 99.5% level.

AT&T-Bell Systems Technical Journal, Vol. 54 — No.5 , May–June 1975 introduced a simple error performance correlation formula. It uses a random error factor instead of a burst error one and provides another shade of white to contemplate. While Table 14-1 doesn't satisfy the technical purist, it blows away the smoke used to cloud one's mind.

Using a 10^{-7} bit-error performance for 56-kbps digital service generates a 99.5% error-free second rate (Figure 14-6). Take this same formula a step further to find the bit-error performance of T-1 lines (Figure 14-7) and 45-Mbps services (Figure 14-8). The first revelation is a bit-error performance level greater than expected. A second discovery is the conservative telephone company supported error performance for the T-1 and 45-Mbps services.

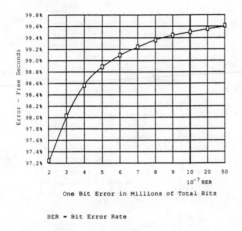

Figure 14-6   56,000 BPS Digital Services Error Performance.

Exponential formulas exhibit one important feature. They only show good data on the "knee of the curve." This area has neither a steep slope nor a very flat rise. All other areas on the exponential's curve are circumspect.

T-1 lines between telephone company central offices exhibit at least a 10^{-8} bit-error performance. Performance for 45-Mbps service

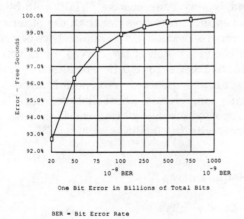

Figure 14-7   T-1 Digital Services Error Performance.

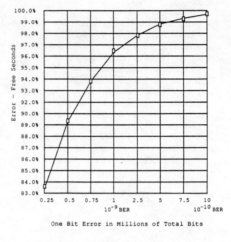

One Bit Error in Millions of Total Bits

BER = Bit Error Rate

Figure 14-8   45 Mega-bit Digital Services Error Performance.

reaches at least a 10^{-10} bit-error level on fiber-optic cable. Plotting curves for the three digital services shows the relation between their error performance levels. We stress the word relation, since block size and error burst characteristics prevent a direct correlation.

Looking at the "knee of the curve" for each exponential curve shows some interesting conclusions. DATAPHONE Digital Service's 99.5% error-free second support is at the upper end of the curve's valid area. T-1 supported 95% error-free seconds is on the steep part of the curve and is very conservative. AT&T's 45-Mbps 92% error-free seconds is even more conservative than the other services.

Comparing error-free second performance between digital services must start with the valid area of the curves. Then you see one value of error-free seconds means three different bit-error rates.

One last thing about supported error performance is that the rate is for a 4,000 mile long circuit. Short-distance circuits should never approach the supported error performance. If they do, there are fundamental problems with the facilities.

Ones-Density Requirements

Reason for Ones-density

For a number of years, the regenerators used in the access lines required a large diet of pulses to sustain life. They quickly degraded

1. No more than 15 zeroes in a row.
2. Windows of 16 bits to 192 bits require at least N number of ones bits according to the following formula.
3. Window = 8 × (N + 1)

   Where N = 1 to 23

Table 14-2   Ones-Density.

without them. Their internal clocks drifted off frequency, and the service suffered.

Newer regenerators and fiber-optic cable installations reduce the ones-density needs. Nevertheless, the requirements in Table 14-2 still stand.

Methods Used

AT&T's PUB 62411 requires the end-user's data to adhere to the ones-density requirements. One T-1 Channel Service Unit manufacturer convinced the FCC that the ones-density was a function of the CSU instead of the end-user. Other manufacturers of CSUs that didn't follow the ones-density rules had FCC fines levied against them and were told to remove their product from the marketplace.

The need for a rigid ones-density requirement with equipment being installed lessens each day. Whatever rules apply should fall to the end-user's data. Indiscriminate insertion of ones bits into a data stream leads to errors and confusion.

Clear Channel Capability (CCC)

Clear Channel Capability (CCC) concerns the unrestricted transmission of data in the 64-kbps time-slot. When the North American digital network began, the ones-density requirements became the responsibility of each of the 24 channels on a T-1 line. The European network developed their system with the ones-density handled at the 2.048-Mbps level. Needless to say, the North American network is just getting around to what the Europeans have had over the years.

Major steps to provide CCC began in 1986 to move the ones-density requirements to the T-1 level. It wasn't until the next year that the Bipolar Eight Zero Suppression (B8ZS) method became the standard method for all T-1 providers.

Other methods furnish clear channel capability until the entire North American digital network converts to the standard. Bell Communications Research standards permit the Zero Byte Time Slot Substitution method as well as the accepted B8ZS.

64-kbps Restricted

64-kbps restricted transmission is another way of saying "it's not my job." It assumes the end user knows all about ones-density rules and never sends steady zeroes. Data compression, inverted code, or scrambling techniques provide ways to meet restricted transmission.

Data compression methods sense long strings of either ones or zero bits. Strings of ones or zeroes reduce to a brief code expressing the number of contiguous bits to reinsert at the receive end. Additional logic needed adds to the cost of the terminal equipment. The additional logic also adds to the delay of the signal.

Inverting all the ones and zeroes assumes never using a character that uses all ones bits. It trades the problem of not sending an all-zero bit string to an all-ones string. There is a very slight change in cost or delay to invert bits.

Scrambling techniques use quasi-random binary numbers to change long strings of zeroes into a random collection of ones and zeroes. There is a remote possibility that the combination of the random data and valid data will create a string of zeroes. Another deterrent occurs when there isn't any end-user data. The quasi-random generator is a repetitive pattern. False framing of equipment results from repetitive patterns

Keep-Alive Signal

Data Service Units (DSU) and Channel Service Units (CSU) provide a clear channel capability. DSUs monitor strings of zeroes and send a control word in its place. CSUs for T-1 services also monitor the data stream and inserts ones bits into strings of zeroes.

Removing the terminal from the T-1 line results in the CSU sending all ones bits as a keep-alive signal. Keep-alive signals maintain access line repeaters timing recovery.

Ones-Bit Insertion

Some T-1 terminal equipment insert a ones bit in every 8th-bit location. This allows some channels to transmit at a full 64,000 bps. While meeting the ones-density requirements, it uses 192,000 bits of overhead out of the T-1 line. Facilities that do not require a ones bit density can transmit the entire data stream without stuff bits.

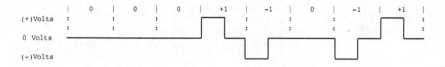

Figure 14-9   Bipolar Eight Zero Substitution Code.

Bipolar Eight Zero Substitution (B8ZS)

Bipolar Eight Zero Suppression (B8ZS) takes the ones-density problem to the T-1 level. A monitor checks the T-1 bipolar data stream for a string of eight zeroes. When eight zeroes register, a bipolar violation code takes its place on the T-1 data stream. Chapter Three on Digital Hierarchy discusses bipolar with N-zero substitution and the European high-density bipolar with n zeroes. The code shown in Figure 14-9 assumes the preceding ones bit had positive polarity. Polarity positions reverse when the preceding ones bit had negative polarity.

Zero Byte Time Slot Interchange

Zero Byte Time Slot Interchange (ZBTSI) looks for all-zero 8-bit bytes within the D4 or Extend Superframe format. Instead of inserting ones bits into the 8-bit byte like other ones-density schemes, they tag the bytes for interchange. Interchanging swaps all-zero byte positions within a special frame format. Ninety-six 8-bit bytes or time slots serially enter a 772-bit buffer. This buffer holds the equivalent of four Main Frames with their four frame pattern bits.

```
96 Time slots  ×   8 Bits    = 768 Bits
                  ─────────
                  Time slot


768 Bits + 4 Frame Bits = 772-Bit Buffer
```

Numbers from 1 to 96 designate each time slot's position. Frame pattern bits still locate in each 193rd-bit position. When using a D4 Frame pattern, one out of four framing patterns bits inverts states if all-zero bytes exist.

An Extended Superframe proposal uses the data link to indicate all-zero bytes present. Since standards committees debate the ESF data link end-user use, the remainder of the explanation concerns only a D4 Frame. Once the 96 time slots enter the buffer, it identifies the all-zero time slots and assigns position numbers. Our ex-

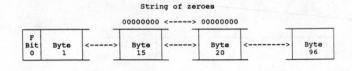

Figure 14-10   ZBTSI Initial Frame Structure.

ample in Figure 14-10 shows a string of all-zero bytes in time-slot positions 15 through 20.

ZBTSI's goal is sending other information in place of the all-zero bytes. All-zero bytes 15 through 20 disappear after identification and leave six 8-bit byte gaps. The remaining time slots move together, leaving six consecutive gaps at the front of the message buffer.

Telling the receive end that all-zero indicators exist rests with the frame pattern bit inversion. Borrowing one out of the four frame pattern bits doesn't adversely affect synchronization. Out of Frame Alarms (OOFs) require four or five errored frame pattern bits before initiating an alarm condition. Received frame pattern inversions return to their original state before entering end-user equipment.

Our example in Figure 14-11 only shows the first frame pattern bit or flag-bit in the special frame format. Three other frame pattern bits exist, but complicate the picture.

The gaps in the front of the special format become the all-zero byte indicators. Each indicator carries a binary code for its time-slot location (Figure 14-12). One needs only 7 bits to binary encode the 96 possible all-zero byte locations. The 8th bit denotes if additional all-zero bytes exist. A zero in the 8th bit position implies more zero byte identifiers to follow. Conversely, a one in the 8th bit position reflects the end of zero byte identifiers.

Decoding this clear channel message at the other end reverses the process. It enters a receive buffer and the inverted flag-bit alerts the presence of bytes with all-zero indicators in the message. The time slots restore to their original configuration. All-zero bytes reinsert back into their original time slots, and the flag-bit changes back to its proper state. Clear channel messages that do not have any all-zero indicators will exit from the buffer unchanged.

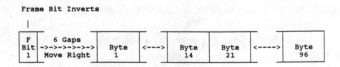

Figure 14-11   ZBTSI Frame Restructure.

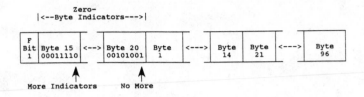

Figure 14-12   Final ZBTSI Frame Structure.

ZBTSI Disadvantages

1. Requires Superframe Integrity from end to end with either D-4 or ESF framing. It cannot pass through a Digital Cross-Connect System, which inserts a new Superframe framing pattern.
2. Additional delay to the data stream since it requires buffers and processing.
3. Borrowing one out of four frame pattern bits reduces the range of the Out-of-Frame (OOF) alarm.

ZBTSI Advantages

1. Doesn't require telephone companies to change equipment in the central offices. B8ZS clear channel implementation is perceived as a costly endeavor.

15

Digital Network Transmission Constraints

Telephone companies have always worked within transmission limits or constraints. Whether you use telephone company facilities or your own, they all have transmission limits. Going beyond those limits leads to unsatisfactory performance. Delay and timing are the dominate factors affecting digital networks. Delay plays several critical roles. One is the response time for data transmission. When implementing a digital network, one needs to know the delay factors that affect data response time.

Most networking computer programs use airline mileage to estimate delay factors. Nevertheless, digital networks travel very specific routes. This results in the actual mileage being two or three times longer than direct distances. The actual facility distance adds unplanned delay to the calculations.

The other delay consequence is the perception of echo on voice circuits. Telephone companies always used echo control in their public network, and it now becomes the end-user's responsibility with private networks.

Timing is the most important factor for digital networks. Analog data transmission always had some timing woes, but not to the degree of digital communications. Services with analog data modems have individual clocks for each transmission line. Digital networks have only one clock. All digital lines either time themselves from one master clock or provides buffers between timing differences.

Another form of timing constraint is the response time to get things done on public digital networks. Telephone company services and maintenance have a different response time when compared to private networks. Public network services are shared with many end-users and often vie for time with the computer operating systems. Just accessing a telephone company operating system requires security checks not found on a private network. They also go through a longer sanity check to verify that the commands given are appropriate and make sense.

Maintenance time of public networks may follow long-standing telephone company procedures. The concept of first come, first served is especially true with telephone offices with trouble ticket dispatchers. There is nothing as frustrating as to find your T-1 line trouble is waiting in line with single voice channel troubles. Agreements between the end-user and the telephone company avoid the "take a number please" concept to assign priorities to high-capacity services.

Echo Restrictions

Telecommunications delay impacts both voice and data circuits. Voice circuit delay slows the returned echo to a point that the talker perceives words coming back. Your brain's first reaction to the echo sound is another person speaking in the background. One's first experience with a satellite circuit without echo control is unnerving. After a few "how are you" — "how are you" and "fine" — "fine," it dawns on you that the voice coming back is your own.

Echo is a complex issue for the telephone companies. They vary transmission levels and use several delay factors for echo control. When should the end-user worry about echo? Any time you connect a 4-wire circuit to a 2-wire circuit, you can expect returned energy. How that impacts on the transmission depends on the delay between events.

Echo Characteristics

Echo occurs when energy returns from the connection between a 2-wire and a 4-wire facility. Perception of the echo occurs when the delay is long enough for the ear to react to the sound.

Maintain a 4-wire circuit from telephone to telephone and there isn't any way energy reflects back. Nevertheless, almost all voice networks use 2-wire loops between the telephone set and the premise switch. This means there is a hybrid somewhere to connect the 2-wire loop to the 4-wire telephone company network.

Going between a 2 and a 4-wire facility requires an impedance matching device called a hybrid. Connecting the two facilities together produces an imbalance of resistive and capacitive values. This mismatch prevents the total transfer of energy from one facility

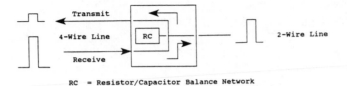

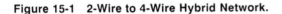

RC = Resistor/Capacitor Balance Network

Figure 15-1   2-Wire to 4-Wire Hybrid Network.

to the other. Energy that didn't transfer has to go somewhere. Figure 15-1 shows a signal entering the hybrid from the 4-wire line. The major portion of the signal transfers to the 2-wire circuit, and a small portion reflects back to the 4-wire's transmit side.

Counteracting the impedance mismatch are a resistor and capacitor combination. While the values closely approximate the ideal hybrid balance, preventing echo with fixed component values isn't feasible. The telephone companies' approach to returned energy or echo takes several courses. One is the hybrid balance networks. Another method is adjusting the circuits power level to reduce the echo's perception value.

Reducing the transmit power level by half (-3 dB) lowers the receive level. This means the energy returned at the hybrid is also cut in half. Received returned energy is cut in half again with adjusted transmission levels. Telephone companies vary their levels with a process called Via Net Loss (VNL) design. Lowering transmission levels is an economical way to handle echo. At some point, lowering signal power becomes detrimental. Besides not hearing too well, the signal-to-noise ratio decreases and modems cease functioning.

Two different echoes exist. One is the talker echo and the other is the listener echo. Figure 15-2 shows the return of reflected energy at the distant end back toward the talker. The talker hears his own voice coming back or data equipment senses unexpected data signals.

Listener echo is the second trip of the talker's original speech (Figure 15-3). A portion of the talker's energy reflects back toward the original source. The hybrid at the talker's end also reflects a portion of the talker echo back again toward the listener. If the circuit follows VNL design, listener echo perception is very remote. Poor hybrid balance, zero-loss circuits, and enough propagation delay could produce listener echo.

Another form of listener echo occurs when high-level energy returns in phase with the original signal. When this happens, either a near-singing or singing condition occurs. Near-singing produces a hollow effect as if the person was talking in a big barrel. Singing produces load screeching sounds.

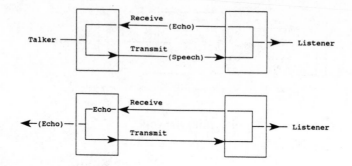

Figure 15-2   Talker Echo.

Echo Perception Level

Echo perception is a combination of returned energy and delay. If the network has 4 to 2-wire hybrids, you can expect echo. Perceiving echo is a function of the ear and the mind to respond to the returned sound. Usually echo is a low-level signal, and not all people will hear it.

Over the years, telephone companies used 1850 miles as a benchmark circuit distance before using echo control measures. They use a combination of circuit design levels up to a point where increased loss is detrimental. After a 45-ms round trip talker echo delay, the telephone companies add echo suppressors or cancelers.

Echo control equipment installation takes place only after adjusting levels and calculating more than a 45-ms echo delay (Figure 15-4). Propagation round trip delay doesn't follow clear-cut parameters, but instead varies with facility and terminal equipment types. Fiber-optic systems have greater propagation delay than wire facilities. Complex multiplexers introduce greater delay than simple digital channel banks, As one can see, the variables make echo control harder than a strict mileage factor.

Echo Suppressors and Cancelers

Echo cancelers are a digital equivalent of the older analog echo suppressors. Echo suppressors added loss to the return path of the 4-

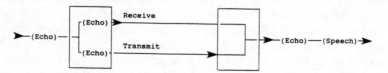

Figure 15-3   Listener Echo.

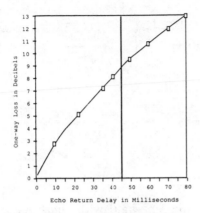

Figure 15-4 Circuit Power Loss vs. Echo Delay.

wire circuit. It looked for voice power in each direction and switched the loss in and out (Figure 15-5).

Echo suppressors' major shortcomings were clipping of the voice and virtually opening one circuit direction. After one talker gained control of the echo suppressor, the listener couldn't stop the talker. The listener had to wait for a pause in the talker's conversation.

Two-wire analog data modems faced other problems. Normal hand-shaking between modems accounted for echo suppressor disabling. If the data stream didn't start within 100 ms, the suppressor would drop back into action. Half duplex transmission required data stuff characters at the beginning just to operate the suppressor's switch.

Echo cancelers (Figure 15-6) estimate the expected returned signal and subtract it from the signal before transmitting. Cancelers act independently on each end and permit simultaneous transmission in both directions. While cancelers do not clip speech, they do use a few milliseconds to arrive at a good estimate.

Cancelers either handle echo on a T-1 level or on a per-channel basis. T-1 echo cancelers provide control for 24 channels at one time. Since telephone companies dedicate digital channel banks to long-haul voice facilities, a T-1 canceler is economical. End-users that in-

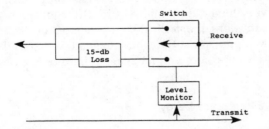

Figure 15-5 Echo Suppressor.

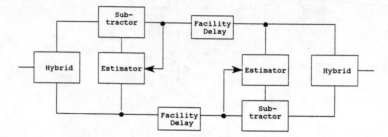

Figure 15-6   Echo Canceler.

tegrate services or mix long-haul with short-distance circuits would opt for individual channel control.

End-User Echo Control Considerations

Telephone companies handle echo by adjusting transmit levels and use echo control equipment as a last resort. End-users should also consider echo cancelers as a last resort. Whatever you do is a trade-off. Lower the transmit level, and the signal-to-noise value decreases, causing a new problem. Add echo cancelers, and some analog modems won't work.

1. Forty-five milliseconds round-trip delay for talker energy to return as echo is the telephone company's bottom floor measurement. They also use a 1850-mile factor, which equals 37-ms round-trip delay. Still another factor is 1150 miles for intermachine trunks. Fiber cable uses a 1250-mile distance for echo control. As you can see, there isn't a single definitive distance or millisecond delay.
2. Telephone companies lower the transmit level to decrease the echo perception level. If your network doesn't adjust levels, you will notice echo with shorter distances.
3. Networks with several switching nodes can create circuits with long delays. Restoration of T-1 lines may also inadvertently make very long delays and require the addition of echo control.
4. Echo cancelers must disable when modems send a disabling tone. Modems must be able to send the standard disabling tone. Few cancelers and modems adhere to the new standard.

Facility and Equipment Delay

Total delay between two points considers the facility's propagation delay and the delay within the terminal equipment. Data response

Airline Mileage Bands	Multiplication Factor
0 – 200	3.0
201 – 750	2.5
751 – 2000	2.0
2001 – 3000	1.4

Table 15-1 Multiplication Factor to Determine Actual Mileage.

time includes both delays plus time for the terminal device reaction to a query.

Calculating the end-to-end delay takes on the same scientific accuracies as the Salem witch hunts in the 1600s. Airline mileage or the straight-line distance between two points feeds networking architecture computer calculations. No one makes any consideration for the real distance or the type of transmission equipment. Often, true mileage is several times more than airline distance. Each piece of equipment also has its own delay factor.

Telephone companies get around telling you what the real delay is by citing worst-case examples. One example is the 100-ms one-way delay for T-1 lines. Hasty delay vs. distance calculations for the T-1 line approximates a 10,000 mile long circuit. Some ballparks are bigger than others when estimating.

Facility Delay

Propagation delay is the length of time between the transmitted signal and when it reaches the receiver. Every wire, cable, and equipment adds a delay factor. For that matter, even radio waves through the air have a delay factor.

Knowing the exact mileage between two points gives a close approximation of the delay. If you lease facilities from telephone companies, ask the right people for the real distance. Telephone company engineers and maintenance personnel know the exact distance and the type of facilities. Marketing and sales groups only know the airline mileage between locations and have no idea about the facilities.

AT&T Technical Reference PUB 43202 provides insight into the difference between airline and actual mileage. The multiplication factors computed facility mileage for analog multipoint circuits (Table 15-1). These factors are averages of a large analog circuit data base.

Integrated digital facilities multiplication factors are almost inverse in their ratios. T-1 facilities follow limited corridors across the country. Telephone companies and fiber-optic services compete for

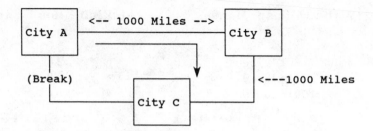

Figure 15-7   Reconfiguration Delays.

the same service between major telecommunications centers. A T-1 service between Chicago and Phoenix could travel by way of California to follow the digital corridors. One service travels 750 miles to get between two locations 75 airline miles apart.

Knowing the exact distance between points lets you closely approximate delay. Since delays differ between facility types, a factor of one millisecond for each 100 miles is an acceptable multiplication factor.

$$500 \text{ Mile Circuit} \times \frac{1 \text{ Millisecond}}{100 \text{ Miles}} = 5 \text{ Milliseconds}$$

Equipment Delay

Telephone office equipment use multiplexers to efficiently pack high-speed transmission facilities. Every time the signal enters another multiplexer, additional delay occurs.

End-users compound the delay problem by stringing more equipment in line. Every piece of equipment enters some delay. A millisecond here and a millisecond there all add up to real-time delay.

Ask each vendor about actual delay you can expect from their equipment. Total equipment delay with facility delay to arrive at the expected time interval.

Reconfiguration of Facilities

Ring or large nodal networks stand the greatest chances for surprise delays. They are surprises if restoration or reconfiguration plans don't go under the same scrutiny put into the main network.

Double or triple the Figure 15-7 ring network and reconfiguration delay troubles also multiply. The distance between each city is 1000 miles and shows no cause for echo concern. A break in the T-1 line between City A and City C requires restoring those circuits through City B's multiplexer. Network control signals reconfigure all the multiplexers. Service between City A and City B restores to find the data circuit's round-trip delay doubled, and the voice circuits need echo cancelers.

Timing Differences

Integrated digital networks are timing-clock-oriented. Clocks open and close logic gates to expected data pulses. When two clock sources appear in the same network, confusion abounds and errors ensue. Staying within one network only lessens the problems encountered. Your main concern is to reduce timing difference to a minimum, and thereby limit the number of bit slips in the network. There are several ways to reduce the clock differences. One method is adequate buffering between equipment and facilities. Another is slave-timing analog portions of your network to the main clock source.

Tracing Clock Sources

After completing the planning for the initial digital network, your first chore is tracing the clock source through every piece of equipment. Designate each piece of terminal equipment as to the type of clock it uses.

Internal — Supplies its own clock.
External — Clock source has separate lead.
Loop or Slave — Recovers clock from data stream.

Remember that connections to telephone company services require the terminal equipment to slave or loop time. If the telephone company is a clock source, mark the serving telephone office with a (S) for source. Mark any other clock source with the same (S) marking.

Figure 15-8(a) shows a simple point-to-point arrangement that uses internal (I) clocking for transmitting data to the other end. This small system basically has two sources that are totally independent of each other.

Figure 15-8(b) shows a simple network with end-user premise multiplexers connected through a Digital Cross-Connect System. In this case, the (DCS) is a master clock, and all other equipment recovers clock from this source.

Figure 15-8(c) gets a little complicated but is still quite simple when compared to some end-user networks. In the upper-right portion, a collocated analog modem receives external timing from the

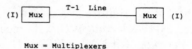

Figure 15-8(a) Point-to-point Timing.

multiplexer. The distant analog modem loop- or slave-times to the frequency. We labeled the DCS with the source (S) clock and loop-timed the connecting multiplexers. The multiplexer in the upper-left corner loop (L) times to the DCS and sets its internal (I) clock to this frequency. This clock now feeds the transmit data stream to the lower tier of equipment. If the PBX in the lower tier was another DCS, there would be two source (S) clocks in the network. The multiplexers on the left side require additional buffering to help compensate for the clock differences.

If two clock sources appear on your planned layout, make changes in the design to eliminate all extra sources. Once you have reduced your clock sources to one, the next step determines what happens during a disaster. Equipment failure or that backhoe cutting through your access cable could eliminate the master clock source. The rest of your network begins to free-run and synchronization falls apart. Planning for a disaster builds restoration plans that swing a new clocking source into the system. And having restorations plans calls for computer data base systems or written procedures for every possibility.

Buffering

Buffering provides a way to reduce the number of slips between two clock sources. It doesn't eliminate slips, but instead delays when they will happen. The best way to describe a buffer is to use the comparison of the proverbial bean jar (Figure 15-9). A write clock (one source) opens the bean jar and lets bits drop in one after another. At the bottom of the bean jar there is an outlet controlled by a read clock or second source. If the read clock is slower than the write

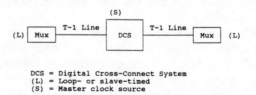

Figure 15-8(b) Simple Network with Telephone Company Source Clock.

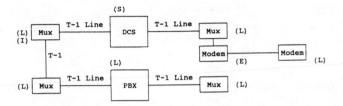

Figure 15-8(c) Small Network Clocking.

clock, the bits build up in the bean jar until a bit slips out the over-flow chute. The difference between our bean jar and a buffer is that the buffer process starts over and the bean jar doesn't. When the read clock is faster than the write clock, there comes a time when the bean jar doesn't have any bits to give. Instead of a bit spilling out the overflow, there is a bit gap in the data output. Bit gaps also become bit slips.

Buffers have a major drawback of adding delay. Increase the buffer's size to extend the interval between bit-slips, and it increases the delay of the equipment.

Going Between Networks

At one time, the entire North American Network had only one master clock source. This single master clock source existed through the first few years of the Bell Systems divestiture. All the individual telephone companies derived their clock from some AT&T office. One new telephone company synchronized their network clock from Digital Data System's clocks at three different locations across the country. Now, some telephone companies are installing their own atomic driven clock source to improve the accuracy of their own clock sources.

Going between telephone company networks and private networks requires some buffering. The size of the buffering depends on the accuracy of each network's clock. Accurate atomic clocks in both net-

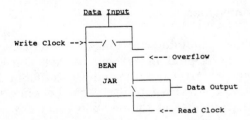

Figure 15-9 Buffering with Two Clocks.

works call for a bit or two buffing for phase differences. Networks based on crystal-driven clocks need large buffers to reduce the bit-slip interval.

Going to Analog Services

Analog modems must use the external timing option and receive clock from the digital service (Figure 15-10).

The modem at the remote end uses loop or slave timing to clock the transmit data back towards the digital end. Besides the external timing lead option, the collocated modem needs a small buffer on its receive side for phase differences in the signals.

End-User Controlled Telephone Services

End-user controlled telephone company services are inherently slow. They are commonly user based and demand extensive security checks. Dialing into an operating system finds procedures of identification codes and passwords to get by. After determining you may be who you say you are, the computer drops the call and dials a telephone number from its data base.

Once into the operating system, you run into sanity systems built into the program. Is the end-user's command valid? Can they really do it now? Better check that switch before we do anything. Are you sure the other end understands a switch order is under way? Let's make the switch and then check to see if everything is good before telling the end-user.

Compounding the slowness of security and sanity checks, there is another time delay. End-user controlled telephone company services use parts of internal operating systems already in place. The end-users operating systems must interface with the normal operating system without slowing down the internal telephone company use. This means all internal system work has the highest priority over end-user requests.

Telephone Maintenance

Telephone company maintenance tends towards centralized testing centers. They save capital investment by reducing the number of testing locations. Nevertheless, the end-user suffers from centralized testing locations. Centralized testers lack the same understanding that a local testroom has of the end-user's network. End-users become another number in the line at the supermarket instead of being known by name at the local store.

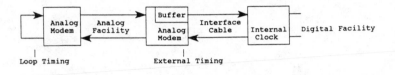

Figure 15-10   Timing Analog Modems from Digital Services.

Being caught up in the telephone maintenance mill is lessened by agreement between the end-user and the telephone company.

1. Everyone should agree on how the telephone company will handle T-1 or higher rate digital facility troubles. Since the high-speed digital facilities carry a disproportionate amount of low-speed services, telephone companies should treat them with higher priorities.
2. When a facility fails, you want to know how soon you can expect restored service. Calls to a centralized test center often get a dispatcher who writes trouble tickets and doesn't supply answers. Obtain telephone numbers that supply answers.
3. Meetings between the end-user and the telephone company should take place at both locations before final agreements. Understanding the other party's goals and needs brings about a lasting friendship. After installation, have other meetings to discuss what went wrong and how to prevent problems the next time.
4. Push for T-1 lines with Extended Superframe (ESF) capability. It is a proven winner to locate intermittent problems.
5. Long distance T-1 facilities should have ESF monitors at locations between the end-offices. Monitors are particularly important at locations where T-1 lines change types of facilities. Sectionalizing troubles to specific routes and equipment improve your chances for service rerouting to good facilities.
6. Push for Bipolar Eight Zero Substitution (B8ZS) on all your facilities. Getting to 64,000 bps clear channel capability means increased usage of your T-1 lines.

16

Integrated Services Digital Network Architecture

ISDN — A Telephone Company Service

Mystery surrounds ISDN and what it will do for the end-user. It has gotten to a point where people are making up new names for what ISDN stands for. They all seem to reflect a general concern about the delays in ISDN processing.

Making long-range ISDN plans has the same success rate as nailing jelly to the wall. Various North American and CCITT standards groups still argue about interfaces for the Basic Access. Meanwhile, new groups debate Broadband ISDN or B-ISDN to handle very high digital speeds.

Nevertheless, ISDN has captured the minds of telecommunications people around the world. When you realize ISDN isn't the future panacea for telecommunications, its scope reduces drastically. It doesn't provide the ubiquitous or utopian communication system for all people.

We treat ISDN differently from other books that deal with the communications messages and software. This chapter approaches ISDN from a network and transmission viewpoint instead. ISDN makes sense for telephone company provided services. The additional overhead and call-processing information creates a vehicle to consolidate telephone office equipment. It also eases the transfer of information from one telephone company network to the other. From the telephone company and many end-user's view, ISDN supplies information that aids in billing for the service.

ISDN Basic Access

Initially, ISDN has two access methods: the T-1 rate, called the Primary Access, and a lower rate access called the Basic Access. A Basic Access is the first line of transmission from the integrated voice/data terminal to a local switch. The limited distance between the terminal and the switch is an important fact to remember about the Basic Access channel.

ISDN Basic Access Channels

The term 2B + D is the popular name for ISDN Basic Access. Each B channel uses 64,000 bps digital time slots indiscriminately for voice or data services. Transparency to the type of information transmitted is a better definition than calling it integration. A D channel contains either signaling information or end-user data communications in a 16,000 bps time slot.

Information in the B channels has the same fundamental format that all the other digital services use. Eight-bit bytes transmit at an 8000 bps rate for a 64,000 bits per second time slot. Data in the D channel uses the X.25 Packet format and occupies a 16,000 bps time-slot. The 16,000 bps packet channel transmits signaling and control information between terminals. Its capacity is so large that the end-user can also transmit other data over the same D channel. Signaling and control information, running at full tilt, would use only an eighth of the D channel's capacity.

ISDN Basic Access Transport

ISDN Basic Access remains a controversial issue. Interfaces haven't reached complete agreement between the various standards groups. Cutting through all the debate on interfaces and operating systems, one finds a little discussed transmission item. Bell Communications Research's original documentation referred to ISDN Basic Access being served from little islands. The islands in turn were connected by ISDN Primary Channels.

Basic Access for ISDN runs at a 160,000 bps rate, and its Nyquist Frequency is 80,000 Hz. This transmission speed can drive only a couple of miles from its equipment, since there aren't any repeaters to extend the service. Signal attenuation on metallic facilities limits the terminal to slightly over three miles from the exchange termination.

Figure 16-1 shows the Bell Communications Research proposed Basic Access 2-wire transport system. Unlike the alternating transmission scheme of Switched 56-kb service, ISDN Basic transmits

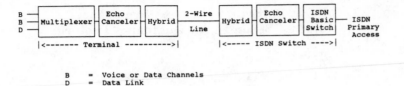

Figure 16-1   ISDN Basic Access Transport.

simultaneously in both directions with a little magic. Each end of the 2-wire facility has a hybrid to change to a 4-wire interface. Echo cancelers in turn negate the energy returned from the hybrid. Transmission magically allows both ends to talk at the same time and only lets them hear what the other says.

Figure 16-2 shows the echo canceler and hybrid combination. The echo canceler monitors the digital pattern and inverses the expected signal returning from the hybrid. Adding the inverse of the expected digit to the actual signal cancels the echo. Theoretically, both data streams travel across the 2-wire facility, and each end only recognizes valid information.

ISDN Basic Access Signal

Chapter Three described the various digital signals in the digital hierarchy. Basic Access introduces a new transmission method called Two-Bit for One Quatenary Symbol (2B1Q). Quatenary refers to the resultant code of four symbols for the two-bit combinations shown in Table 16-1.

The transmit quatenary symbol factors modifies a nominal pulse's size and polarity. Figure 16-3 shows the relative position of these modified pulses with a maximum transmit level of 2.5 volts (V).

If the data stream contained a repetitive signal, a direct-current charge could build up and cause noise. A 23-stage scrambler counteracts the chance of transmitting repetitive signals. Scrambling

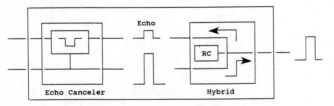

RC = Resistor/Capacitor Balance Network

Figure 16-2   ISDN Basic Access Interface Equipment.

Bit Pairs		Symbol
First	Second	Quatenary Factor
1	0	+3
1	1	+1
0	1	-1
0	0	-3

Table 16-1 ISDN Basic Access Quatenary Symbol Factor.

also ensures an even spectral distribution of the quatenary symbol pulses.

ISDN Basic Access Frame

The ISDN Basic Access frame has four major aspects. Figure 16-4 shows the basic block containing an 8-bit byte from each B Channel and 2-bits from the data link. Next, Figure 16-5 shows combining the basic blocks into a basic frame format. Figure 16-6 then combines the basic frame into a superframe format. Lastly, Figure 16-7 shows the offset between transmitting patterns.

At this point, we convert the end-user information from bits to bauds or quatenary symbols. Moving up from the basic block of 18 bits to a basic frame combines data from 12 basic blocks.

$$\frac{18 \text{ Bits}}{\text{Block}} \times \frac{12 \text{ Basic Blocks}}{\text{Frame}} = 216 \text{ Bits per Basic Frame}$$

$$216 \text{ Bits} \times \frac{1 \text{ Quatenary Symbol}}{2 \text{ Bits}} = 108 \text{ Quatenary Symbols}$$

A synchronization word (Table 16-2) heads the end-user data, and a maintenance control word completes the basic frame. When the

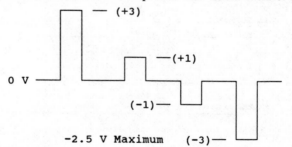

Figure 16-3 ISDN Basic Access Quatenary Signal.

```
┌─────────────┬─────────────┬──────────┐
│ 8-Bit Byte  │ 8-Bit Byte  │ 2 Bits   │
│ B Chan. 1   │ B Chan. 2   │ D Chan.  │
└─────────────┴─────────────┴──────────┘
│<----------- 18 Bits ------------>│
```

Figure 16-4   ISDN Basic Access Building Block.

basic frames combine to make a superframe, the first synchronization word logically inverts to indicate the beginning.

Eight Basic Frames constitute a Superframe. The maintenance
word (M Word in Figure 16-6) provides performance information as
well carrying a 12-bit cyclic redundancy check for error detection.

ISDN Basic Access Superframe Offset Time

A 60-symbol offset between transmitting superframes improves the
transmission scheme. Had both ends started transmitting at the
same time, the echo cancelers would subtract from good data instead
of returned energy.

Two-Wire Transmission Limitations

Two-wire transmission between the end-user's integrated digital terminal and the first ISDN switch assumes metallic wire facilities. As
such, the gauge of the wire plays a critical part in the distance allowed between locations. One must plan for the worst-case scenario
of 26 gauge wire with the greatest loss to the signal. Therefore, a
limit of 2.55 miles of 26-gauge wire is a marginal transmission point.
Facilities with heavier gauge wire would extend the distance to 3.4
miles.

Just before 1983, the Bell System surveyed the local telephone
company loop facilities. This survey showed that 80–90% of the
facilities were less or equal to 2.8 miles in length. If one agrees
ISDN isn't for everyone, it wouldn't make sense to propose other
ways to transport Basic Access circuits beyond this distance. The
market for devices to transport Basic Access beyond 2.8 miles is minimal at best. This then becomes a vicious cycle when the prices go up

```
┌───────────┬───────────────────┬─────────────┐
│ 9 Symbols │    108 Symbols    │ 3 Symbols   │
│ Sync Word │  Data Information │ Maintenance │
└───────────┴───────────────────┴─────────────┘
│<--------- 1.5 Milliseconds --------------->│
```

Figure 16-5   ISDN Basic Access Frame Format.

+3	+3	−3	−3	−3	+3	−3	+3	+3	Quatenary Symbol

10	10	00	00	00	10	00	10	10	Paired Bits

Table 16-2   ISDN Basic Access Synchronization Word.

because of the small market, which in turn causes a drop in the remaining market.

Basic Access Transmission Requirements

Besides the frame format and patterns used, the Basic Access must supply the following items.

1. The line rate should be 80,000 baud (quatenary symbol rate) plus or minus five parts per million. End-user tests for this accuracy calls for specialized unit interval measuring devices.

$$80,000 \text{ Baud} \times \frac{5}{1,000,000} = 0.4 \text{ Baud}$$

2. Jitter shall not exceed 0.1 peak-to-peak Unit Interval (U.I. = 1/80,000 baud).
3. An ones bit idle code fills time slots that do not contain end-user information.
4. Timing source will come from the telephone company network.

Frame 1	ISW	End-User Data	M Word
Frame 2	SW	End-User Data	M Word

⋮

Frame 7	SW	End-User Data	M Word
Frame 8	SW	End-User Data	M Word

<-------------- 12 Milliseconds -------------->

```
ISW     =  Inverted Synchronization Word
SW      =  Normal Synchronization Word (Figure 16-2)
M Code  =  Maintenance and Operation Code
```

Figure 16-6   ISDN Basic Access Superframe.

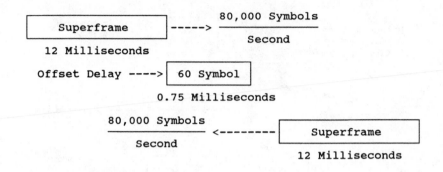

Figure 16-7 ISDN Superframe Transmission Offset Time.

Other Proposed Basic Access Transport Systems

Siemens Components Inc. introduced an integrated circuit (IC) chip in 1987 that provides a ping-pong method over 2-wires. This method limits the distance between the terminal and ISDN switch to just 2.18 miles.

At the same time Siemens announced their new IC, N.V. Phillips introduced an IC that uses an echo canceler. Their system is different from the Bell Communications Research proposed quatenary signal. Phillips method combines 4 bits of information into ternary bits. Their claim is a signal that is 120,000 bauds per second instead of 160,000 bps. The limit claimed between the end-user terminal and the ISDN switch is 4.97 miles. Since they didn't specify what gauge wire this signal transmitted over, one must assume a 19-gauge wire instead of the typical 26 gauge used in local wiring.

ISDN Basic Access via T-1 Time Division Multiplexer

Transporting the ISDN Basic Access beyond 18,000 feet needs the next level in the hierarchy. While the next ISDN hierarchal level is the Primary Access, the following methods employ multiplexers to transport a number of Basic Access services over a T-1 line (Figure 16-8).

Using the Bell System's 1983 local loop survey as a guide, one sees 10–20% of the total Basic Access circuits not reaching the local switch. Bell Communications Research's engineers proposed using multiplexers to provide access for these remaining circuits. The first proposal uses the normal time slots one sees with a typical digital channel bank. Each B channel occupies a complete 64,000-bps time slot. Each 16,000-bps D channel also occupies a full 64,000-bps time slot.

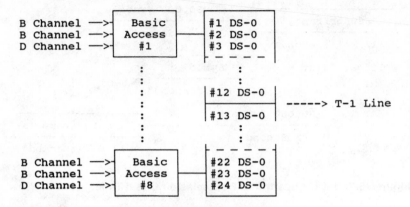

Figure 16-8   ISDN Basic Access Via T-1 Multiplexers.

Time division multiplexing isn't efficient since it yields only 16 information time slots. Eight time slots or 512,000-bps bandwidth carries the signaling and control for these 16 channels. When one wants to cite a case of overkill, this example should take first place.

ISDN Basic Access via T-1 Statistical Multiplexing

A statistical multiplexing proposal by Bell Communications Research would increase the number of Basic Access B channels over a T-1 line. They propose a limitation of 68 D channels over a single 64,000-bps time slot (ISDN E-Channel). If we take the Basic Access ratio of two B channels for each D channel, the total number of information channels is 136.

Statistical multiplexing has the inherent problem of variable delay resulting from different traffic loads. It assumes the end-user will use the vast majority of the circuits for strictly voice. Use of analog modems over the voice circuits would increase the delay.

One only has to pick up the latest telecommunications magazine to see the introduction of faster and cheaper analog modems. A number of these modems pop right into personal computers and eventually will replace the millions of 212-type units in use today.

ISDN Basic Access Serving Area

An ISDN Basic Access configuration appears like a lot of other end-user premise networks. What sets it apart is the location of the first ISDN switch. Private Branch Exchanges (PBX) can have a ISDN option or the local switch is in the local telephone company's office. A

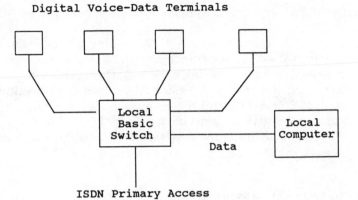

Figure 16-9   ISDN Basic Access Serving Area.

telephone company ISDN switch resembles the familiar CENTREX installation that hauls all the local loops into telephone office.

ISDN Basic Access makes sense if the end-user plans to connect into a telephone company ISDN network. It also becomes significant if the end-user needs the extensive call-processing statements associated with ISDN.

The Basic Access serving shown in Figure 16-9 treats the terminals and the ISDN Basic switch as a little island. Traveling between islands belongs to the ISDN Primary Access or higher rates.

ISDN Primary Access

An ISDN Primary Access accounts for 23 voice or data channels. The 24th time slot in the T-1 frame carries the call-processing information and end-user data on a data link. If two T-1 lines combine into a Digital Signal Level-1C, 47 voice or data channels become available. One time slot combines the data links from each T-1 service.

AT&T's Technical Reference PUB 41459 provides AT&T'S views about the control messages for the Primary Access Channel. When they first issued the preliminary issue in 1985, it was the only reference available. It succeeded in its role in getting people to sit down and finalize a standard.

Changes in the standard will still occur with the time delimiters and messages sent over the data link. The facility requirements will see very few modifications other than clear channel transmission. Adoption of Bipolar Eight Zero Suppression will change the initial proposal to invert the data link's bit structure.

End-user Primary Access equipment requirements are as follows:

1. If the T-1 interface uses a D-4 Framing Pattern, the Yellow Alarm will set the second bit in each time slot to a zero. The B channels and the data link must react to this pattern.
2. Extended Superframe's Yellow Alarm sends a repetitive pattern of 8 ones bits and 8 zero bits in the data link. A Yellow Alarm repetitive patterns transmits for 256 + 4 frames.
3. Time slots without any end-user feed must transmit and all-ones character.

CCITT H_0 CHANNEL — 384-kb ACCESS

At one time the CCITT H_0 channel seemed a logical crossing point between North America and Europe. Each digital system uses the basic time slot of 64,0000 bps. Combining six basic time slots equals one 384,000-bps channel.

North American
$$\frac{24 \ \text{Time slots}}{6 \ \text{Time slots}} = 4 \ H_0 \ \text{Channels}$$

CEPT
$$\frac{30 \ \text{Time slots}}{6 \ \text{Time slots}} = 5 \ H_0 \ \text{Channels}$$

Grouping three time slots is another usable bridge between systems but doesn't provide the same economics. It also doesn't present any need to provide another digital service running at 192,000 bps. Finding communication needs at 384,000 bps is difficult enough.

Other than designating the operating speed for the H_0 channel, ISDN plans don't include a five B channel plus one D channel to fill the slot. One of the few end-user products that could use this channel is a bundle of ADPCM channels. A bundle of 11 ADPCM channels and their signaling could traverse between Europe and North America. Although a supported standard in both Continents, ADPCM doesn't have the internal backing of large telephone companies. Their reluctance to use ADPCM stems from the 9600-bps analog modem limitations.

Broadband ISDN

Broadband or wideband ISDN standards are in their initial stages. Since world standards take years before acceptance, it was wise to get the ball rolling. The fiber-optic industry remains the primary beneficiary for these standards.

Chapter Three on Digital Data System Hierarchy mentioned two Synchronous Optical Network (SONET) data rates. While standardizing these rates for Broadband ISDN is still under way, they are 90% set in concrete.

The first Broadband ISDN data rate is 139,267,000 bps and the second rate is around 500,000,000 bps. These data rates will not have any meaning until the late 1990s, if then.

17

Integrated Telephone Network Architecture

Integrated telephone network architecture takes many forms other than the emerging Integrated Service Digital Network. They are, in some cases, the forerunner of ISDN services with telephone companies. Nevertheless, the following services will remain long after they finalize the ISDN standard.

While telephone companies around the world work on ISDN standards, other groups introduced ways to integrate different services on a common digital service. One major thing that differentiates the integrated telephone network from ISDN is the Digital Cross-Connect System. ISDN facilities connect directly into switching machines.

Integrated telephone services require the Digital Cross-Connect System to direct the various services to right spot. It was a logical use of existing equipment, but other factors led to the design.

Factors Governing Telephone Company Integration

Telephone companies' major factor limiting integrated services provision is accounting for service-specific costs. After years of cross-subsidizing low-profit services with long distance service, the telephone companies now try their best to identify service separations.

While an end-user combines data and voice circuits in the same multiplexer, large telephone companies separate the services into specific service equipment. A small telephone company could prorate the expense of joint equipment usage, but large telephone companies would face an accounting nightmare.

Besides accounting difficulties, the telephone companies' ability to test integrated service is another factor. Combining data and voice services takes the circuit away from the usual test access point in the telephone office.

Both AT&T and Bell Communications Research are working on ubiquitous test operating systems. Eventually, test personnel could access and test any service from a remote test position. Currently, an integrated subrate digital service's testing stops at the last dedicated Subrate Digital Cross-Connect System. Testing the integrated portion stops because the test personnel lack access or responsibility.

Responsible service provision gets cloudy at times. While the various telephone services belong to one company, the telephone company has many groups that have individual responsibilities. These responsibilities end at specific demarcations, and going beyond that point doesn't count for merit incentives or promotion. A total network testing system does away with demarcation points.

Finally, identifying service performance factors for the end-to-end service is a problem. Technically blending performance factors of several services into a new unit of measurement faces many long debates. It's similar to combining different fruits into a new variety with a name no one can pronounce and a taste no one can stomach.

Private-Line Voice Circuits Terminating at a Central Office

Telephone companies integrated Private-Line analog voice circuits first. It was the easiest thing to provide with the least amount of trouble. Digital channel banks were commonplace in the telephone office and didn't present perceived problems. After the initial installations, the testing factor became an issue. End-users thought they bought end-to-end service only to find they had parts of services. Nevertheless, when end-users reported a trouble about one of the integrated circuits, the telephone companies would test only the T-1 line.

While long distance telephone companies deny they encouraged local company bypass, this service has all the appearances of avoiding the local company. End-users bundle their analog circuits between their premise and the telephone company office. At this point, the circuits fan out from the Digital Channel Bank (D-Bank) in the telephone office.

Original tariff charges accounted for a connection charge between the T-1 line and additional cross-connect charges for each voicegrade circuit. Figure 17-1 shows 24 analog voicegrade circuits fanning out to various services.

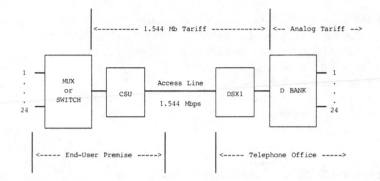

Figure 17-1 Voicegrade Private Line Circuits to a Telephone Company Central Office.

End-User Responsibility

MUX = Multiplexer
SWITCH = Private Branch Exchange or Digital Switch
CSU = Channel Service Unit

Telephone Office Responsibility

DSX-1 = T-1 Central Office Digital Cross-Connect Frame
D-Bank = D4 Digital Channel Bank

End-User Equipment Requirements

Premise equipment must have the following minimum features for compatibility with the telephone company's equipment.

1. The multiplexer or premise switch's T-1 data stream must use 24 8-bit byte formatting.
2. The T-1 line must have either D4 or Extended Superframe framing patterns.
3. Analog to digital conversion must use the North American Mu-Law 255 Pulse Code Modulation coding process.
4. The multiplexer or premise switch must loop or slave time to the T-1 recovered receive clock. Multiple ports should provide buffering for clock and phase differences.
5. Signaling information must use A and B robbed-bit transfer or in-band tones.
6. Loop- and ground-start signaling features at the premise location require special channel cards.

7. Premise multiplexer or switch should respond to Yellow and Blue Alarms from the telephone network. It should also issue a Yellow Alarm when recognizing an incoming failure.
8. Install a Channel Service Unit (CSU) or function if the T-1 service uses metallic wire facilities. CSUs should have a self-powered option in case the local telephone company doesn't furnish line power.

Private-Line Switched Telephone Company Services

Combining Private-Line switched services on T-1 facilities became the next entree for integration. The T-1 service carries either entirely message switching, switched 56-kb, or Wide Area Telephone Service (WATS) type circuits. Full integration of the different services wasn't possible because they lacked mixed service Digital Cross-Connect Systems. There were many Digital Cross-Connect Systems installed around the country, but they were dedicated to other services.

WATS service had the demand to make this arrangement economical. Many people felt T-1 facilities served as a bypass vehicle around the local telephone company's end-office switch. Bypass economics varied from state to state depending on the tariff for particular T-1 access line. Oregon established a T-1 access charge between $200 and $300. Around Chicago, one could expect at least a $1200 charge for a similar length access line.

Access line charges paid to the local telephone companies was a thorn in the long distance carriers' side. Providing switched services over a T-1 service to a long distance switch brought few extra dollars to the switch owners. They would collect the money for the service and turn a good portion back to the local company for access. Reducing the length of the access lines to service access points eventually led to a service node concept.

Service nodes moved access to the closest long distance company's office instead of a distant office with the service. In the past, special services appeared only at a few offices. Routing services to the closest office instead of offices with the service cut access line pay outs to the local telephone companies.

Figure 17-2 shows the connection of the T-1 line directly into the switching machines interface. The prime serving vehicle at first was the Digital Interface Frame of the #4 Electronic Switching System (#4-ESS). It plays the same role that a computer's high-speed interface does by reducing the need for 24 low-speed ports. Nevertheless, each T-1 port carries only one particular service. If the end-user had 12 WATS circuits and 12 switched 56-kb circuits, each service rode separate T-1 lines.

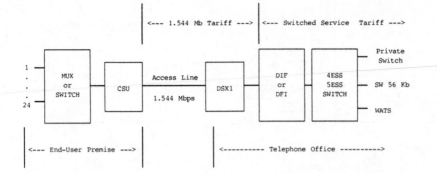

Figure 17-2 **Switched Voicegrade and 56 KB Circuits to a Telephone Company Switch.**

End-User Responsibility

TIE	=	Terminal Interface Equipment Not Shown
MUX	=	Multiplexer
SWITCH	=	Private Branch Exchange or Digital Switch
CSU	=	Channel Service Unit

Telephone Office Responsibility

DSX-1	=	T-1 Central Office Digital Cross-connect Frame
DIF	=	Digital Interface Frame — 4ESS T-1 Port
DFI	=	Digital Facility Interface — 5ESS T-1 Port

End-User Equipment Requirements

Premise equipment must have the following minimum features to interface the telephone company's equipment.

1. The multiplexer or premise switch's T-1 data stream must use 24 8-bit byte formatting.
2. The T-1 line must have either D4 or Extended Superframe framing patterns.
3. Analog-to-digital conversion uses the North American mu-Law 255 Pulse Code Modulation coding process.
4. The multiplexer or premise switch must loop or slave time to the recovered receive clock. Multiple ports should provide buffering for clock and phase differences.
5. Signaling information must use A and B robbed-bit transfer or in-band tones.

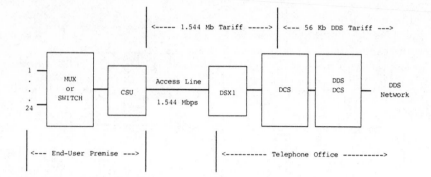

Figure 17-3 56-kb DDS Digital Data Throughput.

6. Loop- and ground-start signaling features at the premise location require special channel cards. Elimination of the local telephone company's end-office switch requires simulation of certain functions. An end-office is the Class-5 office in the switching hierarchy.

7. Premise multiplexer or switch should respond to Yellow and Blue Alarms from the telephone network. It should also issue a Yellow Alarm when recognizing an incoming failure.

8. Bypassing the local telephone company's end-office eliminates off-net or secondary dial tone. Originally, the only option was assuming the switch was ready for signaling information. Software and hardware changes to the some long distance switches provide a new source for secondary dial tone.

9. Install a Channel Service Unit (CSU) or function if the T-1 service uses metallic wire facilities. CSUs should have a self-powered option in case the local telephone company doesn't furnish line power.

10. Switched 56-kbps services require terminal equipment to change data and control signals into A- and B-bit signaling.

56-kb Digital Throughput

56-kbps digital throughput (Figure 17-3) was AT&T's first venture into integrating voice and digital data circuits. Before this, the extent of integration was one specific service on one T-1 line. Digital throughput was a true integration of different services on the same T-1 line.

This is the initial introduction of the Digital Cross-Connect System as a way to separate services within the telephone company's office. The first Digital Cross-Connect System separates digital data circuits from the other services riding on the aggregate T-1 line. After splitting off the digital data circuit from the end-user's T-1 service, it routes the data to a joint-user T-1 port.

Combined digital data services exit the first Digital Cross-Connect System and connect to another unit. This other Digital Cross-Connect System cross-connects only data services bound for Digital Data System's Hub Offices. While convenient to separate services this way, it adds delay and reduces the time to failure.

End-User Responsibility

MUX	=	Multiplexer
SWITCH	=	Private Branch Exchange or Digital Switch
CSU	=	Channel Service Unit

Telephone Company Responsibility

DSX-1	=	T-1 Central Office Digital Cross-Connect Frame
DCS	=	Integrated Services Shared Digital Cross-Connect System
DDS/DCS	=	DDS Dedicated Digital Cross-Connect System

End-User Equipment Requirements

Premise equipment must have the following minimum features to interface the telephone company's equipment.

1. The multiplexer or premise switch's T-1 data stream must use 24 8-bit byte formatting.
2. The T-1 line must have either D4 or Extended Superframe framing patterns.
3. 56-kb service occupies an entire 64,000-kbs time slot. The 8th bit in the time slot remains a data or idle-mode indicator. Terminal Interface Equipment must count 7 data bits and insert the 8th bit for control.
4. The multiplexer or premise switch must loop or slave time to the recovered receive clock. Multiple ports should provide buffering for clock and phase differences.
5. Premise multiplexer or switch should respond to Yellow and Blue Alarms from the telephone network. It should also issue a Yellow Alarm when recognizing an incoming failure.
6. Install a Channel Service Unit (CSU) or function if the T-1 service uses metallic wire facilities. CSUs should have a self-powered option in case the local telephone company doesn't furnish line power.

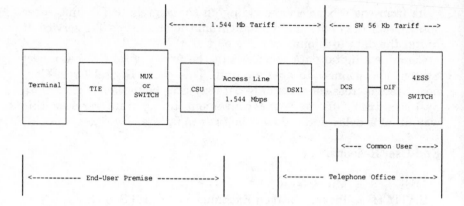

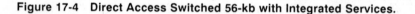

Figure 17-4   Direct Access Switched 56-kb with Integrated Services.

Integrated Switched 56-kb Direct Access

Integrating Switched 56-kb Service was the next logical step. Any switched 56-kb services riding the end-user's aggregate T-1 line splits off at the Digital Cross-connect System and cross-connects to a dedicated T-1 port (Figure 17-4). Other end-user switched 56-kb services also connect to the same common T-1 line going to the nearest digital switch office.

Chapter Eleven discussed switched 56-kb special signaling considerations. When switched 56-kb services rode Digital Data Systems access lines, the signaling indications changed at the telephone office. Integration moves the signaling interchange function to the end-user's premise. 56-kb terminal equipment changes the binary state of the 8th bit of its time slot to pass call information. The multiplexer or premise switch must convert the 8th-bit indicator into A and B robbed-bit signaling.

End-User Responsibility

TIE	=	56-kb Terminal Interface Equipment
MUX	=	Multiplexer
SWITCH	=	Private Branch Exchange or Digital Switch
CSU	=	Channel Service Unit

Telephone Company Responsibility

DSX-1	=	T-1 Central Office Digital Cross-Connect Frame
DCS	=	Integrated Services Shared Digital Cross-Connect System
DIF	=	Digital Interface Frame–4-ESS T-1 Port

End-User Equipment Requirements

Premise equipment must have the following minimum features to interface the telephone company's equipment.

1. The multiplexer or premise switch's T-1 data stream must use 24 8-bit byte formatting.
2. The T-1 line must have either D-4 or Extended Superframe framing patterns.
3. Each 56-kb service occupies an entire 64,000-bps time slot. The 8th bit in the time slot remains a data or idle-mode indicator. Terminal Interface Equipment must count 7 data bits and insert the 8th bit for control.
4. Switched 56-kbps services require multiplexer or premise switch equipment to change data and control signals into A- and B-bit signaling.
5. The multiplexer or premise switch must loop or slave time to the recovered receive clock. Multiple ports should provide buffering for clock and phase differences.
6. Premise multiplexer or switch should respond to Yellow and Blue Alarms from the telephone network. It should also issue a Yellow Alarm when recognizing an incoming failure.
7. Install a Channel Service Unit (CSU) or function if the T-1 service uses metallic wire facilities. CSUs should have a self-powered option in case the local telephone company doesn't furnish line power.

Subrate Digital Throughput

Subrate digital service throughput requires additional Digital Cross-Connect Systems (Figure 17-5). Similar to the 56,000-kb throughput, the subrates split off the end-user's T-1 line at the first Digital Cross-Connect System. Other similar end-user subrates services combine into one T-1 port interfacing a second Digital Cross-Connect System or to a subrate data multiplexer (SRDM) in a DDS Hub Office. Digital channel banks with the (SRDM) optional unit are also possible but require manual connections.

The following assumes someone will eventually eliminate the software bugs that have plagued implementation to date. After entering the second Digital Cross-Connect System, the subrate's time slot splits off again and cross-connects to another T-1 port. This T-1 port now connects to a third Digital Cross-Connect System dedicated to subrate cross-connections.

While it is technically possible to mix data rates within a DS-0 time slot, the telephone companies find it uneconomical. Each DS-0 time slot carries only like speeds digital services.

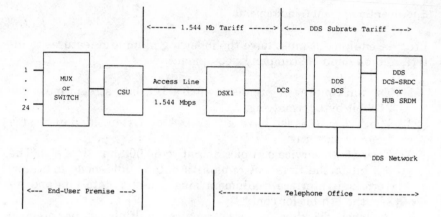

Figure 17-5   DDS Subrate Digital Data Throughput.

Subrate Channel Capacity

5 — 9600 bps per Time Slot
10 — 4800 bps per Time Slot
20 — 2400 bps per Time Slot

All subrate rearrangements complete and route back through the second DCS to get to the Digital Data System network.

End-User Responsibility

MUX   = Multiplexer
SWITCH = Private Branch Exchange or Digital Switch
CSU   = Channel Service Unit

Telephone Company Responsibility

DSX-1   = T-1 Central Office Digital Cross-Connect
                        Frame
DCS   = Integrated Services Shared Digital Cross-
                        Connect System
DDS/DCS   = DDS Dedicated Digital Cross-Connect
                        System
DDS/DCS/SRDC = DDS/DCS/Subrate Digital Cross-Connect
DDS/HUB-SRDM = Hub Office Subrate Digital Multiplexer

| 0 | DDDDDDC OCU 1 | 1 | DDDDDDC OCU 2 | 1 | DDDDDDC OCU 3 | 0 | DDDDDDC OCU 4 | 0 | DDDDDDC OCU 5 |

D = Data Bits   C = Control Bit

Figure 17-6   SRDM Framing Pattern for 9600 bps.

End-User Equipment Requirements

Premise equipment must have the following minimum features to interface the telephone company's equipment.

1. The multiplexer or premise switch's T-1 data stream must use 24 8-bit byte formatting.
2. The T-1 line must have either D4 or Extended Superframe framing patterns.
3. Each group of subrate speeds occupies an entire 64,000-bps timeslot (Figure 17-6). The 7th bit in the each subrate remains a data or idle-mode indicator. Terminal Interface Equipment must count 6 data bits and insert the 8th bit for control. It also must include a framing pattern (Table 17-1) to provide synchronization between the transmit and receive equipment.
4. The multiplexer or premise switch must loop or slave time to the recovered receive clock. Multiple ports should provide buffering for clock and phase differences.
5. Premise multiplexer or switch should respond to Yellow and Blue Alarms from the telephone network. It should also issue a Yellow Alarm when recognizing an incoming failure.
6. Install a Channel Service Unit (CSU) or function if the T-1 service uses metallic wire facilities. CSUs should have a self-powered option in case the local telephone company doesn't furnish line power.

Subrate Digital Throughput via Digital Data System #2

Subrate digital throughput by direct access requires Digital Data System #2 facilities. Digital Data System #2 is the DDS service with a secondary channel and has a higher transmission rate. The higher bit rate of 72,000 bps handles the subrate's framing and control bits.

Each 9600-bps data channel becomes 12,800 bps with the normal framing pattern bits. Five times 12,800 bits equals 64,000 bits. This

9600 bps — 0 1 1 0 0
4800 bps — 0 1 1 0 0 1 0 1 0 0
2400 bps — 0 1 1 0 0 1 0 1 0 0 1 1 1 0 0 0 0 1 0 0

Table 17-1   SRDM Framing Format patterns.

leaves a remaining 8000 bps for even more framing pattern bits to locate the subrate frame.

As soon as the Hub Office recognizes the subrate frame, it strips the extra framing bit from the pattern. Normal connections at the Hub Office combine the DS-0 time slot to a T-1 Digital Multiplexer (T1DM). The the regular DDS Network transports the subrate frame to a Subrate Digital Cross-Connect (SRDC) location (Figure 17-7). The (SRDC) function may never happen if software problems still exist. Once they solve the mystery, the developmental costs will put an oppressive burden on implementing the unit in the first place.

End-user terminal equipment is very specialized with the additional framing patterns and its 72,000-bps output. Digital Data System #2 facilities depend on the local telephone companies and the end-user location being within 3.4 miles from a Hub Office.

End-User Responsibility

MUX   = Multiplexer
SWITCH = Private Branch Exchange or Digital Switch
DSU   = Data Service Unit

Telephone Company Responsibility

OCU   = DDS Office Channel Unit
T1DM   = T-1 Digital Multiplexer
DDS/DCS   = DDS Dedicated Digital Cross-connect
                        System
DDS/DCS/SRDC   = Dedicated Sub-Rate DDS/DCS
DDS/HUB-SRDM = Hub Office Sub-Rate Digital Multiplexer

End-User Equipment Requirements

Premise equipment must have the following minimum features to interface the telephone company's equipment.

1. Terminal equipment must form equal speed subrate services into special frames. See Figure 17-6 and Table 17-1 for control signal and framing pattern locations.

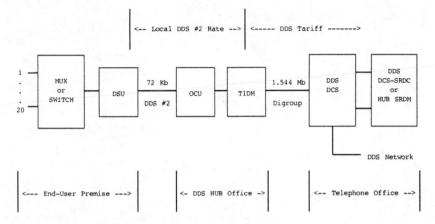

Figure 17-7 DDS Subrate Multiplexing via DDS-#2.

2. The terminal or Data Service Unit must loop or slave time to a 72,000-bps recovered receive clock.

Integrated Private-Line Voice and Digital Data Circuits

Integrating analog voice and digital data services over the same T-1 line may never progress much past this method. While ISDN includes all the call-processing messages to successfully move between networks, it doesn't meet major communications interests. ISDN answers telephone companies' needs for standardization. End-user multiplexers and digital switches perform many integrated preliminary functions and perform rapid reconfigurations. Like all names they quickly change to some other along the way.

The first Digital Cross-Connect System separates the integrated services and splits off the digitized analog services from the combined services (Figure 17-8). It then cross-connects these to a T-1 port that interfaces a digital channel bank (D-Bank). The D-Bank returns the channels back to an analog signal. Individual analog circuit connect to various dedicated services.

All digital circuits cross-connect at the DS-0 Level in the first Digital Cross-Connect System. A T-1 port interfaces the first DCS to a dedicated DDS Digital Cross-Connect System. If the digital service is 56,000 bps, the circuit cross-connects to an outgoing T-1 port to the DDS network. Lower-speed digital services cross-connect to a T-1 port interfacing a third Digital Cross-Connect System. The third DCS does all the low-speed digital services cross-connections. After completing these connections, the low-speed services return to the second Digital Cross-Connect System and the DDS network.

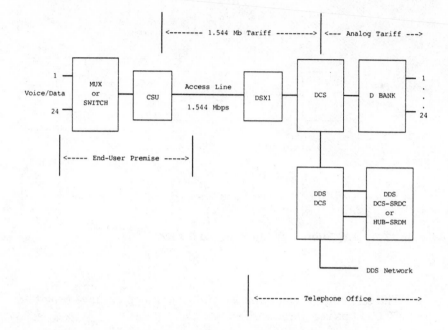

Figure 17-8   Integrated Analog Voice and Digital Data Circuits.

End-User Responsibility

    MUX   = Multiplexer
    SWITCH = Private Branch Exchange or Digital Switch
    CSU   = Channel Service Unit

Telephone Company Responsibility

    DSX-1   = T-1 Central Office Digital Cross-
                        Connect Frame
    DCS   = Integrated Services Shared Digital Cross-
                        Connect System
    D Bank   = D4 Digital Channel Bank
    DDS/DCS   = DDS Dedicated Digital Cross-Connect
                        System
    DDS/DCS/SRDC = Dedicated Subrate DDS/DCS
    DDS/HUB-SRDM = Hub Office Subrate Digital Multiplexer

End-User Equipment Requirements

Premise equipment must have the following minimum features to interface the telephone company's equipment.

1. The multiplexer or premise switch's T-1 data stream must use 24 8-bit byte formatting.
2. The T-1 line must have either D4 or Extended Superframe framing patterns.
3. Analog to digital conversion use the North American Mu-Law 255 Pulse Code Modulation coding process.
4. The multiplexer or premise switch must loop or slave time to the recovered receive clock. Multiple ports should provide buffering for clock and phase differences.
5. Signaling information, other than in-band tones, must use A and B robbed-bit transfer.
6. Loop- and ground-start signaling features at the premise location require special channel cards.
7. Each 56-kb service occupies an entire 64,000-bps time slot. The 8th bit in the time slot remains a data or idle-mode indicator. Terminal Interface Equipment must count 7 data bits and insert the 8th bit for control.
8. Each group of subrate speeds occupies an entire 64,000-bps time slot. The 7th bit in each subrate remains a data or idle-mode indicator. Terminal Interface Equipment must count 6 data bits and insert the 8th bit for control. It also must include a framing pattern to provide synchronization between the transmit and receive equipment.
9. Premise multiplexer or switch should respond to Yellow and Blue Alarms from the telephone network. It should also issue a Yellow Alarm when recognizing an incoming failure.
10. Install a Channel Service Unit (CSU) or function if the T-1 service uses metallic wire facilities. CSUs should have a self-powered option in case the local telephone company doesn't furnish line power.

Bell Communications Research Low Bit Rate Voice
AT&T Bit-Compression Multiplexer

Low Bit Rate Voice (LBRV) transcoders or multiplexers are ANSI or CCITT standard Adaptive Differential Pulse Code Modulation (ADPCM) signals. Initially the telephone companies oriented the ADPCM transcoder towards voice circuits only. As such, the channels divided into four bundles. Each bundle had 11 32,000-bps voice channels and a signaling channel.

Bundles made sense if Digital Cross-Connect Systems entered the network to efficiently pack the T-1 lines. A voice only configuration used an option called Template 0 (zero) and allows only 44 circuits. Figure 17-9 shows the first Digital Cross-Connect System splitting two bundles for a total of 22 circuits off and connecting to a collo-

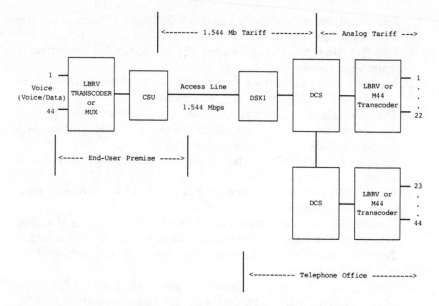

Figure 17-9   ANSI/CCITT ADPCM Integrated Voice and Data Circuits.

cated LBRV multiplexer. The second two bundles transfer to a T-1 line interface a distant Digital Cross-Connect System. Again the two bundles interface another LBRV multiplexers.

Integrating digital data circuits with the ADPCM voice circuits requires different multiplexer options or templates. The digital data circuits follow the same architecture shown in Figure 17-8. Dedicated Digital Cross-Connect Systems for digital services handle the data.

End-User Responsibility

LBRV MUX	= ANSI/CCITT ADPCM Transcoder or Multiplexer
CSU	= Channel Service Unit

Telephone Company Responsibility

DSX-1	= T-1 Central Office Digital Cross-Connect Frame
DCS	= Integrated Services Shared Digital Cross-Connect System
LBRV or M44	= ADPCM multiplexer with voice only option

End-User Equipment Requirements

Premise equipment must have the following minimum features to interface the telephone company's equipment.

1. The ADPCM transcoder or multiplexer must use meet the ANSI and CCITT September 1986 Standard.
2. The T-1 line must have either D4 or Extended Superframe framing patterns.
3. Final analog to digital conversion after conversion from ADPCM to PCM must use the North American Mu-Law 255 Pulse Code Modulation coding process.
4. The transcoder or multiplexer must loop or slave time to the recovered receive clock. Multiple ports should provide buffering for clock and phase differences.
5. Signaling information, other than in-band tones, must locate in the twelfth channel in the associated bundle.
6. Each 56-kbps service occupies an entire 64,000-bps time slot. Terminal Interface Equipment must count 7 data bits and insert the 8th bit for control. The 8th bit in the time slot remains a data or idle-mode indicator.
7. Each group of subrate speeds occupies an entire 64,000-bps time slot. The 7th bit in the each subrate remains a data or idle-mode indicator. Terminal Interface Equipment must count 6 data bits and insert the 8th bit for control. It also must include a framing pattern to provide synchronization between the transmit and receive equipment.
8. Premise transcode or multiplexer should respond to Yellow and Blue Alarms from the telephone network. It should also issue a Yellow Alarm when recognizing an incoming failure.
9. Install a Channel Service Unit (CSU) or function if the T-1 service uses metallic wire facilities. CSUs should have a self-powered option in case the local telephone company doesn't furnish line power.

Disaster Restoration

Disaster restoration plans call for bundled transfer of service to another site. Restoration of service takes two major directions. One, the data services head towards a central computer site and switch to a computer restoration company. Second, data between two locations can switch to another end-user location.

Switching between end-user locations at the T-1 rate uses a transfer switch in the telephone office. The end-user has control of the transfer switch through a key-switch closure. Some telephone companies also offer switch control by an ASCII terminal through a dial-up connection. Our example shows the Transfer Switch with three different outputs. A basic transfer switch can switch one line to either one of two different lines or telephone functions. Cascaded basic switches provide additional choices. The choice shown in Figure

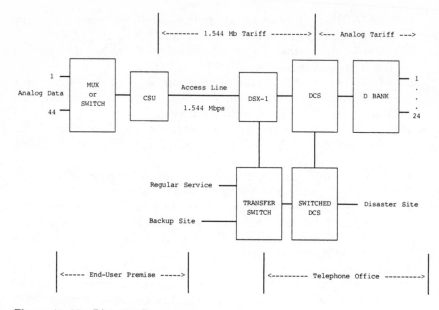

Figure 17-10 Disaster Restoration.

17-10 switches between end-user locations and an alternative common-user disaster restoration service.

Computer site disaster restoration services use the switched T-1 service for economy. Remote end-user services homing on a central computer site can quickly switch to alternative computers. Since up to 24 analog services share the same T-1 line, a Digital Cross-Connect System makes one switch to move all circuits to a new site.

Computer restoration services often use several computer back-up locations. Using a switched T-1 service to reach these sites makes sense. Low-usage sensitive charges and flexible site locations makes it desirable.

End-User Responsibility

    MUX   = Multiplexer
    SWITCH = Private Branch Exchange or Digital Switch
    CSU   = Channel Service Unit

Telephone Company Responsibility

    DSX-1   = T-1 Central Office Digital Cross-Connect Frame
    DCS   = Integrated Services Shared Digital Cross-Connect System

D Bank   = D4 Digital Channel Bank
Switched DCS   = T-1 Switch Digital Cross-Connect System
Transfer Switch = End-User controlled T-1 Switch

End-User Equipment Requirements

Premise equipment must have the following minimum features to interface the telephone company's equipment.

1. The T-1 line must have either D4 or Extended Superframe framing patterns.
2. Terminal equipment cannot require superframe integrity if the system uses a Digital Cross-Connect System. A new superframe framing pattern changes any relationship the original frame had with the pattern first sent.
3. The multiplexer or premise switch must loop or slave time to the recovered receive clock when connected to a Digital Cross-Connect System. Clocking must change back to internal clocking when bypassing a Digital Cross-Connect System.
4. Premise multiplexer or switch should respond to Yellow and Blue Alarms from the telephone network. It should also issue a Yellow Alarm when recognizing an incoming failure.
5. Install a Channel Service Unit (CSU) or function if the T-1 service uses metallic wire facilities. CSUs should have a self-powered option in case the local telephone company doesn't furnish line power.

Video Teleconferences

Video teleconference equipment furnishes adequate television pictures using the latest video compression units and T-1 services. Studio- quality video transmission uses the higher DS-3 or 45-Mbps rate facilities.

Figure 17-11 shows video equipment connected to a switched T-1 service Digital Cross-Connect System. End-users or the telephone company have control of the switching operation. AT&T offered end-user control of the DCS with Customer Controlled Reconfiguration and under their control with Reserved 1.5 Service.

Video signals often include long strings of zeroes in the data stream. A special Digital Cross-Connect System interface port reacts differently to video signals than other digital signals. While a normal interface interjects ones bits after sensing a short zero-bit string, the special interface allows greater latitude. Scrambling techniques also overcome the concern about long zero-bit strings.

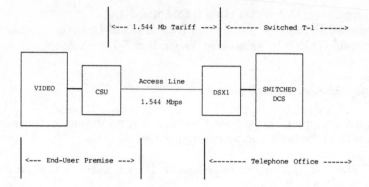

Figure 17-11 Video Conferences.

End-User Responsibility

    Video = Video Terminal Equipment
    CSU   = Channel Service Unit

Telephone Company Responsibility

    DSX-1   = T-1 Central Office Digital Cross-Connect
                           Frame
    SWITCHED DCS = T-1 Switch Digital Cross-Connect System

End-User Equipment Requirements

Premise equipment must have the following minimum features to interface the telephone company's equipment.

1. The T-1 line must have either D4 or Extended Superframe framing patterns.
2. Terminal equipment cannot require superframe integrity if the system uses a Digital Cross-Connect System. A new superframe framing pattern changes any relationship the original frame had with the pattern first sent.
3. The video terminal equipment must loop or slave time to the recovered receive clock when connected to a Digital Cross-Connect System. Clocking must change back to internal clocking when bypassing a Digital Cross-Connect System.
4. The video terminal should respond to Yellow Alarms from the telephone network. It should also issue a Yellow Alarm when recognizing an incoming failure.

5. Install a Channel Service Unit (CSU) or function if the T-1 service uses metallic wire facilities. CSUs should have a self-powered option in case the local telephone company doesn't furnish line power.

6. Maintaining ones-density and keep-alive signals is the responsibility of the video terminal. Introduction of ones bits by the CSU distort video signals.

18

Combining Digital Services Into One Network

So far we have looked at the telephone digital services, end-user equipment, and facilities. Now is the time to see if the gestalt principle is right that the final system has properties not found by sum of the parts.

Testing the premise equipment on a test bench lessens the surprises later. Testing the equipment with the facilities is even better. The final proof of the pudding is putting the complete system through its paces. Anything less than full testing is like sending for a mail-order bride with no idea of the compatibility. When you marry for better or worse, it helps knowing just how bad the worse really is.

Doing your own tests with your own test equipment is ideal. It is an indication of the commitment of upper management to provide the technical personnel and tools to maintain excellent communications. Test equipment rental companies also have the specialized equipment needed to perform compatibility tests.

If you do not have the technical expertise to make the system's acceptance tests, there are other people around that can. One way is to use the telephone companies and the manufacturers to jointly make tests of the system. They are receptive to spending time and money for tests if the combination of equipment and facilities has never been tried before. It provides information they can't get any other way and looks good in advertisements if it works. Successful tests will solicit requests for customer endorsements.

When your system resembles others already working, the equipment and service providers will not want to spend their time and money on tests. They may elect to provide the testing on a cost or small profit basis instead. This still beats your third testing option of contracting with a consultant. Your first difficulty is finding a telecommunications consultant that knows about transmission testing. Consultants with a data hardware communications background understand transmission principles better than voice-oriented groups. Your last option, of course, is trusting to luck. There are people who have a good track record with just plan old intuition. If the intuitive powers also rely on a strong technical background, there is a greater chance for success. When the intuition points to a questionable performance, there a good justification to make tests.

Testing Equipment After Connection to Facilities

System testing should experience the most demanding trial one can think of. You stress test the premise equipment and the facilities as a complete system in their worst light. Simple things like the time of day make a difference in the tests.

If you selected telephone company facilities and services, then plan testing time around their busy period. The telephone companies busy periods are between 9:30 and 11:30 a.m. and 1:00 and 3:30 p.m. And if you are really lucky, a test period on Mother's Day will furnish the ultimate in stress. Also, making tests during the worst period of microwave radio fading will provide good indications.

We keep emphasizing the need for stress testing to see if there are problems under a full load. It is like stepping on the accelerator of your car to avoid an accident and finding out your engine doesn't respond to the need. You don't wait until an emergency happens to find out the limitations.

Initial Tests of Premise Equipment and the Facilities

The goal of stress testing is loading the equipment and facilities with the greatest amount of power. Testers use a variety of things to load circuits down for tests. Using voice or music from the local radio station is convenient, but a white-noise generator loads the voice channel the best. White-noise generators load a wide bandwidth of frequencies with a steady power. It also simulates an analog modem's output over the message circuits. Those individuals that have listened to a data circuit in operation understand the similarity of white noise to the output of a high-speed modem.

Data testing over the years used random data generators to simulate a wide variation of end-user data transmission. Two problems arise from using quasi-random signals. First, the majority of end-user data has a preponderance of only a few characters. If the content of the data messages is numerical, there are only 10 characters. The second problem arises with digital equipment getting confused with repetitive patterns. This confusion centers on the equipment always searching the data flow for the framing pattern. If it spots a repetitive pattern that simulates the framing pattern, the equipment will resynchronize on the data instead of the true framing pattern. One problem with a telephone company digital system occurred when a long string of ones bits charged a capacitor. When a single zero in the stream of ones bits appeared, the capacitor discharged back into the data stream creating a ones bit in its place.

Each end-user's installation is different, and the following tests are only suggestions. While listed as separate tests for voice and data, they run concurrently just like a true integrated world. Tests on switched telephone company services require dialing up connections to off-net quiet terminations or tone supplies. Most local telephone companies use the NXX-999X series of available numbers to dial milliwatt tone supplies and quiet terminations to check for noise. NXX stands for the three numbers identifying a local telephone exchange. Trial- and-error dialing will find the last number in the NXX-999X. Numbers between six and nine are the first choices. An alternate choice uses the telephones on-net that will hold the switched connection during the tests.

Voice Circuit Stress Testing

I assume you completed all equipment transmission testing during your equipment selection process. Results from that test bench testing serve as benchmark reference points with the following tests. You should have records of the transmission characteristics of circuits boards without facilities attached. A couple of words of caution when comparing transmission measurements between bench readings and real life. Transmission measurement values may be logarithmic, root-mean-square, or linear. Adding or subtracting values often requires translating units into common bases for comparison.

Figure 18-1 shows a white-noise generator connected to the transmit port of one voice channel. Adjust the power from the generator to read -13 decibels (db) at a zero test level point (TLP). Since decibels are ratios, one must know the TLP of each interface point. If the TLP for the interface is +7 db, set the generator's output to -6 db.

```
       -6 db       0 db     +7 db
       t_____ 13 db _____t
```

Voice circuits carry other things besides voice conversations. Analog data modems are faster and cheaper than anything in the

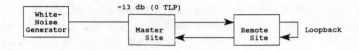

Figure 18-1   Voice Circuit Loading.

past. Inexpensive circuit boards for personal computers make the concern even greater in the future. These tests check for the presence of high-speed modem output as well as their effect on normal voice conversations.

1. Put all the remote channels cards into a loopback condition. While a few impairments clear when the circuit loops back, others become very obvious. The ideal arrangement is testing simultaneously from both ends, but this requires additional test equipment and personnel. If the tests point out questionable results, we recommend end-to-end tests to pinpoint problem areas.

2. Connect white-noise generators to almost all voice circuits. Set the output of the generator to provide a -13 dbm level (0 TLP) to all inputs. This will load down all the channels not under direct test.

3. Connect a tone generator(s) to the remaining circuit(s). Other viable test equipment send and measure a comb (many single frequencies in the voice band) of tones. Vector oscilloscopes or P/AR (Peak-to-Average Ratio) test the whole circuit's bandwidth. Several companies make a spectrum analyzer that provides a graphic picture of the frequency gain characteristics.

4. Record various phrases that contain harsh sounds and soft sounds with different pitched voices. Chapter Seven on Coding Methods suggests one phrase with a distribution of sounds. Vivid imaginations can always substitute different phrases that seem appropriate for the environment. When recording, use high-quality or crystal microphones instead of the typical built-in unit that may band-limit the voice frequencies.

5. Connect the tape player to the transmit side and regulate its power to deliver a 0 dbm level (0 TLP). Since the voice power varies continuously, setting the power level may be only an approximation. If the voice power is too high, the coding will take place on the outer edges of the compander and may overload the system.

6. Connect another tape recorder to the receive side of the same circuit. The circuit loops back at the remote end and doubles

the transmission distance. Recordings of the taped phrases after traversing the system makes it easier to analyze later.

7. Run the series of taped phrases and record with the system under full load. Open the transmit aggregate line for three seconds and then close the connection during the recording. This should provide an idea what happens during the recovery period of a hit on the line.
8. Run the same series of tests with no load on the other circuits.
9. Make echo return tests with the voice circuit connected to a quiet termination. This means terminating the circuit in 900 ohms (2-wire connection) to ensure a noiseless connection. Leave the transmitting tape player and recorder connect to the same circuit. Remove the loopback at the remote end and terminate the 2-wire section. Any echo content heard in the recordings will duplicate real-life situations. Disregard this test if the voice circuits remain 4-wire from end to end.
10. Tests run on large networks should also run tests with the network configured in its worst disaster restoration layout. This will provide some insight on the need for echo control.

Data Circuits Stress Testing

Data testing over the complete system also requires the same amount of pushing the circuits to their limit. Imagine your company is a large department store chain. Your network has to respond the traffic expected during the Christmas shopping surge. While one can reconfigure the network for peak demand periods, it pays to find out what the network can take. You'll also take these precautions once you find that equipment acts very different under a full load. Sometimes manufacturers will underestimate the internal bus capacity and power requirements. The following tests will help find the limitations of the system. Once you have found the system's limit, you can safely operate under that level. Operating near the limitation level will lead to a higher error performance.

1. If testing from just a central site, loop each data circuit back on itself. Looping the remote equipment at the high-speed side doesn't test all the equipment properly.
2. Connect bit-error test generator(s) to as many digital data circuits as possible. If the equipment has an internal test generator with a selective test pattern, use that on the remaining circuits. We emphasize a selective pattern instead of the usual quasi-random generators. A repetitive test pattern with either strings of ones or zeroes provides a better test.

3. Connect a bit-error measuring device to the receive side of a circuit under test. Open the transmit side momentarily or inject an error to verify you are testing valid data. Restore the circuit and make 15-minute tests of the data transmission.

4. If you can't regulate the bit-error test pattern to send strings of ones and zero bits, then use a dotting pattern. This pattern is alternating ones and zeroes found on nearly all sets. A dotting pattern is better than a quasi-random pattern but not as good as strings of ones and zeroes (ones bits with a few zero bits and vice versa).

5. Open the transmit aggregate line for three seconds and then close the connection during the recording. This should provide an idea what happens during the recovery period of a hit on the line.

6. Run the same series of tests with no load on the other circuits.

7. Tests run on large networks should also run tests with the network configured in its worst disaster restoration layout. This will provide some insight on the need for adjustments to data response monitors.

Analysis of the Results

Recordings of a loaded and nonloaded system assist in the overall analysis of your completed system. Several people can listen to the results at the same time and render an objective opinion. Its objective if the majority of the listeners agree to what they heard.

The following are a few items to listen for in the voice recordings and the data transmission results.

1. Under full load, check for voice clarity and low background noise. High-pitched voices sound comparatively the same as transmitted. Clipping is nonexistent or relatively minor in nature.

2. Listen for strange sounds when the aggregate high-speed line opens for several seconds during the test. Time the recovery time after reconnecting the high-speed line. Listen for any strange noises during system recovery. Determine if strange sounds are too loud or will cause users concern.

3. Echo return test doesn't require a looped circuit since the energy reflection is a loop already. The tests used a straight-away circuit connected to a quiet termination. Any echo perceived by the listeners is a true indication of the end-to-end service. Tests for echo from circuits on a worst-case restoration con-

figuration are very important. Echo on voice circuits prompts either echo control or rerouting to off-net facilities.

Service Node Concept or Virtual Network Concerns

Up to now, the telephone companies used separate testing groups to handle each type of communication. Order a T-1 line to integrate services, and you talked to the high-speed digital facilities people. Order connections into a WATS network, and you also talked to the switching people. Add a DDS circuit, and you got to speak to the Hub Office.

Integrating end-user circuits into a T-1 line and connecting them to telephone company's services often found access problems. Digital data serving locations were only located in a third of all telephone company offices. They could very well situate in cities many miles away from the end-user's associated analog voice circuits.

Combining digital services into one network has started to take shape cloaked under different names. What remains is a new commitment on the part of the telephone companies to offer administration and maintenance of integrated services. This is a major change in implementation and testing philosophy.

Technically connecting the parts is the easy portion of integrating digital services. If the various digital services followed all the standards, they should fit together. Nevertheless, administration and something as simple as how to bill for the service often cancel the best plans. One service proposed using a pair of wires to connect two telephone company interfaces together. There wasn't any way to install the pair of wires since there wasn't a way to officially call it something. And if you can't assign a circuit number to it, you can't bill the customer. No bill means no service — the simple determining factor of telephone company service.

End-User Premise Networking Controls

End-user's network control of data communications equipment lean either to computer or facility orientation. Computer orientation assumes that network and facility control rest with message retransmission and response times. It assumes the facility transparency if the messages get through correctly. Facility-oriented network control assumes computer transparency if the facilities look good.

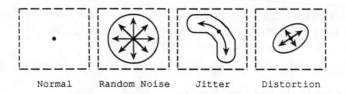

Figure 18-2 Analog Modem Transmission Impairment Measuring.

As the integrated networks grow in size, their complexity also grows. One still finds difficulty trying to blend the various network control reports into something helpful in running the system.

Adding Analog Modem Testing to Network

Analog data modems offered network control for many years. Depending on what you wanted to pay, one could get anything from basic to grandiose. When you opt for the grandiose you may end up with the ludicrous instead. Systems that provide instantaneous measurements of analog transmission impairments are borderline at best.

Some units provide transmission measurement readings by making snap decisions from the receive data. After making a one-second check of the signal, they claim definitive values. The trouble is that one wouldn't see the values shown during a standard 15-minute period specified for the tests.

End-users should question the dependability of the other measurements if based on speedy modem evaluations. There are too many transmission interactions that produce false readings. Figure 18-2 shows the modems decision area for just one symbol or baud signal. When no transmission impairments exist, the symbol appears in the center of the imaginary decision area. Random noise positions the symbol in a circular pattern. Jitter swings the symbol back and forth along an arc equal to the degree of jitter around the axis. Inter-modulation distortion moves the symbol around in an ellipse. Other impairments do different things to the symbol's position. Nevertheless, one impairment like noise has several interpretations by the modem.

Review of Overall Concerns

Know exactly what you are getting. Assume nothing and verify everything. And when you can't verify, make sure all claims are in writing. Memories may fade, but signed papers have a lasting effect.

Complete Understanding of Support

One needs a complete understanding of how the telephone companies will support the combined services. Since they propose integrating several services under one umbrella, there should be one point of contact for trouble reports.

After you get one point of contact for all integrated services, obtain the second, or their level management contact. Just as telephone companies have their own trouble escalating process, the end-user should also know where to get results. Excessive use of these contacts will lead to irritation instead of response.

Error Performance Supported

Since several error performances exist with the various services, the telephone company should specify what you should expect for end-to-end error performance. End-user service covers the entire network. You should receive a consistent error performance level and not have to calculate between error units.

The telephone companies first approach to an ubiquitous error performance is applying the worst-case principle. They add the sum of the parts and arrive at a figure one wouldn't wish on a competitor. Adding error performances from several different types of facilities is enough to boggle anyone's imagination.

AT&T-Bell Laboratories did studies on the various error performances. They could approximate the expected performance level on mixed facilities and services. Computer programs could easily determine expected error performances for every situations. It remains one thing to arrive at an expected performance and another to support the figure.

Every circuit could have a reasonable (for the telephone companies) and realistic (for the end-user) supported performance (Figure 18-3). If your service is under 100 miles, the performance support should match the actual distance. Right now that length circuit has the same backing as a 4000-mile-long facility.

Error performance should have one term of error performance. The most acceptable error performance is the bit-error rate. While not embraced by the technocrat as a true error performance description, it is a common definition recognized by the end-user.

Restoration of Service Concerns

Service failures will tell the strength of the system. And strengths come from preparing for the worst. It is knowing what to do when the master clock source for the network no longer exists. You play

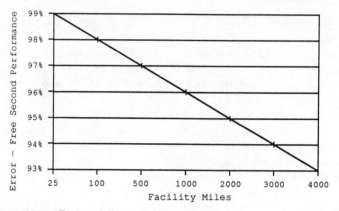

Figure 18-3   Rational Error Performance.

"what if" games until you run out of things. The following are but a few reminders of what could go wrong in a system.

1. Master clock source: Plan to connect a new clock source to system when master clock fails. Plans include changing timing options around the network to meet the new clock's origination point.
2. Delay: Excessive delay will affect data response times and introduce echo to the voice circuits. Plans include changing the computer's maintenance program times. Instruct the PBX to switch voice circuits to use alternate routing during failure period.
3. Channel priorities: Each circuit must have several priority settings. When several facilities go out and premise sites fail, the remaining facilities will save only a portion of your network. This information resides either in the network control equipment or is kept in a handy binder for the maintenance personnel.
4. Data performance: Restoration of service results in longer facility distances. If error performance deteriorates too much, you should plan on alternate transmission means until service returns to normal.

Future Concerns

Future concerns revolve around the trends for the next digital evolution. The next chapter reviews some of the directions and the factors that will help or kill the idea. Thoughts about an evolutionary process should find a spot in the back of your mind, because as soon as you complete the installation of one network, it is time to work on plans for its replacement.

19

Digital Evolution

At first there was a digital revolution, when high-speed digital technology started in the 1960s. End-users didn't feel the impact until AT&T issued the first T-1 service tariff in the early 1980s. Then the real revolution gripped the communications world and changed the operating methods used for the past 100 years.

A lot of things have happened since the first T-1 tariff. End-user networks that started small now rival some small telephone companies. T-1 multiplexers also started out small, and now their complexity has peaked in the changes they can offer. During this transition period, telephone companies watched the demand for high-speed digital services slant towards the end-user's premise. Today they are in the best position for the next digital evolution.

Digital Services Evolution

During the early days of the 1980s digital revolution, many established manufacturers fought standardization. It was a common practice to build proprietary designed equipment for the end-user. Their main objective was locking the end-user into a single-source design. Every installation was different, and each unit became customized for the end-user. Custom configured multiplexers always returned to the factory before being used again in other installations.

Telecommunications equipment manufacturers began to see the light when end-users demanded equipment that had compatibility to telephone company services. Disaster restoration plans used the Digital Cross-Connect Systems and prompted many manufacturers to meet the frame structure common to telephone companies. This was their first recognition of the need for standards.

Computer hardware and software companies saw the need for compatibility several years ago. Open network architecture meant being able to talk to an IBM, DEC, Wang, or whatever computer. Systems were getting too large to paint the end-user's locations totally blue. While large computer networks found the demand for openness and standards, personal computer manufacturers produced clones of the major suppliers. The personal computer boom also pointed out the need for compatibility and portability from one system to another.

Coexistence, compatibility, and portability all rely on standards to find mutually agreeable ground to stand on. Telecommunications personnel must also agree to standards that will provide an open network architecture. The full potential of the next digital evolution depends on how well the services and products interact when connected together.

Evolution Direction

The evolution of digital services rests with the telephone companies and how swiftly they respond to the opportunity. While they are spending a lot of time with Integrated Services Digital Network (ISDN) architecture, it is only a small portion of the total integrated digital services evolution.

ISDN requires some dramatic equipment changes and doesn't reflect an evolutionary process. Modifying existing equipment and offering innovative ways to connect services is a clearer picture of evolution. Nevertheless, telephone companies will waste their chances without the following steps.

1. Increase end-user controlled capability of telephone company services.
2. Improve the speed of the computer operating systems controlling digital services to a real-time basis. This may mean separating the end-user controlled services away from internal telephone company operations.
3. Develop access to the data link channel of the Extended Superframe pattern and the ISDN Access Channels.
4. Develop translators to reconcile the differences between the individual data link packet streams. While each data link follows a generic X.25 packet protocol, the addresses and data information contain individual traits.
5. Develop other translators to reach an open network architecture for end-user and telephone company operation in a reasonable time frame. There are too many network manage-

ment operating systems on the market to lead to an early resolution of an ubiquitous standard.

6. Automate trouble reporting and clearance of telephone company services. Automate facility failure reporting back to the end-user and provide estimates of restoration or clearance of trouble. Telephone companies would seem to be partners with the end-user instead of giving the old "mother knows best" attitude.

7. Offer digital multiples of 64,000 bps between telephone company offices. While local access requires a T-1 line for local transport, sharing of facilities between cities is possible with minor administrative changes.

8. Offer 19,200-bps digital data service local access. Don't spend added time and expense creating a system that can extend to the outer reaches of local access. Offer the service within the loss distance for a 9600-Hz Nyquist frequency.

End-user Control of Telephone Services

The Bell System often sent misleading information to the end-user. One group pushed end-user premise equipment, and another group pushed central office services. Divestiture confused the end-user even more when telephone company sales force competed against itself. It wasn't long before the telephone companies realized they were shooting themselves in the foot.

Reorganization brought direction to the sales force. Reorganization also brought telephone company office services that complemented the premise products. Telephone companies began to offer the end-user limited control of some Digital Cross-Connect Systems. While the original concept for customer control revolved around voice message reconfiguration, the end-user applied it for data service restoration. Digital Cross-Connect System response to a switch request took an inordinate amount of time. Data communications people wanted demand switching capability.

Premise switching multiplexers recognized the problem and provided almost instantaneous reconfiguration of circuits when a facility failed. Nevertheless, in their haste to get a product in the marketplace, they didn't take time to understand the impairments covered in previous chapters.

Offering end-user controlled telephone services requires a fast reaction to their demands. Voice message circuits never had a demand for quick restoration. Most PBXs have alternate routing options. When a facility fails along the route, the calls redirect to off-net operations. The facility failure could last a long time before reaching a deep concern about the extra routing cost. Data communications can mean millions of dollars to the financial community if a facility fails for any period of time.

Increased end-user control of telephone company integrated digital services depends on the following.

1. Decrease interval to initiate Digital Cross-Connect System switches to a few minutes or subminutes. Activate fast switching over dedicated lines between the end-user and the operating system by providing access via the data link on T-1 lines. Dial-in connections still need extensive security checks to screen unauthorized entry.
2. Connect the various digital services offered into a common Digital Cross-Connect System. Reduce the amount of equipment needed for complex integration to one local access area. This would decrease the propagation delay and improve the reliability.

Data Link Merging

Data links from the various digital services all use X.25 Packet protocol. Unfortunately, there are enough differences between the services to restrict direct interconnection. Arriving at a common packet protocol is a major step towards merging the data links together. By a common protocol, we refer to the content of the messages and not the X.25 Packet protocol each uses.

Translators between the systems are technically feasible. Given the engineer's plea of enough time and money, interface converters remain a minor detail. Nevertheless, administration of data link packet network is a massive job. Assigning and maintaining a packet address list has the same scope as issuing telephone numbers to a small country. Issuing and maintaining multiple address lists is an even more complex administrative job.

Figure 19-1 shows the basic block diagram for merging the data links associated with an ISDN Primary Access and Extended Superframe (ESF). As the T-1 line enters the telephone company office, the ESF Equipment pulls off the data link associated with the frame pattern. The 4000-bps data link contains error performance, control signals, and end-user data signals. This system uses the simplified BX.25 (Bell X.25) packet protocol without frame sequence numbering, message acknowledgment, or flow control.

Next, the ISDN Primary Access enters a Digital Cross-Connect System for cross-connection. Here the data link is 64,000 bps and contains signaling information as well as end-user data. This data link follows a normal X.25 packet protocol.

Both packet interfaces connect to a packet translator that reformat the data into new packets. Since each system had its own origination

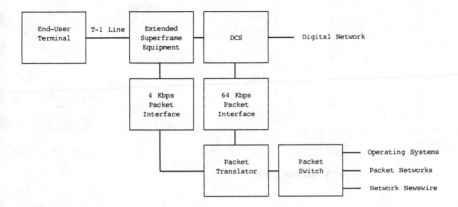

Figure 19-1   Data Link Merging.

and destination addresses, the translator changes the destination address to traverse the packet network. The new destination address is the far-end translator where it changes back to the original address.

To be truly effective, telephone companies must be able to translate other packet and end-user information. Minor adjustments to packets allows transport over a common packet network. Different operating systems would have a way to communicate to each other. While being a software problem to change from one operating system to another, there is a fundamental question about protocol converters. Previously, the Federal Communications Commission ruled against the telephone companies changing customer data in any way. It was a clear demarcation line that set telephone carriers apart from value-added carriers.

Telephone company operating systems exist for Extended Superframe (ESF) facility monitoring information. They also have trouble reporting operating systems that also contains historical information. Digital Cross-Connect Systems used to integrate digital service have even other operating systems. Everything the end-user would ever want to know about their network exists in some form of operating system.

Full-blown facility failures always had their individual alarms at the collocated offices. These alarms never went anywhere else until someone sent the information over an electronic mail system. This information showed up only after they felt a hard failure would last for a long time period. Now ESF offers the telephone companies the first real-time indication of pending facilities failure. If the ESF alarms passed to a central data base, it could notify end-users of specific circuits failures.

Lastly, the packet interface would allow end-users to access packet network sources without dedicated data rate (i.e., 2400 bps) port

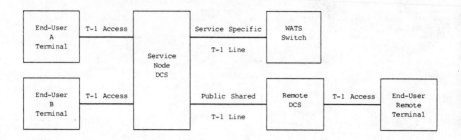

Figure 19-2   64 kb by N-Channels.

charges. This would provide a lower-cost option for the end-user with limited packet network traffic.

Bell Communications Research Gamma Transfer Service

Recent Bell Communications Research work proposes a service concept called Gamma Transfer Service (GTS). GTS is a packet transfer station between local services and network services. This proposal shows the serious intentions by the Bell Operating Companies to standardize a packet transfer between services. Its main purpose is as follows.

1. Provide a bridge between ISDN and a growing number of Local Area Networks (LANs).
2. Serve telemetry applications such as meter reading, alarm reporting, credit card validation.

Digital Transmission Speeds

64,000-bps Times N-Channels

If telephone companies tout the service-node concept to serve integrated digital service, they must also offer a new interoffice bandwidth. Figure 19-2 shows two end-users accessing the same service node Digital Cross-Connect System. Service-specific services like WATS or DDS strip off the dedicated T-1 access line coming from each end-user. It then connects to a service specific line going to the particular function. At the same time, 64,000 X N channels also strips off the dedicated T-1 accesses. They in turn connect to a public shared facility going to a remote location. A similar arrangement ap-

Data Rate	Data Bits	ECC/CRC	Filler	Stuff Bits	Loop Speed
1,200 bps	192	85	192	17	3,500 bps
2,400 bps	192	85	0	17	3,500 bps
4,800 bps	384	85	0	17	7,000 bps
9,600 bps	384	85	0	17	14,000 bps
19,200 bps	384	85	0	17	28,000 bps
32,000 bps	320	85	64	17	56,000 bps
38,400 bps	384	85	0	17	56,000 bps
64,000 bps	Unformatted				72,000 bps

Table 19-1   Advanced Digital Network Data and Line Rates.

pears at the remote DCS to connect service back on to dedicated T-1 access to the end-users location.

Providing segments of a T-1 line is an administrative extension of the initial integration concepts. While technically feasible to do, it is a matter of developing a suitable tariff. Rates would approximate a fill level between a 70 and 80 percentage level of the T-1 line plus an administrative charge.

```
$1,000 T-1 Rate  = $1,333 Fill Price
      75%
```

```
$1,333 Fill Price + 15% Surcharge = $1,533 New Rate
```

```
$1,533 Shared T-1 Rate = $64 Per Segment
      24 Channels
```

Pacific Bell's Advanced Digital Network

The Pacific and Nevada Bell Companies announced a new Advanced Digital Network with their Technical Reference PUB L-780056-PB/NB. This service proposes a range of digital data rates never offered before. Table 19-1 shows the end-user rates and their associated line rates. The difference between the user rate and the line rate includes error control and stuff bits.

Figure 19-3 shows a generalized version of the frame structure. The first 16-bit block carries the synchronization pattern for the frame. Next, a 16-bit block carries commands for network functions

16 Bits Sync	16 Bits Command	16 Bits Address	8 Bits Rate	2 Bits Signal	User Data	16 Bits Reserved

<----------------------------- 560 Bits Per Frame ----------------------------->

Figure 19-3   Advanced Digital Network Frame.

like loopbacks. The address code designates which equipment within the network will perform the function shown in the command field. After the address code, a rate and loopback status field carries information only when telephone company request a status. The 2-bit signaling field and the reserved field at the end of the frame have no purpose for the initial offering.

In reality, the frame structure also includes stuff bits and an error correction block. The stuff bits raise the operating data rate up to an even line rate figure. Error Correction/Cyclic Redundancy Check (ECC/CRC) codes throughout the frame structure permit greater tolerance to errors caused by noise. This in turn permits longer transmission distance between the premise and the telephone office.

Figure 19-4 shows stuff bits and the error detection and correction bits inserted into the frame structure. The frame's format uses a pattern of 16 bits — 1 stuff bit — 10 bits — 5 ECC/CRC before it repeats the same format.

19,200-bps Digital Services

Nine years ago, a 19,200-bps digital data service proposal had the backing of several marketing surveys. It didn't survive at the time because of the Bell System's divestiture. Now renewed interest in a service between 9600 and 56,000 bps has prompted new proposals. One method discussed was the Pacific Bell's Advanced Digital Network.

This speed has a lower appeal than other priorities and will always find its way to the bottom of the pile. The other anchor to providing the service is the lack of agreement on how to do it in the first place.

16 Bits Sync	1 Bit Stuff	10 Bits Command	5 Bits ECC/CRC	6 Bits Command	10 Bits Address	1 Bit Stuff	6 Bits Address 4 Bits Rate	5 Bits ECC/CRC

Figure 19-4   Stuff Bit and Error Detection Bit Locations.

Synchronous Transmission — SYNTRAN

SYNTRAN will make a minor impact on the overall digital transmission. The telephone companies will receive greater returns by offering a synchronous Digital Level-3 network or service. End-users would benefit from very accurate timing sources and should see a reduction in systematic jitter.

Synchronous Optic Network — SONET

SONET promises some sanity to the fiber-optic world by standardizing the operating rates. Look forward to the introduction of new end-user interfaces to meet these new formats.

Wideband Packet Voice Transmission

A lot of work is under way towards packetizing voice circuits onto a T-1 line. While a novel approach to multiplexing voice circuits, it must overcome major obstacles. Some of these obstacles are inherent to packet switching, and it faces a battle for acceptance.

1. Packet transmission has variable delay. Variable delay happens with different route selections and during the conversation if there is a high traffic load.
2. Analog data use would dramatically increase the wideband packet's traffic load. Traffic load would delay voice communications to an undesirable level.
3. Telephone company office packet switches are service specific, and equipment costs remain entrenched.
4. Economics would limit wideband switch locations. End to end service would travel great distances just for local service.
5. End-users would also require new equipment.
6. New standards are needed to arrive at only one design. Present methods are not compatible.

New standards for wideband packet are important to provide direction of this transmission medium. Since it can't gracefully blend into the existing network, a lot of work is ahead of the wideband advocates.

Figure 19-5 shows the telephone company interface needed to change from a wideband packet service into the regular digital network. The first device at the telephone company is a wideband packet switch. This separates the calls off the packet network and directs them to the regular digital network circuits. The second block returns the packetized voice channels back to an analog signal or

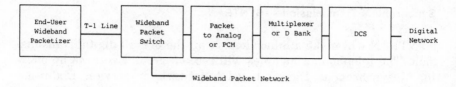

Figure 19-5   Wideband Packet Interfacing the Digital Network.

Pulse Code Modulated (PCM) signal. Some wideband packetizers already have an internal stage to change the analog signal into a PCM digital code.

Barring any additional design work, analog signals would appear on the normal output of the wideband packetizer. These signals then feed a regular digital channel bank (D-Bank) to combine the individual channels into a T-1 data stream. Now the output of the D-Bank can interface a Digital Cross-Connect System to distribute the individual channels to their destination.

Residence Communications Evolution

One fascinating residential communications proposal concerns a fiber-optic system. This particular proposal involves a new development and the installation of a fiber-optic network connecting the homes to a central site.

At first blush Figure 19-6 doesn't appear to be anything new. What separates this proposal from others is the connection of cable TV services from a common central location. Normally, subscriber TV services power all their analog video services over a coaxial cable. This proposal would supply only one digital video channel to a subscriber. The user instead selects one video channel out of the ones offered to watch. The desired channel selection travels back to the central site, and the particular video channel switches to the subscriber's line.

This proposal poses no threat to the majority of residence telecommunications, but offers some insight into what is possible. Video transmission by digital signals will show improved quality. Pay television specials on a per-show basis are practical. Nevertheless, one TV service into a household of multiple sets may kill the project. Satisfying everyone's viewing habits with just one normal video feed isn't realistic. It certainly wouldn't happen when a children's show, a soap opera, and sports programming were available at the same time. After trial thinking calls for a minumum of four video channels.

One thing that will make this type of service fly is expanded and higher-definition television. If the quality of the video signal was

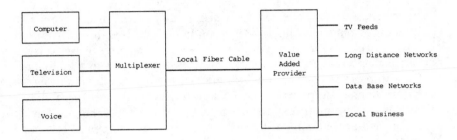

Figure 19-6   Residence Communications Evolution.

drastically better, the household could adjust to other means for multiple viewing.

Factors Affecting Evolution

Glut of Fiber-Optic Facilities

A glut of installed fiber-optic cables is one thing. When the wavelength division multiplexers triple their facilities' bandwidth capabilities, one will know what overabundance is all about. The AT&T investment plans for a nationwide fiber-optic network may be a reaction to offset US Sprint's advertised all-fiber system. Whatever the reasons for their decision may be, the investment has the following impact on the end-user.

1. Telephone companies will reduce cost of digital facilities. T-1 lines and higher-rate services will see the greatest price reduction.
2. Independent long distance fiber-optic companies will merge to protect their own investment. Only a few mergers will withstand the price wars that will result between the giants of the industry.
3. Telephone companies will offer a greater variety of integrated services to entice the end-user to use their facilities.

Slowness of Telephone Company Response to Evolution

If the telephone companies react in their normal manner to change, the evolution potential may slip through their fingers. Merely offering integrated digital services isn't enough to entice the end-user to invest time and money.

The end-user has obtained network management from premise equipment. It responds quickly to reconfiguration demands. Graphic displays provide every imaginable network map, circuit response, and error performance a user could want. Everything is available except one important part of their system — control over the facilities.

The telephone company holds the key to the total picture. If they do not respond to merging data links and operating systems, uniform evolution will never happen. Large companies will implement custom installations if telephone companies do not present a partnership attitude.

Federal Communications Commission Response

The FCC must revise their decision about telephone companies changing end-user data found on data links. It is one thing to prevent telephone companies from providing value added services. If the FCC uses the same reasoning to block protocol translators, the integrated digital evolution will drag out longer than it should.

Glossary

ABATS — Automatic Bit Access Test System (ABATS) remotely tests the DATAPHONE digital service. This system accesses individual low-speed digital data from a composite T-1 data stream. Some Hub Offices also test the local access lines with a system previously called Line Access Test System (LATS).

ADPCM — Adaptive Differential Pulse Code Modulation (ADPCM) is a 32,000-bps digital transcoder. As the term suggests, the primary coding method is Pulse Code Modulation. By looking at the differences between the PCM codings, the transcoder reduces the 8-bit byte PCM code into a 4-bit nibble ADPCM code.

AMI SIGNAL — Alternate Mark Inversion (AMI) is another name for the bipolar return-to-zero digital signal. (AMI) refers to the alternating polarity of the ones bit (a mark signal). Zero bits (a space signal) equal a zero voltage and appear only as a time deviation.

ASYNCHRONOUS TRANSMISSION — Asynchronous transmission is serial binary data with a start and stop bit added to identify the character. Over the years, people have bent the original meaning to cover data transmission that doesn't have a synchronous format.

BASIC ACCESS CHANNEL — The ISDN designation for the access line between the end-user and the first ISDN switch. Often referred to as 2B + 1D, signifying two voice/data circuits plus a data link.

BAUD — A unit of information or symbol transfer. In the case of 9600-bps modems, they use a 2400 bauds per second symbol rate. Each symbol represents a specific combination of four bits.

BELL COMMUNICATIONS RESEARCH — An organization that provides technical advisories to the various Bell Operating Companies. After divestiture of the Bell System, they furnished the technical expertise that AT&T supplied them in the past. See Chapter Twelve on Equipment Selection for access to technical advisories.

Bit-Interleaved — Bit-interleaving describes the method of assembling information from many channels and forming them into one composite or aggregate data stream. If all low-speed channels have the same data rate, the multiplexer selects one bit from each channel before starting the selection process over again.

Bits — A contraction for a *BI*nary dig*IT* which is either a zero or a one bit representation.

Bit Stuffing — A process to add nondata bits into the composite data stream to compensate for timing differences.

Bipolar Signal — See Alternate Mark Inversion.

Bipolar Violation — Bipolar violations are controlled violations of the coding practice to use alternating mark (ones bit) polarity. While the higher digital use a violation code for ones-density, DDS uses additional violation codes at the lower rates for control signals.

Bipolar Zero Substitution — A method to handle ones-density requirements on the T-1 and higher digital speeds. It uses bipolar violation codes to replace all zero bytes.

Blue Alarm — An alarm that informs down-line switching machines that a facility failures occurred beyond normal Yellow Alarm notification.

Burstiness — A description for the error performance of digital signals that combines errored bits in groups or bursts. This is converse of analog transmission, which has random errors that dribble errored bits.

Byte-Interleaved — Byte-interleaved describes the method of assembling information from many channels and forming them into one composite or aggregate data stream. Bytes or characters from many channels multiplex together instead of bit-interleaving.

CCITT — The International Consultative Committee for Telegraphy and Telephony. An international group of telephone companies seeking to find a common ground for telecommunications standards.

CEPT — The Conference of European Postal and Telecommunications Associations. Similar in operation to North America's Exchange

Carriers Association, which seeks standards for telecommunications standards.

Channel Service Units — Channel Service Units (CSU) serve as the interface between the digital data cable facilities and the end-user premise equipment. Major functions of the CSU are maintenance loopbacks and impedance matching between equipment and facilities.

Companding — Originally the *CO*mpression and ex*PANDING* properties of some analog transmission systems to lower the noise content. At the transmit end, the volume variations compressed into fewer variations. When the signal arrived at the receive end, the signal variation expanded to appear like the original. All noise content picked up during transmission became very low after expansion. Companding in the digital world means compressing the coding segments and steps for very-low-volume signals in comparison to high-volume signals.

Critical Angle — The angle of light (optic) hitting the boundary between the fiber's core and the cladding surrounding the core. Light hitting the boundary at an angle less than the critical angle permits light to enter the cladding and reduce the final received light signal.

Cyclic Redundancy Codes — Cyclic redundancy codes (CRC) provide error detection for blocks or frames of data bits. Data at the transmit equipment end assigns a distinctive digital code for all the data preceding it. The receiving equipment also checks the incoming data and checks the derived CRC against the CRC sent with the data stream. Differences between the derived and sent CRC often initiates message retransmission.

CVSD — Continuously Variable-Slope Delta-modulation is another name for Adaptive Delta Modulation, which samples the analog signal at a very high rate. Most commercial multiplexers sample the analog signal at a 32,000-bps rate and codes the direction of the sample in reference to the previous sample. A positive deviation from the previous signal assigns a ones bit for the coding and a zero bit for a negative direction.

Data Link — Data link refers to the packet circuit embedded in the Extended Superframe pattern or the D channel of ISDN Access lines.

Digital Data System (DDS) — Digital data systems (DDS) refer to the generic digital hierarchy. It can transport DATAPHONE Digital Service, T-1 services, or any other digital service.

Dataphone Digital Service (DDS) — An AT&T registered Service Mark for a digital data service for speeds between 2400 and 56,000 bps.

Dataport — A channel card that fits into a digital channel bank like the D-4 or D-5-Bank used to extend a digital data service from the Hub Office to an end-user's location.

Data Service Units (DSU) — Data Service Units (DSU) are used only with the digital data rates between 2400 and 56,000 bps. They change the bipolar signal output from the CSU into a typical end-user interface. It also recovers receive and transmit clock from the incoming data stream.

Digital Cross-connect System (DCS or DACS) — Digital Cross-Connect Systems (DCS) or Digital Access Cross-Connect Systems (DACS) provide electronic connections between DS0 (64,000 bps) time slots of many T-1 lines. When 24 DS0 time slots connect or switch between T-1 ports, the DCS acts like a T-1 switch.

DSI — Digital Speech Interpolation looks for speech inactivity and uses the "dead time" between conversations to transmit other conversations in its place. It relies on gaps between voice conversations to allow additional channel to have access to the aggregate line.

DSX — Digital Signal Cross-Connect ("X" means cross-connect) points exist in the telephone company offices to manually connect the various facilities and equipment together. Usually seen with a number suffix to designate the level of cross-connection. DSX points may also be the only point in a telephone company office for maintenance access.

Duty Cycle — Duty cycles describe the portion of the time interval for a unit pulse that has some amplitude or value. A 50% duty cycle has energy in only half of the full unit's time interval.

Echo Canceler — A digital cancellation of a predicted digital echo signal from a remote location.

Echo Return — Echo return is reflected energy usually from 2 to 4-wire hybrids. Any time there is an impedance difference (imbalance) between facilities and equipment, a small amount of energy reflects back.

Extended Superframe — Extended Superframe refers to framing pattern with a CRC code to check data and a data link. The pattern is extended since it uses 24 Main Frames instead of 12 before it repeats the pattern structure.

Frame Format — A frame format is a contiguous sequence of bits or bytes formed serially in a periodic structure.

Framing Pattern — Framing patterns are a sequence of bits that appear at the start-stop bit positions used to indicate a frame.

Ground-Start Signaling — Used to extend the range of end-user signaling when compared to loop-start signaling. A function normally found at the telephone company's end-office.

Integrated Services Digital Network (ISDN) — A complex call-processing system that allows interchangeable voice and data use of the same time slot in the digital stream.

Intersymbol Interference — When energy from consecutive pulses spreads into the time domain of the other, the equipment misinterprets the dispersed energy for valid data.

Isochronous Transmission — Serial binary transmission where the digital terminal equipment recovers timing from the received pulses.

Jitter — A transmission impairment that modulates the phase of the desired signal.

Launched Signal Power — The maximum light power delivered at the transmit end of a fiber cable.

Link Budget — The difference between the launched power and the optic receiver's sensitivity.

Main Frame — A Main Frame combines 24 DS0 (64,000 bps) time slots for a total of 192 data bits. Usually shown with a framing pattern bit that equals 193 total bits for an 125 microsecond time interval.

Loop-Start Signaling — A signaling process that closes the local access loop.

Multipoint Junction Unit (MJU) — Multipoint Junction Units are the digital equivalent of the analog split-bridge. Multipoint data services have a central or control site that broadcasts information to all remote terminal locations. Responding terminals answer on a point-to-point basis back to only the control location.

Nyquist's Frequency — Nyquist's frequency says the analog equivalent (in Hz) to a digital data stream is one-half the bit rate of the digital signal. A Nyquist frequency of 772 kHz becomes the test signal for T-1 facilities.

Numerical Aperture — A value assigned to the coupling efficiency of the light source (optics) to the fiber cable.

Off-Hook — A term referring to the user accessing the telephone network by lifting the handset off its cradle. Old-time telephone sets used a hook to hold the earpiece when not in use. This also served as a switch to close the connection. When you wanted to use the telephone, the user lifted the earpiece or went off-hook.

Office Channel Unit — The interface unit between the telephone company DDS equipment and the facilities.

On-Hook — The opposite operation for off-hook when you wanted to use the telephone. After finishing your call, you would return the old-time earpiece to the switch hook and open the circuit.

Ones-Density — A term referring to the need of digital equipment to see enough ones bits to maintain the timing recovery circuits.

Ping-Pong Transmission — Ping-pong transmission is sending data in alternating directions over a 2-wire facility, much like the ping-pong ball going back and forth. The resultant end-user signal appears to be full-time transmission without the delays for alternating signals.

Polar Binary Signal — Polar binary are 100% duty cycle digital signals that use positive polarity and negative signals for binary bit indications.

Primary Access Channel — An ISDN designation for the T-1 line with 23 voice or data time slots and one data link.

Quantizing — The process of assigning digital codes for the sampled analog signals or differences between digital codings.

Quatenary Signal — This refers to a signal with four different levels.

Red Alarm — When T-1 receive equipment senses a facility failure, it issues a Red Alarm. Locally, the Red Alarm sounds audible and visual alarms and starts a Yellow Alarm back to the transmit end.

Refraction Index — The quality of the fiber cable to bend or refract light. The difference between the refraction indexes of the fiber core and its cladding reflect light.

Robbed-Bit Signaling — A means to use in-band signaling within a DS0 (64,000 bps) time slot. It robs the 8th bit in each time slot in every 6th Main Frame and inserts a signaling indication.

Subrate Data Multiplexer — Subrate data multiplexers divide a DS0 (64,000 bps) time slot into a number of subrate DDS circuits. They can split a DS0 time slot into 20 2400 bps circuits. Used to interconnect integrated digital service into the DDS network.

Superframe — A D-4 Superframe has 12 Main Frames; an Extended Superframe has 24 Main Frames.

Superframe Integrity — The receive equipment must see the exact superframe pattern in relationship to the frame format as sent by the transmit end.

Synchronous Transmission — Serial binary transmission where the digital communications equipment recovers timing from the received pulses and supplies clock to the terminal equipment.

Time Slot — The time domain of the basic building block of an 8-bit byte sent 8000 times a second. Time slots refer to the DS0 level or 64000-bps digital signal.

Unipolar Signal — A digital signal with only one polarity in reference to a zero voltage. Binary ones bits have a positive voltage (typical equipment voltage is +5 V), and zero bits have near-zero voltage.

Yellow Alarm — After the T-1 receive equipment senses a facility failure, it issues a Yellow Alarm back to the transmit end to notify it to stop sending. D-4 frame-oriented units will force the second bit in each time slot to a zero-bit indication. Extended Superframe carries the Yellow Alarm in the data link.

ZBTSI — Zero Byte Time-Slot Interchange is one method to meet ones-density requirements on a T-1 line. It eliminates all zero-byte time slots in the T-1 signal and replaces them with identification codes. The codes tell the other end where to reinsert an all-zero byte.

References

AT&T, Technical Reference PUB 60110, Digital Synchronization Network Plan, December 1983.

Aydin Monitor Systems, VQL A Technique for Digitally Encoding Voice at 32 Kbps, Product Note #9222-0003, Fort Washington, PA.

AT&T Bell Telephone Laboratories, Transmission Systems for Communications. Indianapolis, IN, AT&T, Fifth Edition 1982.

Bell Communications Research, Technical Advisory TA-TSY-000253, Synchronous Optical Networks (SONET), May 1987.

Bell Communications Research, Technical Advisory TA-TSY-000304, Synchronous DS3 Digital Switch Interface, May 1985.

Bell Communications Research, Technical Advisory TA-TSY-000393, ISDN Basic Access Digital Subscriber Lines, March 1987.

Bell Communications Research, Technical Advisory TA-TSY-000393, ISDN Basic Access Digital Subscriber Lines, March 1987.

Bell Communications Research, Technical Advisory TA-TSY-000397, ISDN Basic Access Transport System Requirements, Issue 2, May 1987.

Clarke, P., Primer on Fiber-Optic Digital Data Links,Lightwave, January 1986.

Corning Glass Works, One Size Does NOT Fit All, Guidelines, November 1987, Volume 3, Number 4.

Pacific Bell, Technical Reference PUB L-780056 PB/NB, Advanced Digital Network, March 1987.

Index